Africans and the Holocaust

This book is an original and comparative study of reactions in West and East Africa to the persecution and attempted annihilation of Jews in Europe and in former German colonies in sub-Saharan Africa during the Second World War.

An intellectual and diplomatic history of World War II and the Holocaust, *Africans and the Holocaust* looks at the period from the perspectives of the colonized subjects of the Gold Coast, Nigeria, Sierra Leone, Kenya, Tanganyika, and Uganda, as well as the sovereign peoples of Liberia and Ethiopia, who wrestled with the social and moral questions that the war and the Holocaust raised. The five main chapters of the book explore the pre-Holocaust history of relations between Jews and Africans in West and East Africa, perceptions of Nazism in both regions, opinions of World War II, interpretations of the Holocaust, and responses of the colonized and sovereign peoples of West and East Africa to efforts by Great Britain to resettle certain categories of Jewish refugees from Europe in the two regions before and during the Holocaust.

This book will be of use to students and scholars of African history, Holocaust and Jewish studies, and international or global history.

Edward Kissi is an associate professor in the Department of Africana Studies at the University of South Florida, United States.

Routledge Studies in the Modern History of Africa

This series includes in-depth research on aspects of economic, political, cultural, and social history of individual countries as well as broad-reaching analyses of regional issues.

Themes include social and economic change, colonial experiences, independence movements, postindependence governments, globalization in Africa, nationalism, gender histories, conflict, the Atlantic Slave Trade, the environment, health and medicine, ethnicity, urbanization, and neocolonialism and aid.

Forthcoming titles:

Power, Culture and Modernity in Nigeria
Beyond the Colony
Oluwatoyin Oduntan

African Testimony in the Movement for Congo Reform
The Burden of Proof
Robert Burroughs

Human rights in Sierra Leone, 1787–2016
The Long Struggle from the Transatlantic Slave Trade to the Present
John Idriss Lahai

Miscegenation, Identity and Status in Colonial Africa
Intimate Colonial Encounters
Lawrence Mbogoni

Displaced Mozambicans in Postcolonial Tanzania
Refugee Power, Mobility, Education, and Rural Development
Joanna T. Tague

Africans and the Holocaust
Perceptions and Responses of Colonized and Sovereign Peoples
Edward Kissi

For a full list of titles in this series, please visit www.routledge.com

Africans and the Holocaust
Perceptions and Responses of Colonized and Sovereign Peoples

Edward Kissi

LONDON AND NEW YORK

First published 2020
by Routledge
2 Park Square, Milton Park, Abingdon, Oxon OX14 4RN

and by Routledge
605 Third Avenue, New York, NY 10017

First issued in paperback 2021

Routledge is an imprint of the Taylor & Francis Group, an informa business

© 2020 Edward Kissi

The right of Edward Kissi to be identified as author of this work has been asserted by him in accordance with sections 77 and 78 of the Copyright, Designs and Patents Act 1988.

All rights reserved. No part of this book may be reprinted or reproduced or utilised in any form or by any electronic, mechanical, or other means, now known or hereafter invented, including photocopying and recording, or in any information storage or retrieval system, without permission in writing from the publishers.

Trademark notice: Product or corporate names may be trademarks or registered trademarks, and are used only for identification and explanation without intent to infringe.

British Library Cataloguing-in-Publication Data
A catalogue record for this book is available from the British Library

Library of Congress Cataloging-in-Publication Data
A catalog record for this book has been requested

ISBN 13: 978-0-367-77749-4 (pbk)
ISBN 13: 978-0-367-19537-3 (hbk)

Typeset in Bembo
by Apex CoVantage, LLC

For Daphne, Frank, Akosua, and their grandparents,
as well as Jean and Frank Chalk

Contents

List of figures		viii
Acknowledgments		ix
	Introduction	1
1	Jews in East and West Africa before the Holocaust	18
2	Africans and Nazism	44
3	Africans and World War II	75
4	Africans and the Holocaust	101
5	African and British proposals on Jewish refugees	143
	Conclusion	175
	Bibliography	179
	Index	186

Figures

2.1 (a) *Gold Coast Spectator* photograph of the boxing match between Joe Louis and Max Schmeling; (b) photographs of Joe Louis and Max Schmeling in the *Gold Coast Spectator*, 16 July 1938 — 57
2.2 Front-page headline, *West African Pilot*, 10 January 1939 — 58
2.3 Advertisement for Hitler's *Mein Kampf*, in the *West African Pilot*, 15 July 1939 — 61
3.1 Enlistment advertisement in the *West African Pilot*, 13 October 1941 — 82
4.1 Confidential British document detailing Nazi persecution of Jews prior to the war, also sent to British colonies in Africa — 109

Acknowledgments

The initial idea for this book came from an endowed Kent Family Lecture that I delivered on "The Holocaust and Africa: Africa and the Holocaust," in March 2002, as a visiting assistant professor at Clark University, in Worcester, Massachusetts. Thanks to Roman and Hannah Kent and my colleagues Deborah Dwork and Tatyana McAuley for that honor. Like many thoughts that come to mind in auspicious moments, the idea of exploring the lecture topic further for a manuscript dissipated quickly. It was not until March 2006, when I participated in a symposium at the Florida Holocaust Museum, at the invitation of Noreen Brand, and Ula Szczepinska, on the Legacies of Nuremberg, that thoughts about African responses to the Holocaust (and the Nuremberg trials) returned to my mind. Central to that interest was my own dismay at the absence of African voices and perspectives in Holocaust historiography, as well as the equal absence of Holocaust content in African historiography. I committed myself to starting something at the intersection of African and Holocaust historiographies. This is the product.

I could not have succeeded in this quest without the help of the University of South Florida (USF) where I teach and of the many people and institutions beyond it. The research money for this book came from USF's Humanities Institute and Creative Scholarship Grant in 2008 and 2010, respectively. With these internal research funds and through intermittent summer research between 2009 and 2012, I completed preliminary research at the United States Holocaust Memorial Museum, in Washington, D.C., and the Public Record Office of the British National Archives, as well as the British Library Newspapers in Colindale in the United Kingdom. I could not have found my way through London's complicated underground and overland transportation networks or survived the city's weather conditions, without the help of my brother Alexander Oppong, who accommodated me in his home and accompanied me during his nonworking days to the Archives. I also thank Michael Haider, an Austrian diplomat I met at a conference in Salzburg, in 2012, for sharing some important information about Ethiopia's relationship with Germany in the 1930s with me and for recommending key literature and contacts that opened new avenues of knowledge on the subject-matter of this book.

A semester research leave granted by the Department of Africana Studies, with the support of my colleague Chair Deborah Plant, in 2013, allowed me to travel to Ghana, Liberia, and Ethiopia to conduct the remaining archival research for this book. In Ghana, I enjoyed the hospitality of my brother Emmanuel Ofori and his wife Rhodaline Ofori who demonstrated the significance of our Ghanaian concept of family by accommodating me at no cost in their house during my three months of research at the Ghana National Archives. There, I was fortunate to have the assistance of the Archive's staff, among whom Bright Owusu and Juliet Akuettey deserve special mention and gratitude. They searched for every file I requested and, in the toughest of circumstances, found new and relevant materials that I never thought even existed there. Beyond archival research, life in Ghana was made much more comfortable with the help of my friends George Adu, who took me to the archives daily in his taxi, and Lucy Tetteh and Mercy Gyekye, who lent their moral and material support.

My friend A. B. Assensoh deserves particular mention for putting me in touch with Ora Garway, editor of *The Punch* newspaper in Liberia. My research in Monrovia could not have been successful without her assistance and the generosity of her sister Evon Garway. Ora and Evon picked me up from the airport, found me a place to live, introduced me to people I needed to meet, and took me to the places I needed to go. Equal appreciation goes to the staff of the Africana Room at the Library of the University of Liberia, especially Library Assistant Nimadeh E. Bright, who found valuable information for my research. I am also grateful for the help I received during my research in Ethiopia from Hirut Abebe-Jiri, a human rights activist and a colleague with whom I worked on establishing the Ethiopian Red Terror Documentation and Research Center in Addis Ababa.

I am especially grateful to Emeritus Professor Rhoda Howard-Hassmann for the keen interest shown in this project and also for reading a draft of the manuscript and offering detailed editorial suggestions that improved the structure and analyses of the book. Emmanuel Akyeampong at Harvard University drew my attention to new research on archives that any historian reconstructing aspects of the past from colonial archives needed to read. A statement of appreciation is deserved for my daughter Akosua Tenkoramaa Kissi, who provided me with technological help, and information on publishing outlets and insisted that I complete this work before she left for college. My colleagues at the University of South Florida—Martin Schonfeld, who helped in translating some key documents in German for me; Alex Levine and Roy Kaplan, who read drafts of the manuscript; Cheryl Rodriguez, and Steve Tauber, who supported my request for a Sabbatical leave to complete the writing phase of this book—deserve particular acknowledgement.

Finally, I thank Acquisition Editor Leanne Hinves for her steady interest in the manuscript and Editorial Assistant Henry Strang for answering quickly the many questions I asked on the preparation of the final manuscript for submission. To all the people at Taylor & Francis who made the production of this book possible, the reviewers who took time to read it, the staff at the library of the U.S. Holocaust Memorial Museum, British National Archives, the British Library Newspapers, and the Ethiopian National Library, who assisted me in diverse ways, I remain thankful for your part in the completion of this work. If this book makes any new contribution to knowledge, I share the credit with you.

Introduction

On 27 January 1945, Allied soldiers liberated Auschwitz-Birkenau, the concentration and extermination camp that the Nazi regime had built in Poland in 1941 after the German invasion of that country in 1939. About 1.3 million people including Jews, Roma and Sinti, non-Jewish Poles, and Soviet prisoners of war had been deported by the Nazi government from all parts of Europe to this particular death and labor camp. Here, the Nazi regime murdered nearly 1 million Jews and an unknown number of non-Jewish prisoners in gas chambers. Auschwitz-Birkenau has now become the symbol of the Holocaust, the attempt by Nazi Germany to exterminate German and other European Jews, as well as other groups of people, in order to create a "racially pure" German nation without Jews, Blacks, Gypsies (Roma and Sinti), homosexuals, and people with mental and physical disabilities. In November 2005, the United Nations General Assembly designated 27 January of every year as International Holocaust Remembrance Day, a day on which all nations must remember victims of the Holocaust.

Today, the Holocaust forms part of our contemporary memory of Nazi Germany and what took place beyond the battlefields of World War II. About 1 million Africans in colonial Africa and in sovereign Ethiopia and Liberia are estimated to have fought with the Allied Powers (Britain, France, the Soviet Union, and the United States), voluntarily and by conscription, in that war against Nazi Germany at various battlefronts. At the home front, millions more contributed money and labor to the Allied war effort. In *Fighting for Britain: African Soldiers in the Second World War*, David Killingray and Martin Plaut estimate that West Africa alone supplied "more than 200,000 soldiers and labourers for military service" in East and North Africa between 1940 and 1943. After 1943, some of these soldiers engaged in various military services in Asia. From the British colonies of Uganda, Tanganyika (now Tanzania), Nyasaland (now Malawi) and Northern Rhodesia (now Zambia), in the then East and Central African territories, came another "324,000 men" recruited after September 1939. Most of these men served in the Ethiopian campaign against Italian forces.[1]

The expanding literature on World War II relating to Africa has deepened our knowledge of the role that the people on the continent played in the eventual Allied victory over Nazi Germany. However, to the extent that scholars of the war have ventured to examine the thoughts that people in Africa expressed about that global conflict, their discussions have followed four mutually reinforcing military and political paths of analyses. First is the conscription and mobilization of African colonial subjects and sovereign troops as loyal or self-interested combatants, supporters, and other service providers for the war. Second is the heroic exploits of colonial African troops at particular battlefields in Africa, Europe, and Asia and the nature of military service. Third is the fate of Black African POWs in Nazi internment camps. Fourth is the role of returning African soldiers in the development of anticolonial nationalism in Africa.[2] These historiographical trajectories tend to celebrate the fighting skills of Africans in the service of Empire, to the point of obscuring how Africans thought about and interpreted the meaning and global implications and symbolisms of the war.

It is now part of mainstream historical knowledge that "the systematic mass murder of European Jewry by the Nazis," as Michael Marrus has defined "The Holocaust," occurred in the course of World War II.[3] Thus, World War II was both a declared conflict in which Nazi Germany attacked and occupied sovereign nations in Europe and colonial territories in North Africa and a hidden war against Jews and other groups waged by the Third Reich. But did the colonial subjects and the sovereign troops from Africa who participated in the declared war or who contributed to it at the home front know anything about the hidden one (the Holocaust)? Killingray and Plaut are very skeptical about what "African soldiers fighting with British forces" in World War II knew about "the global significance of the war in which they were involved." Their view that these colonial troops may have had "little idea" about what they were fighting to uphold on a global scale is understandable, in view of the careful management of information about the war and the Holocaust by colonial administrators.[4] But how about the people the soldiers left at home, the educated elite, the editors of newspapers, curious ordinary people, and traditional chiefs who sat on the legislative councils of colonial administrations and who had the leisure to read about the war from the local and foreign press, as well as Allied and colonial war bulletins? If these civilians at the home front knew about the Nazi persecution and extermination of European Jews as a major war aim of Nazi Germany, how did they become aware of that, when, and what did they say or do about it? If they were not aware, why did the Holocaust as a concurrent war in the early 1940s escape their attention? These questions, rarely asked and answered in the major Africanist literature on World War II, and in the major works on the Holocaust, seek to unravel some of the "unknown" elements in World War II and Holocaust historiographies from an African perspective.

This book explores what *Africans* knew about the destruction of European Jews by Nazi Germany during World War II and how they reacted to it. Research reveals that colonial subjects and sovereign peoples in Africa knew much about the Holocaust, as an undercurrent of World War II, and reflected on it in complex ways. Their initial expectation of a Nazi victory in the war triggered intense reflections about the purpose of the war itself and the implications of the Nazi persecution of European Jews for their own humanity and survival in a Nazi-controlled postwar world. Their reflections also touched on the relationship between the Holocaust and the claims of Europeans as the embodiment of civilization and enlightenment in colonial discourse. Thus, colonial subjects and sovereign peoples in Africa did more than fight for Great Britain and its Allies as able combatants and silent loyalists. They read about Nazism, perceived the fate of the Jews in Europe during the war, and thought about what these meant for their own fate, dignity, and survival in any transition from colonial racism and exploitation to Nazi racism and genocide.

Nazi racial ideology of the 1930s had cast the Jews of Europe and the peoples of Africa as "inferior races," although Africans and Jews faced different fates in the Nazi campaign of violence.[5] As people who had borne the brunt of prejudice, discrimination, and persecution in their related histories, Africans and Jews had long forged bonds of kinship and constructed similar narratives of endurance and survival.[6] Between 1939 and 1945, African subjects in Britain's colonies were not only summoned to enlist for combat against Hitler and the Nazi regime but also asked to offer land and resources for the settlement of Jewish refugees who fled or survived the anti-Jewish atrocities of the Nazi state. Louise London has studied the ambivalent attitude of Great Britain to the influx of Jewish refugees to that European country in the course of the Holocaust.[7] She has also alluded to Britain's request and pressure on its overseas dominions and colonies to accept, for permanent settlement, a large number of Jewish refugees in transit in Britain. What London omits is how Britain's African colonies and the sovereign nation of Ethiopia responded to that request and pressure. This book restores that missing element in the transnational history of the Holocaust. Certainly, a study of how the Holocaust tested the bonds and narratives of kinship between Africans and Jews can unravel some of the hitherto unexamined paradoxes in the history of World War II and the Holocaust.

Holocaust historiography has been surprisingly silent on what Africans knew and thought about Nazi Germany's planned total extermination of European Jews in the course of World War II. The redeeming element in that historiography, as far as Africa and the perspectives of Africans are concerned, is its allusions to the anti-African structural racism in Nazi ideology as a counterpart of Nazi structural anti-Semitism. To that end, some scholars who study the Holocaust point to the roles that the anti-Jewish and anti-African ideologies of the Nazi regime played in the attempted physical destruction of European Jews and the sterilization of Afro-Germans in Nazi Germany. The closest that any study relating to Nazi Germany and the Holocaust has come to focusing on the thoughts and actions of peoples of African descent are the few explorations of three intersecting experiences of African-descended peoples variously identified as "Africans," "Blacks," "Afro-Germans," "European Blacks," "African Americans," or "Arabs" in and outside of Nazi Germany. The first intersection is how these groups were treated as a despised segment of Germany's population. Second is the treatment they received in German prisoner of war camps during World War II. Third is their role as rescuers of persecuted Jews during the Holocaust. On these subjects, the works of Hans Massaquoi, Clarence Lusane, Raffael Scheck, Robert W. Kesting, and Robert Satloff are the most prominent.[8]

Hans J. Massaquoi's *Destined to Witness* is a memoir of his life as the grandson of Liberia's consul general to Hamburg, Momolu Massaquoi, during the Weimar Republic. It is, as the author describes his memoir, a "rather different perspective on the Holocaust."[9] Undoubtedly, the memoir offers a unique African view of the Holocaust from the experiences of "a black youngster growing into manhood and surviving in Nazi Germany" and one who was also "an eyewitness to, and frequent victim of both Nazi racial madness and Allied bombings.[10] Born, in January 1926, to an African father and a German mother, as Hans-Jurgen, Massaquoi was seven when the Nazi regime took power. Thus, he grew up in a Germany "consumed by racial arrogance and racial hatred" and a nation "openly committed to the destruction of all "non-Aryans"."[11] His identity as a Black German represented what the Nazi regime regarded as the "cardinal sin" of the German nation: the "pollution of Aryan blood with 'inferior' non-Aryan blood."[12] His status as the grandson of Liberia's consulgeneral in Hamburg, "the first official representative" of a sovereign African nation to Germany since World War I, could not insulate Hans-Jurgen Massaquoi against racial prejudice.[13] He attributes his escape from "extermination, sterilization, or medical experimentation," the fate that Nazi Germany assigned to Germans of African descent like himself, to the confluence of two factors. One, that Blacks in Germany were so few in number compared to Jews, with whom they shared the same identity as non-Aryans, that Blacks were "relegated to low-priority status" among the groups the Nazis targeted for extermination. Two, the military successes of the Allied assault on Germany kept the Nazi regime and its murderers preoccupied with their own survival, and the eventual Allied victory came very quickly before the Nazi regime could complete its program of racial cleansing.[14]

Massaquoi's memoir is distinctive in its quality as a chronicle of an African perspective on the Holocaust from the location of the crime. His view of the Holocaust transcends the various attacks on and persecution of that atrocity's primary victims, the Jews of Germany (and elsewhere). He sees the similar assaults on the lives of Black people like himself and Germany's Roma and Sinti population as part of the Nazi regime's preoccupation with racial purity.[15] Massaquoi's experiences in Nazi Germany make the question that this book seeks to answer even more pertinent: Did people on the African continent, and more so in the Liberia that his grandfather represented as an African diplomat in Germany, know and say anything about Nazism or about what the author describes as "modern history's most extensive, [and] most systematic mass murder scheme" orchestrated by Nazi Germany?[16] At the age of eight, Massaquoi had his early encounter with Nazi racism at a children's playground in Hamburg where he could not play as an African and a non-Aryan. His early education on Nazi racism had come from his German mother. But, as he grew up, he also became aware of Hitler's views of Blacks, particularly the well-educated, in his *Mein Kampf* and what other Nazi officials such as Richard-Walther Darre, the Nazi party's minister of agriculture, had also written about the German children of the Senegalese soldiers whom the French had brought to occupy Germany's Rhineland after the end of the First World War. The minister had openly advocated for the extermination of the "leftovers from the black Shame on the Rhine," a genocidal campaign against a segment of Germany's population he declared had to be carried out soon.[17]

Beyond his own experiences of racial prejudice, Massaquoi had also observed Nazi atrocities against Jews. He recalls the nationwide attacks on the temples, synagogues, and shops belonging to German Jews, and the deliberate murder of about 91 Jews and the arrest of thousands of them on 9 November 1938, a day that has earned its infamy in the history of the Holocaust as the day of *Kristallnacht* [Night of Broken Glass].[18] As an African in Nazi Germany, he had become familiar with all the preludes to the Holocaust that came in the form of Nazi party propaganda, films, and newspaper articles demonizing Jews and presenting them as plagues and diseases whose eradication was necessary to restore the health of the German nation.[19] Memoirs like Massaquoi's, written by Africans or people of African descent who lived in Germany under the Nazi party, that offer firsthand perspectives on the Holocaust are very rare in African and Holocaust historiographies. In their stead is historical research on the experiences of African soldiers who fell into the hands of German soldiers in World War II. Clarence Lusane's *Hitler's Black Victims*, Raffael Scheck's *Hitler's African Victims*, and the research of Robert W. Kesting on African Americans in Nazi Germany are part of that historiographical genre.

Lusane's book focuses on the experiences of "Afro-Germans and other Blacks" in Nazi Germany and the contradictions of Nazi anti-Black racism. It is relevant to the topic that this book explores in one of several key respects. The book examines, among other issues, the "history of contact" between Germany and "people of African descent both in Africa and in Germany" before World War I and throughout the Nazi period.[20] It offers instructive insights into how two groups of Africa-descended peoples in Germany experienced Nazi racism. They were "Afro-Germans," children of unions between Africans and Germans who, by citizenship and cultural immersion, lived in Germany and identified themselves as German nationals, and "Africans," people from the African continent who were distinguished from "Whites of African descent" by virtue of their black skin color.[21] The theme of Nazi anti-African or anti-Black racism in Lusane's book is consistent with Hans Massaquoi's reflections on his own childhood experiences as both an "Afro-German" and an "African." Where Lusane's historical study diverges from Massaquoi's memoir is Lusane's argument that while the Nazi regime's prominent leaders espoused a virulent form of "antiblackness and Negrophobia," their treatment of Blacks, in practice more than in rhetoric, was "complex, fluid, and contradictory."[22] Comparatively, the Nazi regime did not treat Afro-Germans and Africans with the same unyielding determination it demonstrated in deporting Jews from German soil and in exterminating them from the beginning of their ascent to power in 1933 to their demise in 1945. While Jews in Germany were not allowed to attend school or work, Afro-Germans and Africans could do so, at least, initially. After deciding against the extermination of Germany's Afro-German population, the Nazi regime consigned this group to a fate of sterilization.[23] On this issue of the sterilization of Blacks by the Nazis, rather than their extermination, Massaquoi's and Lusane's work converge. But Lusane is correct about the fluid and contradictory nature of Germany's relationship with its colonial subjects.

Germany and Africa had a peculiar relationship. German Chancellor Otto von Bismarck and German missionaries and trading companies had brought Germany into the European imperial dalliance with Africa, in the nineteenth and early twentieth centuries, by acquiring as colonies Togo and Cameroon in West Africa, Tanganyika (present-day Tanzania) and Rwanda in East and Central Africa, and South-West Africa (present day Namibia).[24] Germany also had diplomatic and commercial relations with Africa's only two sovereign nations in this period, Ethiopia and Liberia.[25] Thus, Germany's colonial empire in Africa made millions of Africans Germany's colonial subjects. As was typical in nineteenth-century imperial and diplomatic relations, Germany's colonial subjects in Africa, as well as the citizens of sovereign nations with which Germany had relations, entered metropolitan Germany in sporadic numbers. They came, like Massaquoi's grandparents, as diplomats. Others arrived as teachers of various African languages allowed to enter Germany to prepare Germany's colonial administrators for service in their nation's new African empire. They were followed by students, traders, entertainers, workers, and ex-soldiers who had fought on behalf of Germany during World War I.[26]

The experiences of two Africans—Johnny Williams and Leopold Sedar Senghor, which Lusane examines in his book—highlight the contradictions of Nazi racism in practice that Lusane emphasizes. Williams was the prototype of many Afro-Germans of the Nazi period. His mother came from the then French colony of Ivory Coast in West Africa, and his father from Alsace, in France. Williams had migrated to Alsace in 1922. At the age of 22, he worked at a factory in Montlucon. In 1940, the factory was attacked and seized by the Germans. Four years later, when he and other former workers at the factory returned there, in apparent defiance of a German order not to do so, Williams was arrested and deported by the Germans to the Neunengamme concentration camp. Williams testifies to a concentration camp life of "daily killings by gassing, shooting, and hangings."[27] Williams survived that concentration camp ordeal, and his survival points to the different fate that the Nazi regime assigned to Africans and other Blacks compared to Jews. According to Lusane, Nazi SS soldiers who saved Williams from certain death at Neunengamme, found black skin pigmentation a natural curiosity. They sometimes took Africans out of camp inmates to examine their skin by rubbing it "to see if the color would come off." One of the SS men "who decided that Williams and [other Africans at the camp] should not be killed" had concluded that "Blacks were good athletes." According to Lusane, Williams believed that the victories of Black athletes at the 1936 Olympic Games, in Munich, Germany, and the victory of the African American boxer Joe Louis over the German and Nazi boxing icon Max Schmeling in 1936 and 1938, earned him and others, in the eyes of these SS men at the camp, "enough respect, even if indirectly, to rescue them from a terrible death."[28]

Leopold Sedar Senghor (who became president of Senegal in West Africa in 1960) had a similar experience. He had been enlisted in the French colonial force from Senegal (*tirailleurs senegalais*) in 1939 and deployed for military service in World War II in the service of France. On 20 June 1940, Senghor was captured by the Germans. As a prisoner of war, Senghor spent time in many POW camps, including the camps at Charite-sur-Loire and Romilly-sur-Seine, that the Nazis constructed to hold African POWs. These were mainly labor camps. As Lusane notes, African POWs in these camps worked on farms while others served as the personal and domestic servants of German military officers. According to Lusane, this "type of work assigned to the Africans" in Nazi internment camps showed the difference between how the Nazis viewed Africans and how they viewed Jews and Gypsies. Nazi "visceral hatred" for Jews and Gypsies meant that none of them could become the personal servants of any Nazi officials.[29] The issues that yearn for examination are how the Africans who received quasi-humane treatment at the hands of some Nazi officials viewed the Nazi regime and what they thought about the Nazi persecution of German Jews.

Like Clarence Lusane, Raffael Scheck looks at the fate of a wide range of peoples of African descent in German camps in his book *Hitler's African Victims: The German Army Massacres of Black French Soldiers in 1940*. He cautions that despite the "improved treatment" of Black Africans by some of their German captors, "it would be wrong to conclude that the lives of black Africans in German POW camps were easy and safe for the remainder of the war."[30] Scheck's study is, perhaps, the most notable of the surveys of the experiences of captured colonial troops from the African continent in the throes of Nazi violence. As Scheck notes, historical sources on the fate of "Black," "African," or "colonial" troops are often difficult to assess because they do not differentiate among these categories of fighters. Colonial soldiers in the French or German archival records could mean soldiers from all French colonies, which could also include "white" colonial troops. While the *tirailleurs senegalais* have always been seen as soldiers from France's West African colony of Senegal, other "Black" soldiers in the service of France came from its colonies in Central Africa, French Somalia, Madagascar, North Africa, and the Caribbean.[31] Despite this conundrum, it is indisputable that one of the primary targets of the German army's persecution of "lower" races of people in the German racial obsession was the contingent of Black African soldiers from West Africa. Scheck argues that German officers "showed more respect toward North Africans" because of their "generally lighter skin color." Some German military officers even entertained the hope that the North African soldiers would defect to the German side in the war.[32]

France had declared war on Germany on 3 September 1939 in reaction to the German invasion of Poland at the beginning of that month. About 63,300 "Africans" from France's West African colonies volunteered to fight alongside French troops. Some of the recruits expected a military career to bring economic and social rewards to them. Others hoped that the sacrifices that came with military service could be compensated by France through the grant of French citizenship to ex-soldiers who demonstrated their loyalty on the battlefield. While the precise number of France's colonial troops who died in defense of France on French soil is impossible to know, the atrocities that these troops suffered at the hands of the German army, because of their identity as Black Africans, have been carefully documented.[33] They were "singled out for particularly harsh treatment" during the war, and between their deployment in war against the Germans in May 1940 and the fall of France in June 1940 when the German army attacked and subsequently occupied much of France and took large numbers of French troops prisoners.[34] The *tirailleurs senegalais* bore the brunt of the German occupation. They were killed in brutal and intentional massacres and in summary executions ordered by officers of the German army. Many African troops, along with the white French officers who commanded them, were brutally murdered in transit and in the camps themselves. Others were starved to death and exposed to inclement winter weather and diseases. The harsh brutality that German soldiers visited upon French troops from Senegal and Black troops from other parts of Africa, fighting under French colors, stemmed from the German disapproval of the recruitment and deployment of Black African troops, by France, in war against Europeans on European soil and, worse still, the liberal French practice of promoting some of their distinguished African soldiers to officer ranks.[35]

German war propaganda portrayed African soldiers as wild and aggressive and as "an inferior race" of people who did not deserve "to do battle with such a civilized race as the Germans."[36] As Scheck notes, "The German hatred and fear of Tirailleurs Senegalais continued after the battle."[37] Their status as prisoners of war did not protect the French troops from West Africa against rampant summary executions and degrading treatment. German soldiers seized or destroyed the military tags of African soldiers, thus preventing their corpses from being properly identified. They also issued special orders forbidding the burial of dead African soldiers.[38] Furthermore, German soldiers and reporters who photographed and filmed Black African soldiers did so in the most degrading manner. Black African POWs "had to perform a strange dance" at the end of these films intended to portray Africans as exotic creatures.[39] The condition of the West African POWs changed "in the summer of 1940." Permanent camps and better rations and treatment were offered in accordance with the Geneva Conventions mandating improved and humane treatment of POWs.[40] In the view of Scheck, this improved situation was politically motivated. The Nazi regime had started to nurture hopes of reclaiming Germany's former colonies in Africa and concluded that continuing such inhumane treatment of West African soldiers could breed anti-German feelings in that part of

Africa after the war. Here, Scheck agrees with Lusane that better treatment of West African prisoners of war must have been based on Germany's interest in reclaiming its colonies in Africa after the end of the war.[41] But Scheck affirms his central thesis that improved conditions did not mean the end of the brutal and degrading treatment of African troops in German-occupied France. In fact, German physicians who were engaged in research on drugs against tropical diseases found captured West African soldiers convenient specimens for medical experiments, while German anthropologists also used them for research.[42] Despite this persistent degrading treatment of captured African soldiers, Scheck does not see any evidence of a "general order" from the Nazi High Command to massacre Black POWs. In fact, the majority of these soldiers were not killed after their capture. Rather, under the deadly circumstances of war in the 1940s, each German officer, under stress, acted on his own, albeit inconsistently, to kill or not to kill African POWs in the service of France.[43]

Robert W. Kesting, a former archivist at the United States Holocaust Memorial Museum, was among the first researchers to broaden the study of the Holocaust by integrating into it the experiences of "Black victims" of the Nazi regime. His research notes on "Blacks" as forgotten victims of the Holocaust examine the experiences of "blacks from Europe, Africa, and the United States" who, like "Jews, Gypsies and others," were oppressed and destroyed by "Adolf Hitler's irrational racial philosophies."[44] Like Lusane and Massaquoi, who wrote after him, Kesting acknowledges that the number of Blacks (Africans and African Americans) who lived in Nazi Germany or in Europe and who fell victim to Nazi racism on the Rhineland, to eugenics in Germany, or, as prisoners of war, to brutality at the hands of Nazi military officers, were "minimal" compared to the losses of life that Jewish victims of the Holocaust suffered. Nevertheless, the "torment and suffering" that Black people endured in Nazi Germany "were no different" from what Jews and other victims of the Nazi state experienced.[45] Kesting bewails the neglect of "the story of blacks in the Holocaust." However, his effort at ameliorating this problem in Holocaust historiography is a preliminary chronicle of only "allegations" of the murder of thousands of "Afro-American and Black African soldiers and airmen" during the Nazi era.[46]

Robert Satloff takes the study of the Holocaust, as it relates to peoples of African descent, away from the story of Afro-Germans, Africans, and African Americans as comparable victims of the Nazi regime in Europe during World War II to the study of Arabs as persecutors and also rescuers of Jews on the African continent. Satloff's *Among the Righteous: Lost Stories from the Holocaust's Long Reach into Arab Lands* is significant in its apt observation that the history of World War II cannot be divorced from "the fate of North African Jewish communities during the war," especially "the stories of Arabs who saved Jews and Arabs who collaborated with Europeans who came to persecute the Jews" of North Africa.[47] Satloff notes that in the course of World War II, the Nazi regime and its collaborators in Vichy France, as well as the Fascist regime in Italy, exported their anti-Jewish policies to France's and Italy's colonial possessions in North Africa. There, they found willing participants in their atrocities against North African Jews among many Arabs in Algeria, Tunisia, Morocco, and Libya.

These local Arab collaborators of the Nazi and Vichy regimes took advantage of the German repression of the Jews of North Africa, after the German defeat of France in May 1940. On the orders of Nazi military officers and sometimes acting in their own interest, many Arabs seized the homes and properties of Jews, pressured "thousands of Jews ... to wear the Star of David," and assisted in the arrest and deportation of local Jews to "more than 100 forced labor camps set up throughout" the North African desert and controlled by the Nazi regime.[48] Jews in Tunisia suffered the worst of these Nazi-ordered atrocities during the six-month German occupation of Tunisia from November 1942 to May 1943. Here, "about 5,000" Jews ended up in "forced labor camps throughout Tunisia," and hundreds of them died if not in similar, then at least related circumstances as Jews who perished in Nazi concentration camps at Auschwitz and Buchenwald in Europe.[49] But, as Satloff notes, "some Arabs" distinguished themselves in their refusal to participate in the European-engineered pogroms of this period in North Africa. These "righteous Arabs" protected their Jewish neighbors, saved their property, and hid them from their persecutors in a remarkable demonstration of human empathy and solidarity.[50]

What Satloff characterizes as "the Holocaust's long reach into Arab lands" underscores one abiding fact of African and Holocaust history that this book seeks to explore in relation to Africa south of the Arab lands: that the history of the Second World War and of African participation in it cannot be written in isolation of the Holocaust. And neither should the Holocaust be studied independently of the African experience of it and reaction to it. Satloff has captured the North African connection to the Holocaust even more persuasively in his argument that:

> [t]he Holocaust was almost exclusively a European ordeal. Both its perpetrators and victims were principally, predominantly, overwhelmingly European.... Europe was the nesting ground for the ideology of hate that brought devastation to the Jewish people.... But, even so, the Holocaust was not solely a European story. From the outset, German plans to persecute and eventually exterminate Jews extended throughout all lands Germany and its allies hoped to conquer, which included a great Arab expanse, extending from Casablanca to Tripoli and onward to Cairo ... home to more than a half-million Jews.[51]

The scarcity of published works on the connection of the non-Arab lands of East and West Africa to the Holocaust may falsely suggest that the people of these regions must have been oblivious to the Nazi regime's other objective in World War II: the annihilation of European Jewry. Given their own historical experience of racial discrimination and European disdain for their religious beliefs and rituals, along with their awareness of what Adolf Hitler and the Nazi party had planned for them and the Jews, it is not unreasonable to suppose that Africans collectively as a racialized and dehumanized group in imperial discourse and relations, would have views about the Nazi annihilation of Europe's Jews. Certainly, like their counterparts in North Africa, the colonized and sovereign peoples of East and West Africa, who also lived with Jews during World War II, saw the Holocaust as significant beyond its European setting. For them, the Holocaust was a gruesome outcome of a way of thinking that also targeted Black Africans. Thus, it attracted more than the empathy of colonized peoples in East and West Africa with the Jews of Europe. The Holocaust gave moral legitimacy to the critique of race and imperialism in colonial Africa. This is an important but missing sub-Saharan African perspective on the Holocaust. This book retrieves that unknown and unexamined West and East African connection to and perspective on the Holocaust. It shifts the discussion from where Massaquoi, Lusane, Scheck, Kesting, and Satloff have located it to events and processes in West and East Africa. It seeks to understand how Africans in these two regions viewed and interpreted the Holocaust in Europe, how they treated the Jews who lived among them, and what human empathy and solidarity they showed to the Jewish victims of Nazi persecution and murder in the course of the Second World War.

It is fair to argue that the absence of African voices and perspectives in Holocaust historiography is no different from the similar absence of Holocaust content in African historiography. Therefore, in its broader historiographical significance, this book bridges that existing gap and brings African and Holocaust historiographies into mutual dialogue over what Africans knew and thought about the Holocaust. Integrating the perspectives of colonial subjects and sovereign peoples in East and West Africa into Holocaust historiography expands and also enriches Africanist historiography on the Second World War. It provides that historiography's necessary but missing fifth theme—an intellectual and diplomatic history of World War II that focuses on the views and ideas that people in Africa expressed about the war in the context of the Holocaust and about the Holocaust as the conceptual and moral lens through which colonial subjects and sovereign people on the continent discussed colonialism, civilization, barbarism, racism, and human rights. This perspective expands Holocaust scholarship by adding to it the "unknown" views on the Holocaust from East and West Africa. Those views highlighted the African empathy toward the Jewish victims of the Holocaust and also exposed its inherent contradictions. African perspectives on the Holocaust, therefore, expand the global geographical reactions to the Holocaust beyond what David S. Wyman and Michael Berenbaum and Abraham J. Peck compiled in their respective edited works.[52]

The most challenging part of any African perspective retrieval task is defining *African* and what constitutes an *African perspective* on the Holocaust. A decade ago, some prominent Africanists including Ali Mazrui, Jideofor Adibe, and Kwesi Prah wrestled with the former conundrum in Adibe's edited anthology *Who Is an African?* These Africanists acknowledged that there are three key components of African identity. One, to be African is to be born in Africa, be black in skin color, or to have ethnic or racial (blood) ties to the continent. Two, to be African is to live within the geographical confine called *Africa* or to reside on its soil. Three, to be African is to have a mental connection to Africa or a "commitment to the cause of Africa," even if one were not born on the continent or had never lived there.[53] For the purpose of this work, *African* means more than a person with an ethnic affiliation with any part of Africa. I use *African* as both an ethnic identity and a locational construct. It is a conceptual tool deployed to examine opinions from the African continent and people associated with Africa in temporary residence outside of the continent. Therefore, by *African perspective* I mean views held or expressed by peoples of African heritage living in Africa as colonial subjects or as sovereign peoples and/or in temporary residence abroad as students and travelers, or serving their sovereign nations abroad as diplomats or relatives of diplomats, and opinions that emanated from the African continent even though those who expressed them were not ethnically African.

By expanding the definition of *African* beyond "heritage" or "descent" to include "location" or "residence" in Africa (with some exceptions), I aim to assemble opinions on the Holocaust from a broader cross-section of "African society" (people who lived in Africa) from 1933 to 1945, not just those who looked "African" according to a racial understanding of African identity. This transracial conceptual framework allows me to see views on the Holocaust in the *West African Pilot*, published and edited in Lagos by Nigerians (ethnically African people) and in the *East African Standard*, published and edited in Nairobi by Indian emigres (ethnically Asian people but nonetheless resident subjects of the British colony of Kenya), as representing African perspectives—views from Africa. There are exceptions to the locational concept of Africans used in this work. For example, the views of British settlers in Kenya, Christian missionaries, and colonial administrators there, as well as their counterparts in the Gold Coast or in Tanganyika, who resided in Africa but who formed part of Britain's colonial administrative structure, are not regarded as the perspectives of "Africans" (colonized or sovereign), which is the focus of this book.

This book is based on qualitative and empirical historical research and methodology. I have used five criteria to select the research focus. One, sovereign countries in West and East Africa that had diplomatic ties with Nazi Germany and whose official archives have diplomatic records outlining official positions on the plight of Jews in Germany from 1933 to 1945. Only Ethiopia (in East Africa) and Liberia (in West Africa) were independent nations in Africa with such ties to Nazi Germany during this period. Two, countries with a Jewish population or whose leaders claimed descent from ancient Israel or historical kinship with Jews. Ethiopia is such a country. Three, sovereign nations and ex-colonies that had a local press controlled by Africans (as I have defined this research concept) and whose newspapers reported on the Nazi persecution of Jews in Europe or published editorial and other commentaries on both. Ethiopia, Uganda, Tanzania, Kenya, Liberia, Nigeria, Sierra Leone, and Ghana (in East and West Africa) meet this criterion. Four, post–World War II sovereign states and ex-colonies that actually sent soldiers to fight in World War II and whose veteran soldiers have shared their memories of the war with scholars and journalists who have written about the African role in that global conflict. Ghana, Nigeria, Sierra Leone, Liberia, and Ethiopia fit this criterion. Five, sovereign nations and ex-colonies that were required by Britain to accept Jewish refugees from Europe and whose leaders, elites, and general public have left traces of their reactions to this colonial order in official memoranda and local newspapers. Ethiopia and the former British colonies of Kenya, Uganda, the Gold Coast (now Ghana) and the trusteeship of Tanganyika (now Tanzania) are examples of such nations. Since it is European Jews, particularly the Jewish victims of the Holocaust, whose fate in the course of the war preoccupied the thoughts of people who lived in these colonies and sovereign nations of West and East Africa, it is on those Jewish victims and survivors of the Holocaust that this book focuses its analytical attention.

Archival materials for this book came from intermittent research in five countries over a period of five years (2009–2014). In the United States, the research library of the United States Holocaust Memorial Museum in Washington, D.C., provided useful primary and secondary sources on the Holocaust. The library of the University of South Florida in Tampa supplied relevant microfilms of major newspapers published in West and East Africa from 1933 to 1945, such as the *West African Pilot, Gold Coast Spectator, Gold Coast Times*, and *Sierra Leone Daily Guardian*. In Britain, the Public Record Office of the British National Archives offered important archival information on communications between British policymakers and colonial administrators in West and East Africa, among other materials. The British Library Newspapers in Colindale supplied useful information on the subject of the book from key newspapers published in West and East Africa during the war years. In Ghana, the Ghana National Archives supplied significant primary sources from colonial records, minutes of legislative and executive council meetings, as well as key local newspapers such as the *Ashanti Pioneer* and the *Gold Coast Spectator*. In Liberia, information from the country's national archives in Monrovia and from secondary and primary sources from the library of the University of Liberia offered insights into the perspectives of that sovereign West African nation. In Ethiopia, information from newspapers and relevant government reports available in the national library in Addis Ababa offered important viewpoints from that sovereign East African nation, although efforts to obtain equally relevant diplomatic sources from the country's Ministry of Foreign Affairs failed.

This book is about how people and governments in West and East Africa received and interpreted information about Nazism, World War II, and the German persecution of the Jewish people in the lead-up to the Holocaust and during the Holocaust itself. It is an intellectual and diplomatic history of World War II and the Holocaust from the perspectives of the colonized subjects of the Gold Coast, Nigeria, Sierra Leone, Kenya, Tanganyika, and Uganda, and the sovereign peoples of Liberia and Ethiopia who wrestled with the larger issues of humanity, racially-inspired violence, self-preservation, and empathy that the war and the Holocaust precipitated.

Retrieving an African perspective on the Holocaust is also writing about African reactions to violence perpetrated by Europeans who had presented themselves, in their justification of colonialism, as superior to and more civilized than their supposedly primitive and barbaric African subjects. Therefore, examining African reactions to the Holocaust in Europe, as a manifestation of European barbarism, is understanding how colonial subjects made moral and analytical sense of this paradox. And even more paradoxical is recovering this aspect of African and Holocaust history from European colonial archives. Thus in drawing primarily upon that archive for this work, I am mindful of the emerging scholarship on the limits of colonial archives as sites for the retrieval of knowledge about the past. Anthropologist Ann Laura Stoler is correct that today the archives "once treated as a means to an end" is no longer regarded as such even by historians. The colonial archive is the embodiment of colonial politics.[54] Scholars who are now "thinking archivally," as historian Kirsten Weld put it, have concluded that colonial archives and those of authoritarian regimes are "documents of exclusion" and "monuments to particular configurations of power."[55] As Weld has noted in her study of the archives of the Guatemalan National Police in the Cold War period, archival thinking requires researchers "to look past the words on a document's page to examine the conditions of that document's production: how it came to exist, what it was used for, what its form reveals and what sorts of state knowledge and action it both reflected and engendered."[56] In short, scholars must place the histories and politics of archives at the heart of their research in order to distinguish between the archives as "sites of knowledge production" and the archives as "sites of knowledge recovery."[57]

What colonial authorities saw fit to reveal about African perceptions and responses to the Holocaust, what they classified as confidential, and what editors of local newspapers also found relevant to print about that subject offer important insights into colonial politics. Not least is how the colonial state stoked anti-Nazi feeling in Africa and portrayed the Holocaust as a distinctively Nazi German act and how colonized people used that information to challenge oppressive colonial ideologies and institutions. If colonial archives are repositories of "documents of exclusion" that reveal some facts and hide others or that reflect perspectives of the elite who had the power and ability to write their views into the historical record, so are local newspapers in the colonial period. Even as supplements to colonial archives, newspapers often reflected the voices of the urban elite to the exclusion of the reactions of people at the margins of colonial society to critical moments in history such as the Holocaust. Of particular relevance here is the absence of the views of African war veterans who, as participants in World War II, may have heard about the Holocaust but who, unlike editors of newspapers, never wrote down their perspectives.

I have made a good effort to include the views of Africa's World War II veterans on the Holocaust in this work. Some of the existing documented interviews with African ex-soldiers reveal the role that the contents of Hitler's

Mein Kampf, and the *Fuehrer's* dehumanization of Africans played in military enlistments in wartime Africa. What is often missing in these interviews are the veterans' awareness of Hitler's similar dehumanization of Jews and the impact that it had on their enlistment decisions. That some African veterans of the war remembered Hitler's anti-African racism but not his anti-Jewish prejudices raises questions about the extent of the ex-servicemen's awareness, during the war period, of the Holocaust and of its various phases, as well as the degree to which colonial authorities and newspaper editors documented the veterans' perspectives. It is therefore safe to argue that the African soldier's access to war news, at the war front, about Hitler's views of Jews and about the Nazi treatment of this segment of Europe's population may not have been the same as the diplomats' and newspaper editors' access to that type of information at the home front. Thus, the limited emphasis in this book on the voices of Africa's World War II veterans on the Holocaust is not an intentional exclusion of important voices but rather an acknowledgment of the difficulty of assembling them at this time and an invitation to future researchers to look for and document those perspectives. In that next phase of research, a key question to be asked is how far down to the village level in East and West Africa did information about the Holocaust reach? Answers to that may reveal another layer of perspective on the Holocaust beyond the African city as the domain of elite opinion. What this book offers, in the interim, is a synthesis of the available perspectives of African soldiers, however limited, and those of Africa's colonial elite whose voices dominate the newspapers and the archival records.

Notes

1. David Killingray (with Martin Plaut), *Fighting for Britain: African Soldiers in the Second World War* (Woodbridge, Suffolk: James Currey, 2010), 8, 46, 58. See also John Nunneley, *Tales from the King's African Rifles: A Last Flourish of Empire* (London: Cassell & Co, 2000), 5, 15; Timothy H. Parsons, *The African Rank and File: Social Implications of Colonial Military Service in the King's African Rifles, 1902–1964* (Portsmouth, NH: Heinemann, 1999), 81, 83.
2. For some of these traditional themes in Africanist historiography on the Second World War, see Andrew Stewart, *The First Victory: The Second World War and the East Africa Campaign* (New Haven, CT: Yale University Press, 2016); Judith A. Byfield and Carolyn A. Brown, *Africa and World War II* (New York: Cambridge University Press, 2015); Killingray and Plaut, *Fighting for Britain*; Raffael Scheck, *Hitler's African Victims: The German Army Massacres of Black French Soldiers in 1940* (Cambridge: Cambridge University Press, 2006); Nancy Ellen Lawler, *Soldiers, Airmen, Spies and Whisperers: The Gold Coast in World War II* (Athens: Ohio University Press, 2002); Nunneley, *Tales from the King's African Rifles*; Parsons, *The African Rank and File*; Myron Echenberg, *Colonial Conscripts: The Tirailleurs Senegalais in French West Africa, 1875–1960* (Portsmouth, NH: Heinemann, 1991); Albert Adu Boahen, *African Perspectives on Colonialism* (Baltimore, MD: Johns Hopkins University Press, 1987).
3. Michael Marrus, *The Holocaust in History* (New York: Meridian Books, 1987), 1. See also Michael Berenbaum and Abraham J. Peck, *The Holocaust and History: The Known, the Unknown, the Disputed and the Reexamined* (Bloomington: Indiana University Press, 1998).
4. Killingray and Plaut, *Fighting for Britain*, 2, 7.
5. Adolf Hitler, *Mein Kampf*, Unexpurgated ed. (Delhi: Jaico Publishing House, 2010).

6 Richard Hull, *Jews and Judaism in African History* (Princeton, NJ: Markus Wiener Publishers, 2009).
7 Louise London, *Whitehall and the Jews, 1933–1948: British Immigration Policy, Jewish Refugees and the Holocaust* (Cambridge: Cambridge University Press, 2000).
8 Hans J. Massaquoi, *Destined to Witness: Growing Up Black in Nazi Germany* (New York: Perennial, 2001); Clarence Lusane, *Hitler's Black Victims: The Historical Experiences of Afro-Germans, European Blacks, Africans, and African Americans in the Nazi Era* (New York: Routledge, 2002); Scheck, *Hitler's African Victims*; Robert Satloff, *Among the Righteous: Lost Stories from the Holocaust's Long Reach into Arab Lands* (New York: Public Affairs, 2006); Robert W. Kesting, "Blacks Under the Swastika: A Research Note," *Journal of Negro History* 83, no. 1 (Winter 1998); "Forgotten Victims: Blacks in the Holocaust," *Journal of Negro History* 77, no. 1 (Winter 1992); David Killingray, "Africans and African Americans in Enemy Hands," in Bob Moore and Kent Fedorowich, eds., *Prisoners of War and Their Captors in World War II* (Oxford: Berg, 1996).
9 Massaquoi, *Destined to Witness*, xi.
10 Ibid.
11 Ibid., xii.
12 Ibid.
13 Ibid., 9.
14 Ibid., xvi.
15 Ibid., 21.
16 Ibid., xvi.
17 Ibid., 63, 112.
18 Ibid., 59.
19 Ibid., 53–54, 197.
20 Lusane, *Hitler's Black Victims*, 5–6, 15.
21 Ibid., 13.
22 Ibid., 6.
23 Ibid., 16, 98, 101, 110.
24 Shelley Baranowski, *Nazi Empire: German Colonialism and Imperialism from Bismarck to Hitler* (Cambridge: Cambridge University Press, 2011), 28–34; Helmuth Stoecker, ed., *German Imperialism in Africa: From the Beginnings Until the Second World War* (London: C. Hurst & Co, 1986), 14, 18, 27, 29–38; D.E.K. Amenumey, "German Administration in Southern Togo," *Journal of African History* 10, no. 4 (1969): 623, 639.
25 Bairu Tafla, *Ethiopia and Germany: Cultural, Political, and Economic Relations, 1871–1936* (Wiesbaden: Franz Steiner Verlag, 1981); Massaquoi, *Destined to Witness*.
26 Lusane, *Hitler's Black Victims*, 54–55, 71.
27 Ibid., 164–165.
28 Ibid., 164.
29 Ibid., 172–173.
30 Scheck, *Hitler's African Victims*, 50.
31 Ibid., 59.
32 Ibid., 9–10.
33 Ibid., 7, 53. See also Echenberg, *Colonial Conscripts*, 96–97; Moore and Fedorowich, *Prisoners of War and Their Captors*.
34 Scheck, *Hitler's African Victims*, 60. See also Killingray, "Africans and African Americans in Enemy Hands," 182, 186–187.
35 Echenberg, *Colonial Conscripts*, 19–20, 94.
36 Scheck, *Hitler's African Victims*, 30–31.
37 Ibid., 41.
38 Ibid., 36, 44.
39 Ibid., 45.
40 Ibid., 46.
41 Ibid., 48–49; Lusane, *Hitler's Black Victims*, 99.

42 Scheck, *Hitler's African Victims*, 51.
43 Ibid., 118, 121.
44 Kesting, "Forgotten Victims," 30.
45 Ibid.
46 Ibid., 34.
47 Satloff, *Among the Righteous*, 24.
48 Ibid., 19, 45.
49 Ibid., 18, 50. For further information about Italian atrocities against Jews in the Italian colony of Libya during World War II, see Patrick Bernhard, "Behind the Battle Lines: Italian Atrocities and the Persecution of Arabs, Berbers, and Jews in North Africa During World War II," *Holocaust and Genocide Studies* 26, no. 3 (Winter 2012): 425–438.
50 Satloff, *Among the Righteous*, 99, 101–102, 105, 124, 132.
51 Ibid., 18. Shelley Baranowski makes a similar point that the Nazi genocide against Jews was "not ... limited to the Jews of Europe" but extended also to Jews in "France's North African colonies." See *Nazi Empire*, 336.
52 David S. Wyman, ed. [Foreword by Charles H. Rosenzveig], *The World Reacts to the Holocaust* (Baltimore, MD: Johns Hopkins University Press, 1996); Berenbaum and Peck, *The Holocaust and History*.
53 Jideofor Adibe, ed., *Who Is an African? Identity, Citizenship and the Making of the Africa-Nation* (London: Adonis and Abbey Publishers, 2009), xi, xv, 16–17, 20, 23, 58, 59–60.
54 Ann Laura Stoler, "Colonial Archives and the Arts of Governance," *Archival Science* 2 (2002): 92.
55 Ibid., 96.
56 Kirsten Weld, *Paper Cadavers: The Archives of Dictatorship in Guatemala* (Durham, NC: Duke University Press, 2014), 13.
57 Ibid., 15.

1 Jews in East and West Africa before the Holocaust

Many Africanists may be aware of the legend of Solomon and the Queen of Sheba and its connection to the history of "Ethiopian Jews" in East Africa. In its simplified version, this is a contested story of an "Ethiopian queen" or "princess" who is said to have visited King Solomon of Israel and ended up having a child with the Jewish monarch. Later in his adulthood, the child, Menelik, steals the Ark of the Covenant and other relics of Judaism and flees with them, together with a retinue of loyalists from Jerusalem, to Ethiopia. Hence, the presence of Jews in Ethiopia.[1] Besides this story of Ethiopia's indigenous Jewish population, the documented history of Jews in Africa, from antiquity to the outbreak of World War II, is primarily the story of Jews and Jewish life in North Africa and South Africa. However, there are isolated but nonetheless notable studies of Jewish life and influence in Africa south of the Sahara desert and north of the Limpopo river. This chapter examines the historical evidence for the presence of Jews in this subregion of Africa, particularly the western and eastern parts of it before the Holocaust. It traces, from a comparative perspective, the origins of Jewish settlements in West and East Africa, the activities Jews engaged in, the status they maintained, the types of interactions they had with the indigenous groups they lived with, and how these groups viewed and treated their Jewish neighbors. Examination of these histories and interactions is necessary to assess the dynamics of African–Jewish relations before the Second World War and how they affected African perspectives on the Holocaust in the two regions.

Evidence of the Jewish presence and influence in West Africa has been established in some notable social science studies. Richard Hull's *Jews and Judaism in African History* is one of the most comprehensive of such studies of Jewish life in West Africa. Hull settles on heritage, religion, tradition, and legend for answers to the perennial question of "[w]ho precisely is a Jew and what constitutes Jewishness" and even Judaism. He considers "Jews" as people and groups whose lineage or ancestry connected them directly to the "Hebrews and the Israelites" of the Old Testament and who practice Judaism as a religion. In this mode of establishing Jewish identity, people in Ethiopia, in East Africa whose lineage may not have originated in Biblical Israel but whose legends linked them to it and who practice a very ancient form of Judaism are Jews. And so are those who are Jewish, by descent or lineage, but do not practice any form of

Judaism because they chose to be secular or converted to other religious faiths, voluntarily or by coercion, at some point in their lives.[2] William F.S. Miles has asked a similar question about how to define a Jew in his book *Jews of Nigeria: An Afro-Judaic Odyssey*. He offers what he calls the "longstanding traditional answer" that "a Jew is one born of a Jewish mother or one who has converted [to Judaism] through the Orthodox Jewish rabbinate."[3] Beside Hull's historical work and Miles's from a political science perspective, Labelle Prussin's study, from the prism of art history, is notable in its confident assertion that there is a "Judaic heritage in West Africa," although that historical fact is rarely acknowledged by Africanists.[4] Although this chapter focuses on the presence of Jews, as Hull and Miles have defined them, in West and East Africa, it cannot overlook the documented history of Jews in North and South Africa, the regions of Africa where their story has often been told. A summary of that history is intended here as a backdrop to the main focus of this chapter.

North Africa

Greek, Roman, Arab, and European written records and other historical sources affirm that Jews and Judaism have been an integral part of the history of North Africa for "more than three thousand years."[5] In fact, Judaism was the first monotheistic religion to take root on the African continent before Christianity and Islam. Jews have lived in Egypt, Morocco, Tunisia, and Algeria under various accommodating and hostile indigenous and foreign governments since 332 BCE. These include Greek and Roman rulers of North Africa (ca. 332–146 BCE), various Arab and Muslim dynasties (ca. 640–1550), Ottoman Turkish rule (1550–1830), and French and British colonial regimes prior to the outbreak of World War II (1830–1939). Under the Greek ruler Ptolemy I (305–283 BCE), "a huge influx of Jews into Egypt" made that North African colony of the Greeks one of the major centers of Jewish settlement in the ancient world.[6] By the time the Romans annexed Egypt in 30 BCE, about one million Jews lived in Egypt, and about 100,000 of them resided in the city of Alexandria. This city that Alexander and his Greek army built in North Africa accommodated "the largest Jewish community in the ancient world between the third century BCE and the close of the first century CE."[7] It was under the Romans that the fortunes of Jews in foreign-controlled Egypt changed. Roman preference for polytheism and obedience to the state marked the monotheistic religion of Judaism and the Jews who practiced it as a threat to the Roman empire. This ideological position exposed Alexandria's Jews to "one of the earliest anti-Jewish pogroms in history."[8] After the introduction of Christianity into Egypt from Jerusalem in about 41 CE (the beginning of the reign of Emperor Claudius), and the rejection of this new faith by many of Egypt's Jews, Roman persecution of Jews in this part of North Africa found its unyielding allies among Christians. To retain their own distinctive faith and survive this Roman and Christian onslaught, Jews in Egypt built strong, but isolated communities. In the west of Egypt and along the coasts of North Africa, Jews prospered economically in their communities as minters of gold coins from gold possibly obtained from "the Upper Senegal River Valley of West Africa."[9] It was their economic success, and self-preservationist consciousness that also exposed the Jews of North Africa to various stereotypes as "cunning, avaricious, secretive, exclusivist, and rejecters of Christianity."[10]

Under Roman rule, the lives of Jews in Egypt worsened. They became even more precarious after the failed Jewish war of liberation against the Romans from 66 to 70 CE which led to the Roman destruction of the second temple in Jerusalem in 70 CE, the imposition of a special tax, and other strict Roman regulations on all Jews in the Roman empire. The persecution of Jews by the Romans and their Christian allies in Egypt also marked the beginning of the global dispersion of Jews and the global spread of Judaism.[11] Increased Roman persecution of Jews under Emperor Trajan (98–117 CE) forced many Jews to flee from the west of Egypt (Cyrenaica) into what is today Morocco in North Africa and Mauritania in West Africa. It was after this period of Jewish settlement among the Berbers of North Africa that conversion of some Berber populations to Judaism must have occurred, if it actually happened at all.[12] Arguably, writing the history of North African Jewry in antiquity (Greek and Roman periods), in the absence of reliable historical sources, is, as H.Z. Hirschberg has aptly put it, a task "similar to the restoration of a mosaic from which many stones are missing."[13]

The second most significant challenge to Jews and Judaism in Africa north of the Sahara desert came during the Muslim Arab penetration into this region in the seventh and eighth centuries CE. The conquest of North Africa by Arab armies begun with the invasion of Egypt, in 639 CE. Within five centuries, Islam had become the dominant religion in North Africa. Between the Arab conquest of the region and the beginning of the seventeenth century, Arab–Jewish relations took many twists and turns. Initially, the Arabs depended on Jews and Coptic Christians to administer Egypt. But as the Arab population grew in the course of the eighth century, reliance on Jews and Christians as administrators became unnecessary.[14]

Events outside of Africa also influenced the emigration of large numbers of Jews into Islamic North Africa. Pogroms in Seville and Andalusia in Christian Spain in 1391, sparked by virulent anti-Semitism, took the lives of close to 50,000 Jews. To survive state-sanctioned and religiously inspired anti-Jewish sentiments in Spain, many Jews converted to Christianity. In the late fifteenth century, Spain had a large population of *conversos*, or converted Jews, and Jews of mixed Judeo-Christian heritage. In 1492 and 1496, when Christian Spain and Portugal ordered all Jews within their domains to convert to Catholicism or leave the kingdoms, large numbers of converted and practicing Jews fled these parts of Europe for the relative comfort of now Arab-controlled North Africa, particularly in Morocco. As is typical of immigrant and diasporic communities, migrating Jews brought with them necessary skills as traders, goldsmiths, and carriers of other culture.[15]

Jews who came to Africa, aside from those who were born on the continent to their migrant parents, came from Judaism's two contending traditions: Sephardi and Ashkenazi. Sephardi Jews trace their lineage to Spain and North Africa, particularly Egypt and Morocco. They follow the traditions of Jews who lived in the Iberian Peninsula, many of whom were expelled from the peninsula in the 1492 royal decree. Sephardi Jews spoke Ladino, a Judeo-Spanish and Judeo-Arabic dialect. Ashkenazi Jews, on the other hand, trace their ancestry to Germany, Hungary, Poland, Belarus, and other East European areas such as Lithuania and the former Baltic States. They spoke Yiddish and German, sometimes Italian and Greek, and also Russian.[16]

Jews who arrived in Morocco, in their thousands, from Spain, were mainly Sephardi Jews. In the course of time, they "played important roles in the political and economic life" of the sultanate of Morocco. Some of them managed the finances of the Moroccan city of Fez, the royal mint, and made Fez the center of the production of Hebrew manuscripts. These "Sephardic exiles," as Morocco's prominent commercial diasporic group, influenced the "culture and architecture" of the Moroccan city of Fez, transforming it in the early fifteenth century into a replica of a Spanish city. The early sixteenth century Muslim traveler Leo Africanus found Jews working and living as masons, weavers, goldsmiths, and blacksmiths in Fez.[17] Historical accounts of thriving communities of Jews in Morocco should not obscure the fact that the lives of Jews in Arab-controlled North Africa were no easier than the lives of Jews in Christian Spain and Portugal. In the century before Africanus's visit to Morocco, the prosperity and hard work of Jewish traders and artisans had begun to rile many conservative Muslims in rural Morocco. In 1437, "some Jews were hacked to death in Fez" before the Sultan of Fez intervened to stop any further annihilation of the city's Jewish population.[18] There were "good reasons" for Arab and Muslim monarchs to protect Jews because they depended on them as a source of revenue through the many taxes they imposed on non-Muslims. Jews were also the main producers of the firearms of the royal Moroccan armory. This mutual economic dependence meant that the Islamic trading states of North Africa such as Morocco would have collapsed without Jewish commercial and technical skills. To avoid paying the taxes that Arab rulers in North Africa imposed on non-Muslims, many affluent Jews in the region converted to Islam. However, when some Arab monarchs in the region tried to force Jews to embrace Islam or face eviction and persecution, many Jews fled Morocco in the mid-eleventh century. Some settled in the "market communities of black-ruled western Sudan" in the vast stretches of the African savannah between what is today Mauritania and Senegal in West Africa.[19]

The lives of Jews in North Africa improved significantly in the sixteenth century when much of this region, and parts of Southeastern Europe, came under the authority of the Ottoman Turks. Under Ottoman rule, Egypt, a major center of anti-Jewish persecution in North Africa, became a tolerant and welcoming place for Jews. Political pragmatism and economic expedience explain these cordial relations between Jews and the new Muslim authorities in North Africa. The technical and financial skills of Jews were so essential to the political economy of Ottoman North Africa that by the beginning of the seventeenth century, Jews had become "indispensable" to the functioning of this region in particular and of the expansive Ottoman empire in general.[20] Ottoman Turkish dynasties that governed the region depended on Jews as "administrators, custom officials, tax collectors, treasurers, commercial brokers, physicians, and diplomats." As diplomats to and people with deep ties with European countries, North African Jews served as envoys and "intermediaries between European Christian commercial interests and the ruling political and commercial elite of the various Mediterranean emirates and regencies."[21] As Jonathan Israel has also observed, Sephardi Jews of the Ottoman empire became the cultural bridge between the Ottoman Near East and the Christian West.[22] Yet despite their high status and role in the economy and diplomacy of Ottoman Egypt, most of the "high-ranking Jews," as Hull notes, lived in "ghettoes" that were "socially and culturally separated from Muslim society." As vital as they were to the functioning of Ottoman Egypt in terms of the responsibilities that their Muslim patrons entrusted to them, Jews were, in person and position, both "insiders and outsiders, visible and invisible, influential and insecure."[23] In short, Jews were tolerated but not necessarily integrated or assimilated into Ottoman North African society at this time.

Several things explain this precarious and ambiguous existence. Sheer envy of Jews as able competitors in the economies of Muslim and Christian monarchies that eschewed usury and commerce may be one explanation. But the types of communities Jews built and the nature of their interactions with their host societies cannot be overlooked. Since the fourteenth century, the majority of Jews in Africa outside of Ethiopia and South Africa were Sephardi Jews noted for their uncompromising monotheistic beliefs and resistance to the kinds of acculturation and social integration that they believed could compromise their strict religious observances. It is this desire for distinctiveness among Sephardi Jews that often invited resentment from their non-Jewish neighbors and made them "easy targets for negative stereotyping."[24] Perhaps, more important, the reality of Ottoman Turkish rule in North Africa also accounts for the precarious lives that Jews lived in this region. Under Ottoman rule, the rulers of Egypt, Tunisia, Algeria, and Morocco were nominal rulers who held power at the pleasure of their Ottoman overlords in Istanbul. The rights and obligations of Jews and of all non-Muslims groups in Ottoman North Africa were dictated by Islamic law and custom. As *dhimmis* (protected non-Muslims), Jews were subject to a special poll tax. They were also required by Islamic law and custom to live in "segregated quarters" and wear distinctive clothing that identified them as Jews. As Hull notes, "[O]nly a tiny minority [of Jews and non-Muslims] were given permission to own land."[25] Thus, most Jews were barred from the occupations that medieval societies held in high esteem and also regarded as the most honest of all labor: agriculture (feeding society through the sweat of the brow) and military service (the honor of protecting the state). Amid these humiliating restrictions, Jews in North Africa had some "rights and protections" that their overlords had to honor. They were to be protected from physical harm and dispossession of their property, although this could not always be guaranteed. They were free to practice their religion and answer to their own rabbis and other leaders of their faith but also free to convert to Islam, although reconversion to Judaism carried with it the criminal charge of apostasy. As long as Jews and Muslims lived within these restrictive and humiliating boundaries imposed by Islam, they coexisted peacefully. Islamic-prescribed protections for the subjects of Muslim monarchs in North Africa also kept anti-Semitism from religious demagogues under control. There were occasional pogroms and persistent discrimination that created tension in this relationship, but for the most part Muslims and Jews lived in guarded peace. That served as the context of Muslim-Jewish interactions in North Africa from the seventeenth century until the mid-twentieth century.[26]

From the seventeenth to the mid-twentieth centuries, Morocco, a major terminus of trade between Europe and North Africa and the Mediterranean world, had the largest number of Jews in North Africa. Only a few of them were shopkeepers and petty traders. The majority of Jews in the Sultanate of Morocco were poor and illiterate and survived on such poorly rewarded occupations as weavers, tailors, cobblers, tanners, butchers, and artisans. Morocco's Jewish artisans were, however, master producers of a wide range of blade weapons that served the needs of the royal courts and militaries in the Muslim world. As part of North Africa's impoverished groups, the majority of Jews were "ill-treated, ridiculed and held in contempt by their Muslim patrons."[27] The few prominent Jewish merchants in Morocco controlled much of the sultanate's trade with Western Europe. Until 1680, Moroccan Jews and their Sephardi coreligionists in the Netherlands carried on a "fruitful trade" in cloth, copper, and gold, among other commodities.[28]

Morocco's preeminence as a major trading city declined at the beginning of the nineteenth century as European traders looked eastwards toward Algiers and Egypt for new commercial opportunities. The French conquest of nearby Algeria in 1830 and France's ambitious building of the Suez canal to connect the Mediterranean and Red seas in 1869, "diverted much of the Mediterranean trade toward Egypt." By the 1880s Europe's "scramble" for colonial influence in Africa was gathering rapid pace. British interest in cotton in Egypt and French control of the Suez, and competition between the two imperial powers for a new kind of trade in industrial raw materials, made the lucrative trans-Saharan trade that Morocco had controlled as a transit area obsolete. Railways and trains were gradually replacing camel caravans as conveyors of trade goods. Morocco, Egypt, Algeria, and Tunisia fell victim to the politics of the great powers: Britain, France, and Germany, in the early twentieth century.[29] The building of the Suez Canal and the coming of the French and British to Morocco and Egypt, shaped the fortunes of North African Jews in positive and negative ways. These developments opened up economic and social opportunities that Jews welcomed and by doing so became identified with colonial rule and the Europeans as people of European descent themselves. Antisemitism in North Africa intensified in tandem with local opposition to European-led colonialism.

Richard Hull has noted that "[c]olonial policies in French Morocco largely benefitted the local Jewish communities."[30] The French abolished the humiliating residential restrictions that Muslim clerics and chieftains had imposed on Jews. Jews who could afford it now had the freedom to live outside their restricted quarters known as the *mellahs*. The French also opened all occupations to anyone. The replacement of Arabic with Spanish and French in Morocco and the introduction of Western secular legal systems now brought Morocco within the Western cultural orbit. Colonialism created a wedge between Jews who were favored by the French because of their Western education and technical and financial acumen and the Muslims who "remained in a kind of traditional cocoon."[31] Most urban Jews welcomed French colonial influence in Morocco, from 1912 until Morocco became independent in 1956, as their coreligionists had done in Egypt with regard to British colonial influence. Jews in urban areas who could speak French and other European languages "identified . . . too closely with colonial hegemons."[32] This was typical of the reactions of people throughout colonial Africa who had the language and occupational skills to exploit the unprecedented economic and social advantages that colonialism brought.[33] Many young Jews moved to the new and Westernized cities such as Casablanca and Rabat. Because Jews in colonial Morocco identified with the French and became Westernized in their cultural habits (clothing, job preferences, education, and secularism), their relations with the local Islamic population deteriorated in the course of the twentieth century.[34] As the century progressed, Morocco attracted more Jews from France. Many of them settled in the posh European quarters. By the time World War II broke out and by June 1940 when France fell to Nazi Germany and Morocco became part of the anti-Semitic Vichy regime, Morocco's Jewish population exceeded 190,000. The Vichy regime imposed many anti-Semitic laws in a Morocco that was growing deeply anticolonial and intensely anti-Jewish. For the first time in Morocco's history, "government encouraged local Muslims to harass Jewish neighborhoods and businesses." Jews in Algeria and Tunisia suffered similar treatment at the hands of the Nazi-backed Vichy government.[35]

The situation was different in Egypt, a province of the Ottoman Turkish Empire since the sixteenth century. The Ottoman Islamic regime had eased restrictions on Jews in Egypt, allowing them to move into many occupations. Ottoman accommodation of Jews in Egypt served as the forerunner to the significant transformations of Jewish life in Egypt under the British at the beginning of the nineteenth century. In 1801, the British expelled the French from Egypt where they had held control since their invasion of that Ottoman province in 1798, possibly in reaction to fears of anticipated French sabotage of British commercial interests in India and Central Asia.[36] The construction of the Suez canal made Egypt very attractive to Jews throughout Europe. The canal opened opportunities for employment and investment in cotton production and export, as well as textile and sugar refining. Ashkenazi Jews from France, Poland, Greece, Russia, Italy, and Germany came to Egypt. They were joined by new waves of Sephardi Jewish immigrants from Syria and Lebanon. By the end of 1880, Jews found themselves in every major occupation in Egypt.[37] They welcomed the British occupation of Egypt in 1882 and the seizure of the Suez canal as Jews in Morocco had responded to the French takeover of Morocco. In appreciation of their support, the British granted Jews in Egypt "legal equality with the rest of the population." In the subsequent decades and until Britain granted Egypt nominal independence in 1922, most Jews in Egypt prospered and became prominent in such professions as law, medicine, accountancy, finance, and urban real estate. Jewish immigration to Egypt also rose. By the end of the First World War (1914–1918), about 60,000 Jews lived in Egypt, a number that obviously included Jews who were born in North Africa to parents and generations of Jews who had emigrated there. This represented a sharp demographic rise from 25,000 Jews in 1897. In the mid-1930s, when the Egyptian economy declined and unemployment rose as a result of the global depression of this period, xenophobia intensified. As Egypt's main urban landlords and owners of large departmental stores and factories in the cities, wealthy Jews became the targets of discontent. Prior to the outbreak of World War II, anti-Semitism resurfaced in violent anti-Jewish street demonstrations. Rising anti-Semitism in Egypt in the war years led to the gradual departure of many Jews from Egypt. Some of them ended up in West Africa.[38]

South Africa

The history of Jews in Egypt and Morocco and in North Africa is similar to that of Jews in South Africa in Southern Africa, in one distinctive respect. Jews arrived in North and South Africa as "refugees" or "migrants" fleeing various forms of religious persecution and economic discrimination in Europe. There are scholars who also contend that Southern Africa as a region has had its own indigenous Jews (the Lemba) similar to East Africa's Ethiopian Jews long before any European Jews arrived in the region. But even the scholars who see the Lemba as the Black Jews of Southern Africa concede that, like the more well-known Ashkenazi Jews from East Europe who migrated to South Africa in the nineteenth century, the Lemba were also migrants who came to the border regions of Zimbabwe and South Africa from the Arabian Peninsula in earlier centuries.[39] North Africa's migrant Jews were predominantly Sephardi Jews who arrived in incremental waves of migration from Portugal and Spain from the fifteenth century onward. South Africa's Jews were mainly Ashkenazi Jews who came to the Dutch- and later British-controlled settler colony of South Africa initially from Holland and Britain and then later from East Europe in significant numbers at the turn of the nineteenth century, and from Germany, in relatively smaller numbers, following the rise of Adolf Hitler and the Nazi state in the 1930s. Compared to the history of Jews in North Africa, Jews in South Africa lived in relative peace.

Jews were among the earliest European explorers and traders who visited the southern tip of Africa as far back as the late fifteenth century.[40] However, it was not until 1652, when the Amsterdam-based Dutch East Indian Company established a provisioning station at Table Bay (today's Cape Town) that a small number of Jews began to settle in this part of Africa. By 1850, Jewish families from Germany and Holland could be found in the early white settlements at Table Bay as retail shopkeepers, small creditors, or producers and retailers of household goods and agricultural implements. The number of Jews in the emerging settler colony prior to the 1880s, was, however, "fewer than four thousand."[41] The bulk of Jewish migrants especially from Lithuania arrived in South Africa "between the 1880s and the introduction of restrictive [immigration] legislation in 1930."[42] At this period, the entire southern Africa region experienced "unprecedented waves of new immigrants almost entirely Yiddish-speaking Ashkenazics from eastern Europe" particularly from Russian Poland, southwest Russia, and the Baltic Lithuanian provinces. These Jewish immigrants were "desperately poor peasant refugees" fleeing "a massive Czarist pogrom."[43] In the course of the twentieth century and as their numbers grew, Jews became a major force in the South African economy. From nearly 4,000 in 1880, the number of Jews rose to 50,000 in 1911 in what was then the Union of South Africa, constituting about 3.7 percent of the entire White population in the settler colony.[44] The persecution of Jews in Nazi Germany through deprivation of citizenship and destruction and confiscation of their property had intensified the pressure on Jews to leave Germany. Between 1933 and 1936 "more than six thousand German Jews immigrated to South Africa" with the largest number of Jewish immigrants arriving in 1936. On the eve of World War II, South Africa's Jewish population was about 90,000 constituting about "five percent of the total white population." Of this number about "46,697" were Jews born in South Africa of European parents.[45]

As German Jews entered South Africa in very large numbers "between 1934 and 1936," a Nazi-type anti-Jewish attitude emerged in South African politics.[46] Between the mid-nineteenth century and the beginning of the twentieth, Jews in South Africa enjoyed acceptance and respect in the Dutch Afrikaner settler community as "fellow believers in the Old Testament." However, in the course of the twentieth century White Afrikaners in the Union of South Africa began to see Jews as part of a sinister network of international finance.[47] Although this view of Jews had actually originated from Europe, it gained ground in South Africa because Jewish mining magnates were a prominent feature of South African settler society. Jews continued to enjoy full rights, and some were elected to the first Union parliament. Nonetheless, most Jews were accused of illicit dealings in the diamond trade, and in many towns they were perceived by the state and larger segments of White Afrikaner society as dishonest and exploitative. Many White farmers blamed the disruption of agrarian life and the insecurities of land ownership on the incoming Jews. As Milton Shain has observed, "these hapless victims of czarist oppression and discrimination [in East Europe] soon became the recipients of vicious class and race prejudice [in South Africa]."[48]

The growing Jewish community in South Africa considered itself and was perceived by groups among whom they lived as "a distinct group" within an emerging Protestant (Calvinist) Christian community of "white" and "European" settlers.[49] Indeed, Jews were distinct in their occupational and housing preferences in the South African community of white landowners and farmers. Unlike some of the Sephardi Jews of North Africa, some of South Africa's Ashkenazi Jews were educated-middle-class merchants and artisans from England and Germany. Therefore, the Dutch Afrikaner settler farming community associated this distinct group of immigrant Jews with hegemonic English culture, and saw them as a threat to Afrikaner rural values.[50]

The history of Jews in South Africa (and also in parts of East Africa) highlights a paradox often overlooked. In Africa, there is often the tendency to lump Jews in the same category of "white Europeans." But in reality the Jews of South Africa, perhaps by their occupations and origins of migration, were themselves the targets of the attitudes and prejudices of the Afrikaner Dutch European farming and protestant settler community.[51] In Kenya, in East Africa, Jews were also the target of the patrician and aristocratic attitudes of the British European settler population of that British colony. The growing number of Jews in South Africa, their visibility and success in business, and the intense envy and resentment that they attracted as economic competitors to poor Afrikaners, alarmed the Afrikaner government. Negative images of Jews intensified after 1936 when about 3,614 German Jews arrived in South Africa as refugees fleeing Nazi persecution.[52] Their arrival stirred up unprecedented anti-Jewish feeling mainly from the National Party, the opposition party to the ruling United Party. Shirli Gilbert has argued that the arrival of Jewish refugees from Nazi Germany raised the tempo of anti-Semitism among some of South Africa's influential Afrikaner politicians and intellectuals who opposed the ruling National Party in South Africa. Some of these Afrikaner intellectuals had studied in Germany and had "direct contact with Nazi organizations and in some cases with high-ranking Nazi leaders."[53] To contain the new tide of German Jewish immigration to South Africa and thus mollify its political opponents, the ruling party in South Africa passed the Aliens Act in 1937.[54] The number of Jews arriving from Germany declined "dramatically to 238 in less than a year" as the ruling party tied immigration to the "potential assimilability and employability," as well as the "good character" of prospective immigrants, to be determined by an autonomous immigration Selection Board.[55]

Ethiopian Jewry

Some scholars have long held the view that the most persuasive evidence of Jewish presence in Africa south of the Sahara desert and north of the Limpopo river is about the life and fortunes of Ethiopian Jews in East Africa. However, the origins of this group of Africa's famous "indigenous Jews" have always been mired in a controversial legend of seduction and theft (the Sheba-Solomon love story and Ethiopia as the presumed final destination of the stolen Ark of the

Covenant). In the context of African history, the story of Ethiopia's Jews has also been the probable story of migrants (in this case Jews) who came to Africa from outside the continent or a group of indigenous people who adopted Judaism as a way of life. There is a lingering controversy over whether Ethiopia's Jews are authentic descendants of the ancient Hebrews or simply an indigenous people in Christian Ethiopia who continue to hold on to some Old Testament practices.[56] As Ethiopian sociologist Abebe Zegeye has acknowledged, there are multiple versions of the origin legend of the Ethiopian Jews. They include some that link the Ethiopian Jews to Jewish migrants who entered Ethiopia from "the Arabian peninsula" in what is today Yemen in the "first and second centuries CE" and others that tie them to Greek or Egyptian Jews who came to settle in the northwestern parts of Ethiopia from Egypt in "the mid-third century BCE" or indigenous Agau groups who "resisted conversion to Christianity" in the Christian kingdom.[57] Regardless of their origins, it is undeniable that at some point in Ethiopia's long history, a segment of the kingdom's population adopted an ancient version of Judaism or claimed descent from one of the presumed lost tribes of ancient Israel. Richard Hull regards the "Ethiopian Jews" (sometimes called *falasha* or *beta Israel*) as arguably "one of the oldest diasporic communities in the world" and certainly the "largest and most enduring Jewish community in East and Central Africa."[58]

Some scholars and writers now put the Ethiopian Jews at the "center of Ethiopian history" rather than at the "periphery," which induces the temptation to seek external origins for them.[59] At best, the origins of Ethiopia's Jews, according to Steven Kaplan, "must be understood as the product of processes that took place in the region around Lake Tana between the fourteenth and sixteenth centuries."[60] Undoubtedly, the rise of the Amhara emperors, who established what is often called the Solomonic dynasty in the thirteenth century, put "unprecedented pressure" on large numbers of indigenous groups in the Lake Tana region of Ethiopia. In subsequent centuries, many of these groups, including those we now refer to as Ethiopian Jews or Beta Israel [House of Israel], lost their land and sought survival alliances with "the dominant [Amhara] Christian landholders" as tenant farmers. Others like the Beta Israel left the Lake Tana region for "peripheral areas where competition for land was limited" to eke out a living through pottery making, metalworking, and cotton weaving. Nevertheless, it is what they did for survival as potters, weavers, and blacksmiths in a predominantly agricultural society that exposed the Ethiopian Jews to local suspicion and even demonization. They lived, as Dena Freeman has argued, as a stigmatized group at the margins of Christian Ethiopian society. Many Ethiopians referred to the Ethiopian Jews as *falasha*, a derogatory word meaning an exile or a stranger. Some called them "the hyena people" or *buda* (people with the evil eye). As Ethiopian historian Teshale Tibebu has also noted, Ethiopia's indigenous "Jews" experienced "a religious [rather] than an occupational segregation" in the East African Christian kingdom.[61] Nonetheless, Ethiopia's Jews shared with their coreligionists in Islamic North Africa and in Christian Europe the same social prejudices that many associated with the religious beliefs and practices of Jews if not their economic occupation.

Beyond Ethiopia

Other scholars "believe" that Jews settled in West Africa also from Egypt at the pinnacle of the power of the ancient West African kingdoms of Ghana, Mali, and Songhai (ca. 900–1591). According to this belief, Songhai, for instance, had "several powerful Jewish families" until Askia Mohammed's decree of 1492 mandating the conversion of all Jews in Songhai to Islam drove many Jews out of this West African kingdom.[62] Other claims about the presence of Jews in West Africa have been made from allusions to cultural similarities between particular Old Testament Jewish practices and specific West African customs, practices, and beliefs. These cultural similarities, some scholars argue, constitute the evidence of the Jewish ancestry of some West African groups or of some direct contact between peoples of this region and resident or itinerant Jewish communities.[63] The most controversial of these claims appear in Joseph J. Williams's book published in 1930 and summarized lucidly in K.A. Dickson's article "Hebrewisms of West Africa." Williams had sought to establish evidence of Jewish presence, settlement, and activity in West Africa by documenting the similarities of some Old Testament Jewish beliefs and rituals to traditions and practices—such as circumcision, the preparation of ritual food with unleavened bread, respect for elders, primacy of the mother in the concept of family and descent, naming ceremonies for newborn children, and the holding of feasts and festivals on particular days of the month or year—among West African groups such as the Akans of Ghana and the Yoruba and Igbo of Nigeria.[64] Williams's and other claims of a Jewish heritage in sub-Saharan Africa have come under critical scrutiny in the work of Aomar Boum. Boum contends that "with the exception of Ethiopia," the only place in Africa where convincing evidence exists of "long established Jewish communities with deep cultural and religious roots" is among the "oases above the Sahel." According to Boum, Jews, in their status as "merchant strangers" in African history, needed a particular network of patronage and support rooted in specific religious, political, and cultural arrangements to survive, and the historical evidence supporting the existence of such arrangements in West Africa is so negligible as to rule out any possibility that Jews moved from North Africa, where these support networks from Muslim patrons existed, to the southern shores of the Sahara where they did not.[65] Boum therefore attributes the claims of some groups of people in Uganda in East Africa and in Nigeria and Ghana in Western Africa (indeed outside of Ethiopia and North Africa) to Jewish or Israelite ancestry to "contemporary identity politics" and its "invented ... memories of belonging." This "new social and political reality" in sub-Saharan Africa, as Aomar Boum controversially calls it, includes interest in Israeli citizenship and its associated hope of migrating to Israel or the United States to avoid economic discomforts.[66]

While there is some disagreement among scholars over how and when Jews arrived in Africa, south of the Saharan desert and in Ethiopia, there is hardly any dispute over when Jews arrived and settled in Kenya. Britain declared a protectorate over Kenya on 15 June 1895. In 1903, the British government, with the support of some Anglo-Jewish lobby groups in London, announced a plan to settle thousands of Jewish refugees (victims of pogroms in Czarist Russia) on a strip of fertile land in Kenya that British settlers in the protectorate called the White Highlands. The announcement had been prompted by the massacre of Jews in the Russian town of Kishinev on 19 April 1903 that left 47 Russian Jews dead and hundreds seriously injured.[67] However, the British plan was abandoned in 1905 because it encountered strong opposition from British settlers in Kenya and Zionist militants in Britain. The failure of this particular British-backed pre–World War II resettlement idea did not stop the emigration of Jews, albeit on a small scale, to Kenya prior to World War II. Naomi Musiker has written that Jews like Abraham and Sarah Block, originally from Ukraine, arrived in Kenya from South Africa in 1903 and witnessed the "founding" of Nairobi that would later become the capital city of the British East African colony of Kenya. By 1905 when Britain abandoned its official "attempt to establish a temporary Jewish homeland in Kenya," a good number of Jews had already settled there and become an integral part of the immigrant community in Nairobi.

By 1912, a community of "twenty Jewish families" resided in Nairobi with "flourishing businesses," a burial site, and a synagogue.[68] This earliest community of Jews in Nairobi expanded between 1930 and 1939 with the addition of "100 families" mainly from Germany and other parts of East Europe fleeing "Nazi persecution." Although British colonial authorities helped the Jews to settle in Kenya, that was not done without opposition, especially from British settlers who complained about the alienation of "Crown lands" to "European non-British subjects."[69] This aspect of Jewish life in Kenya will be examined in detail in Chapter 5. The contrast here with the status of Ethiopia's Jews in Imperial Ethiopia is particularly striking. Whereas Ethiopia's Jews could not own land and had to survive on crafts such as weaving and pottery making, the Ashkenazi Jews who sought refuge in Kenya such as the Szlapak family owned land. The family also opened a secondhand clothing store in Nairobi, in 1938. When World War II broke out a year later, Charles Szlapak and his wife Rachel opened a tailoring shop that became noted for its production of military uniforms for British colonial subjects in East Africa who enlisted for the war. The "Nairobi Jews," as Naomi Musiker affectionately calls them, became a "transient" community. By the time Kenya regained its independence from British colonial rule in 1963, many of them had left for the new state of Israel founded in 1948.[70]

Scholars may disagree over some of the origin legends of Jews in East and West Africa but not over the historical and anthropological facts about the settlement and influence of Jews in these two regions. Labelle Prussin sees "Judaic threads" or evidence of Jewish influences in West African art, architecture, literacy, weaving, and trading items besides ritual practices such as circumcision. He also points to "the early presence of Portuguese Jewish traders on the West African coast" and "well-documented Jewish involvement" in the growth and export of sugar in sixteenth-century West Africa.[71] Prussin appears to have drawn such observations from the work of Peter Mark and Jose da Silva Horta. Mark and Horta are even more emphatic than Prussin in their view that a thriving "Jewish diaspora" existed on the "upper Guinea Coast" of West Africa—the region that today houses the West African nation-states of Senegal, Gambia, and Sierra Leone—between 1606 and 1630. They argue that Jews built mutually beneficial "inter-cultural relationships" between themselves and Africans in the region.[72] Jews came here from the newly established Jewish community in Amsterdam as traders and intermediaries between Africa and Europe.

Mark and Horta have examined the "history of two local communities of practicing Jews" in Senegal and their transcontinental trading networks. They note that the first documented description of Jewish presence in what is today Senegal dates to 1607 and 1608.[73] It was the "oppression" and persecution of Jews in Portugal and Holland at the time of the Inquisition that forced many Sephardi Jews to flee from these Christian kingdoms in Europe in the fourteenth century to the Islamic kingdom of Morocco. It was from Morocco that a group of these Jewish refugees fled or migrated to create "three Jewish settlements" in Senegal's Petite Cote (the region along the coast of Senegal between Cape Verde and the Gambian river). Here, they settled primarily as traders in ivory, hides, and blade weapons, particularly swords and daggers.[74] It is clear from Richard Hull's comprehensive and continent-wide study of *Jews and Judaism in African History* and from the works of Mark and Horta, Prussin, and Green, among others, on West Africa, that Jews settled and influenced economic and social life in African societies beyond the oases of the Sahel. What emerges in these studies, as well as those of Kagwanjia, Musiker, and Carlebach, is that Jews came to West and East Africa, first as traders, migrants, and refugees and lived among various African groups as one of several settled immigrant groups. Some scholars even contend that in West Africa the presence of Jews go far back to the era of the trans-Saharan trade in the eleventh century and the period of Portuguese exploration and trading along the West African coast (from what is today Senegal to Sierra Leone) in the fifteen century. In East Africa, particularly in Ethiopia, Jewish presence has a much longer history as far back as the fourth century CE, albeit controversially. What is also noteworthy is that not all those who considered themselves "Jews" or were deemed as such in the two regions arrived in their habitats as migrants, refugees, or itinerant traders. Some, like "Ethiopia's Jews" or some of "Senegal's Jews" appear to have been indigenous groups who converted voluntarily to Judaism or who were converted to the religion by Jews with whom they lived or associated. These facts alone undermine the assumptions made by Boum and some scholars and diplomats that only North Africa had any tangible evidence of the "residential presence" of Jews on the African continent. Several seventeenth-century

Portuguese records point to "resident Jewish" communities on the Upper Guinea coast (West Africa). In fact, like Nairobi in East Africa, three trading towns at the estuary of the Senegal river "Joal, Portudal [sic], and Rufisque" had "synagogues and wealthy resident Jewish families."[75]

From the works of Mark and Horta, we can now conclude that some or many of the "Portuguese" who came from Holland to West Africa, particularly the region that covers what is today Senegal and Sierra Leone, beginning in the fifteenth century, were actually "Jews" who had converted to Christianity to escape the Inquisition in the Iberian Peninsula. West Africa was that place outside of the Iberian Peninsula and beyond the reach of the Spanish and Portuguese inquisition's "Holy Tribunal," where Jews did not have to hide their identity but rather lived freely and safely. Here, the "Portuguese Jews" were very likely home among "friends, relatives and co-religionists, who may have already settled here before 1600."[76] This fact should also allow historians of Africa to reconstruct the history of Jews who arrived on the shores of West Africa on "Portuguese" ships separately from the general history of "the Portuguese in Africa." Apparently, at this earliest period in the history of the Jewish diaspora, some African societies located between North Africa and South Africa also served as a refuge for persecuted Jews looking for new commercial opportunities or to strengthening ties with Jews who had already migrated to West Africa in earlier years from the many Islamic states in North Africa where they had lived, for many years among non-Jewish groups and had enjoyed a mixed status of integrated residents, and marginalized strangers.[77]

Activities and status

Accounts by the early sixteenth-century Muslim traveler Leo Africanus reveal the "multifaceted nature" of Jewish involvement in African economies and society.[78] To Africanus's sixteenth-century Arabic sources on the presence of Jewish communities in North Africa have been added European records of the same period showing deep and extensive Jewish family networks and activities in African societies to the south of the Sahara desert. Portuguese, Dutch, Spanish, French, and British travelers to West and East Africa, from the sixteenth to the nineteenth centuries, highlighted the "diverse, complex, and paradoxical roles" that Jews played on the West African coast. Of particular significance is a Portuguese account of life in the Islamic kingdoms located between "Arguin and the Senegal River," in West Africa. Here, Jewish traders and those who served the royal court as "guides" in this Islamic territory were given full protection by their patrons. Anyone who dared to attack, kill, or unduly exploit any Jewish trader or guide risked retribution from the Wolof people of Senegal.[79] Similar protective social and economic relations between Jews and their patrons appear in other "sixteenth-century European accounts of the West African coast below the Senegal River." One of these accounts is provided by Andre Thevet, "a Franciscan monk" who had visited the court of the king of the West African island of Cape Verde in 1575. Thevet records that the king of Cape

Verde "had slaves of diverse nations, among them a Jew, native of Maroc [possibly Morocco]." This "Jewish slave" in the Cape Verdian court "knew how to speak twenty-eight different languages, and to read and write in each." The "Jewish slave" had other skills of distinction. He was the one who informed all mariners about tides, tempests, storms, and any dangers on the seas. He was also a skillful geographer and fortune-teller.[80] Arguably, this person must have been a court official of some distinguished status, far from a "slave" as Andre Thevet describes him. His knowledge of court protocol, marine science, geography, botany, and biology must have served Cape Verde well and paved the paths of European exploration of the West African coast. Another account from the late sixteenth-century Portuguese trader Almada about the West African coast offers an equally fascinating portrait of Jewish presence in West Africa but with the usual derogatory broadsides that often accompanied Christian European travel accounts of non-Christians. In this particular account, Almada tells us about Joao Ferreira, a Portuguese Jewish trader who was so well integrated into West African society that he assisted a local king to accomplish his quest for control over the Futa Toro region of eastern Senegal. Ferreira not only influenced the politics of this area, he was tied to court life by marrying one of the king's daughters.[81]

It is the activities that Jews engaged in that also determined their status in the regions they lived in. Here, the contrast between Jewish life in Africa and in Europe could not be more stark. Jews in West Africa lived safer and more protected lives "in the service of dominant, sometimes Christianized, and often Islamized, . . . political, economic and cultural entities."[82] Unlike Ethiopia where the Christian kingdom's Jews lived as marginalized and demonized groups, West African monarchs and societies "adapted, absorbed and transformed" their resident Jews into an integral and visible part of their lives. The acceptance and integration of Jews into West African societies as respected members of the community is "exemplified by the multidimensional role" they played in the politically Islamized but also socially syncretic kingdoms in the region. Jews lived in West Africa as skilled traders in the gold, silver, silk, and spice economy and also as scholars, scribes, and interpreters in royal courts that embraced them as able handlers of court protocol and diplomatic relations with Semitic and European emissaries.[83]

The ability to transform raw metals into usable farming blade implements and personal adornments made artisans people of high social standing in many West African societies. Artisans enjoyed significant political patronage and social hospitality. As people who literally "played with fire," blacksmiths, as artisans, were respected and also feared in many societies in West Africa. According to Mark and Horta, Amsterdam's Sephardi Jews who settled among the Wolof and Serer people in the Muslim villages of Joal and Porto de Ale enjoyed the protection and hospitality of their West African hosts for three interrelated reasons. First, the Wolof and Serer Muslims accorded to Jews existing customary protections that Muslim societies had traditionally granted all non-Muslim groups, especially Jews as *dhimmis*—protected people who also happened to be adherents to sacred texts. Second, the Wolof and Serer people of the Petit Cote coastal communities pursued a type of open door policy to all visiting traders that granted Jewish merchants the same freedom not only to visit and trade in these parts of West Africa but also the customary hospitality to settle among and intermarry with local people if these traders chose to do so. Some of the Petit Cote Jews, under their Chief Rabbi or spiritual leader Jacob Peregrino (or Jeronimo Rodrigues Freire) and his son Manuel Peregrino, did intermarry in 1612. Jacob Peregrino brought with him to this coastal part of West Africa, "twelve copies of [the] Torah," other prayer books, and "ritual circumcision instruments."[84] Indeed, by permitting this group of "Portuguese New Christians" to publicly identify themselves as "Jews," the rulers of this region intended to diversify their social and economic interactions. Third, the Jews of these two coastal communities (Joal and Porto de Ale)—about 40 people—succeeded in highlighting the religious beliefs and rituals and practices such as male circumcision, reverence for sacred texts, and opposition to the veneration of religious images that they shared with the local Wolof and Serer Muslims of this region. West Africa's Jews and Muslims also forged a remarkable bond. They were united in their "mutual rejection of Catholic adoration of images."[85] That feeling of religious and cultural kinship created a Jewish-Wolof-Serer social affinity that kept the Jews of the Senegal coast safe and secure from the types of persecution they had endured in Portugal.[86] It seems reasonable to conclude that whereas a type of patron–client relationship, sustained by a poll tax and mixed Muslim attitude toward Jews had regulated the relations between Muslims and Jews in North Africa, in the West Africa region, an indigenous custom of hospitality to all visitors and traders served as the framework of social relations. The king of Porto de Ale granted to all traders, including Jews, the same rights to trade and freedom to practice their religion, convert local people, and even marry them, if they wanted.[87]

On the West African coast, the Sephardi Jews from Amsterdam did more than trade. As escapees from religious and cultural persecution in Europe and from Ottoman taxation and other cultural restrictions in North Africa, Jews were also seeking tolerant havens for cultural and spiritual growth. The quest for both is apparent in the synagogues they built, the religious books and circumcision instruments they kept, the converts they made of local residents, and the theological discourses they had with their Muslim neighbors on idolatry.[88] It was also here that Jews encountered fresh religious conflicts but far from a West African version of the Iberian inquisition. Scholars of West African history have long established that the economies of the kingdoms of the West African Sahel (Ghana, Mali, Songhai) and even those of the forest kingdoms to the south of them (Asante, Bono, Gyaman, etc, in the modern nation of Ghana) were shaped by trade and the cross-cultural interactions that flowed from it. They have concluded that the main activities of this interregional commerce were the production of gold and the exchange of this precious metal for salt and ostrich feathers and other products along networks of trade across the Sahara. The key players in this trade were originally assumed to be Berbers from the north of the Sahara desert who were Muslim by religious faith and Mande, Dyula, and Hausa traders to the south of the Sahara, who had also converted to Islam in earlier years. Some scholars, however, posit that the presumed "Berber" traders from the north may actually have been Jewish merchants from North Africa or "Judaized Berbers," as H.Z. Hirschberg calls them.[89]

Islam forbade practicing Muslims from engaging in particular occupations and activities. They included weaving and "usurious" practices associated with the handling of money, gold, and other metals. Medieval Islam was therefore similar to medieval Christianity in its distaste for lending money for interest, minting, and gold working. Such religious prohibitions on these occupations created the economic space that non-Christians and non-Muslims occupied. It was this occupational space abandoned by Muslims and Christians that Jews and other non-Christian and non-Muslim groups filled and created virtual monopolies.[90] Scholars of West African history associate the spread of Islam and the emergence of Islamic kingdoms in West Africa with the trans-Saharan gold trade between the Islamic kingdoms of the North African sahel and their counterparts in the West African savannah. In Islamic theology, gold and jewelry were viewed as equivalent to money and therefore subject to Islam's proscriptions on usury and money lending. Prussin, therefore, asks that, given the "constraints" that Islam imposed on usurious practices relating to the handling of gold, "what was the actual identity of those who could approach the sub-Saharan gold mines and 'handle' the gold"?[91] Prussin presumes, quite credibly, that Jews did. As gold miners under the Abbasid, Fatimid, Almoravid, Mamluk, and Saadian dynasties in Egypt, Jews must have also developed expertise in gold smithery and coinage. Prussin is also confident that Jews from North Africa introduced into West Africa the designs and embroideries that Jewish silk weavers used in their weaving of shrouds and tunics. These designs included the "basic motifs of circle, triangle, and magic square" prevalent in the indigo cloth patterns that North African Jews wove. Or West African weavers may have adopted these motifs and modified them to suit their own needs. Either way, the West African *grand boubou* (great robe) so iconic in Niger, coastal Liberia, and northern Nigeria and the famous "Ghanaian kente cloth produced by Asante weavers" may have had a historical Jewish influence on their weaving patterns.[92] Prussin argues that Jews who came to sub-Saharan Africa "from the Iberian Peninsula [particularly Spain and Portugal], North Africa and Near East" brought with them "four essential resources." One, "a virtual monopoly" over metalworking, silk weaving, and embroidery. Two, worldwide network of trade facilitated by a network of Jewish families. Three, literacy. Four, better ways of life, including religious practices and rituals that their host societies adopted for their own use.[93] According to Prussin, a closer look at the gold metalworking of Tuareg and Mauritanian goldsmiths in West Africa, particularly its intricate detail, reveals the possible use of extensive "granulation and filigree—techniques ... associated primarily with Jewish workmanship throughout the Mediterranean world."[94] Additionally, some Wolof rituals in what is today Senegal, particularly "feasts" on certain days of the month, and preparation of "bread, without leaven" may also point to Judaic influence.[95]

Sephardi Jews enjoyed a very high status in West Africa as traders, scholars, and silk weavers, embroiderers, and metalworkers in communities that encouraged and respected diversity in ethnicity and occupations. Ashkenazi Jews of Lithuanian and Latvian heritage, who helped to lay the foundations of the urban economy of British-controlled Kenya as jewelers, pharmacists, tailors, butchers, brewers, and hoteliers, did not enjoy similar status in East Africa's indigenous and colonial societies. There, landownership, cattle-breeding, Christianity, and Anglo-Saxon heritage were the marks of higher social and political status.[96] However, in a West Africa region that did not have a tradition of writing, those who could write played significant roles in trading transactions. Jews brought their literacy and skills in writing to the courts of Muslim kings in West Africa just as they had done in earlier years in European courts as "viziers, advisers, physicians, bankers [and] ambassadors."[97] They also made a lasting impression on West Africa's material culture. They brought to the region ideas about the smelting of gold, as well as weaving and embroidery of indigo and cotton cloth, and left traces of Jewish Kabbalah mysticism "such as the use of amulets, charms, number and letter combinations" in the region's religious rituals.[98] The striking similarities between Jewish mysticism and traditional West African religious beliefs made Judaism appealing in West Africa.

While West Africa's Jews lived in trading towns, often along the coast, and formed part of the region's wealthy elite, Ethiopia's Jews, on the other hand, were poor by comparison, were hardly integrated into East African elite society, and lived in isolated rural regions in northern Ethiopia. Their isolated settlements from the majority Muslim and Orthodox Christian populations may have allowed Ethiopian Jews the freedom to keep their Judaic traditions intact even as they shared language and other physical characteristics with their Muslim and Christian neighbors. However, the Jews of Ethiopia regarded themselves and were regarded by their neighbors as a separate and distinct group.[99] That was not the status that Jews who settled in West Africa enjoyed.

Interactions and attitudes

The work that many Jews did and the impact they had in West African societies would not have been possible if they had been a marginalized group in the region as their coreligionists in the Christian kingdom of Ethiopia were in East Africa. The status of Jews in West Africa as traders, scholars, and artisans earned them places of esteem in the region's social interactions. The resulting African–Jewish relations in West Africa appear to have been comparatively positive. Jews did not merely live in West Africa as converted people or adapt to the religion and customs of their host societies; they influenced those societies culturally. Prevalence of Jewish customs such as circumcision among some groups in West Africa suggests adoptions and adaptations shaped by a culture of interdependence that a settled community of Jews and accommodating local populations created. As Mark and Horta have argued, the protection that the Sephardi Jews of the Upper Guinea coast of West Africa enjoyed was "part of an established local tradition of . . . tolerance and cultural [interaction] between diverse peoples."[100] The safety and protection accorded to Jews by African rulers of this region, despite the protests of other "Portuguese Christian-merchants," allowed Jews to profess their faith in public without fear of arrest and persecution and engage in doctrinal conversations that even attacked aspects of Christian religious worship and rituals.[101] The key to understanding this particular process of interaction is that the fluid and flexible local customs in this part of West Africa tolerated integration and assimilation of outsiders regardless of their identity. It may be safe to state, however, that the cordial local attitudes toward Jews in this part of Africa, so far back in history, must have left residues of philosemitism in West Africa prior to and in the course of the spread of protestant Christianity in the region in the nineteenth and twentieth centuries.

Whereas Ethiopian Jews as an indigenous community in East Africa faced their own peculiar home-grown prejudices in Christian Ethiopia, expatriate Jews in Kenya did not face similar prejudices from that British colony's indigenous African population. Although the number of Jews who lived in Kenya prior to the outbreak of World War II must have been small (possibly fewer than 15), these early Jews "encountered little or no anti-Semitism" from the indigenous African population. Julius Carlebach attributes the absence of anti-Semitism among indigenous groups in Kenya in the early years of Jewish settlement in that British colony (the first decade of the twentieth century) to the fact that Jews who came to Kenya at this period were not traders but rather "artisans who were essential to the general community" of peasants in the region.[102] Prussin makes a similar observation about the "complementary and interdependent status of . . . artisans within their various host cultures" in West Africa.[103] Oral traditions in Mauritania also suggest that Jewish artisans (the only group with that status) taught the indigenous nomadic Berber communities of this West African sahelian region how to smelt and produce iron tools. Since Muslims regarded work such as tanning, dyeing, gold or iron smelting as incompatible with their faith, Jews were the people who did these activities in Islamic societies of what is today Mauritania and Senegal.[104] Thus, Kenya, Senegal, and Mauritania had a large group of Jewish artisans who operated under the protection and patronage of royal courts and the larger agrarian and pastoral society.

Crafts and activities that Islamic and Christian societies disdained but that society needed to exist were done by Jews who lived in societies where the so-called nobler crafts such as agriculture required ownership of land to which Jews were not entitled. Yet it is these crafts such as metalworking (and trading) that put Jews in the "paradoxical situation of respect and awe, fear, and denigration."[105] Respect and awe were the natural anxieties that the position of blacksmith or metalworker evoked for a visual reason if nothing else. By the nature of their profession, those who cast and smelt iron literally played with fire, an element that has its own ritual symbolism and cultural resonance in

East and West African societies. Not all anti-Jewish prejudices in Africa, however, stemmed from what Jews did for a living. As we will notice in Chapter 5, anti-Jewish prejudices in Kenya came from the colony's European (particularly British) aristocratic settlers.

The penchant of European colonial administrators for classifying or identifying ethnic groups for purposes of control, education, administration, and taxation created a crisis of identity for Kenya's Jews prior to the Holocaust. Just as the apartheid regime in South Africa had classified people in the settler colony into "White," "Coloreds," and "Black" for similar purposes and had put Jews among the colony's "White" population, the British had also classified people in Colonial Kenya into "European," "Asian," and "African." As Carlebach has noted, the British colonial government in Kenya included Jews in the ethnic category of "Europeans" although the "more old-fashioned British settlers," the colony's most anti-Semitic group, viewed the Jews as an "alien race."[106] Regarded as such by British settlers who profited from the colonization of the indigenous population of Kenya, Jews in Kenya faced pressures and prejudices from this patrician group of Europeans akin to those that Jews in Europe endured. A paradoxical situation existed in West Africa in the twentieth century. For colonial subjects, Jews were "Europeans" by their physical appearance and ethnic identification in the colonial narrative, even if they suffered the same racial prejudices that Europeans harbored against Africans. This challenge of identification of "Jews" with "Europeans" reared its ugly head in colonial East and West Africa in the course of World War II as colonial subjects in Africa struggled to make sense of the Holocaust and its aftermath.

Conclusion

Jews have lived in Africa for as long as historians have kept records of human activity on the continent. Jews lived in North Africa under Greek and Roman conquering armies in the classical period and under various Islamic dynasties throughout the Middle Ages and the early modern period. They became identified with European colonial regimes in the nineteenth and early twentieth centuries. The story of Jewish presence in East and West Africa is also a dual story of the misfortunes of indigenous Jewish populations and the fortunes of foreign-born Jews who emigrated from the Mediterranean world and Europe and settled in Africa. Foreign-born Jews came to Africa as migrants, refugees, artisans, traders, scholars, and advisers to African monarchs. From the fifteenth century to the outbreak of World War II, East and West Africa became home to some of Europe's persecuted Jews. They were sometimes viewed as outsiders or sojourners but sometimes as part of the society in which they lived. In West Africa, in particular, they retained a status as groups of people whose presence and occupations grounded their host societies firmly in their own survival.

What makes the presence of Jews in West and East Africa (Kenya in particular) a significant story in itself is that the Jews who came to these parts of Africa arrived from Europe. By cultural heritage and physical appearance, they were white and European like other white European settlers in Africa. They were, however, distinguishable from the majority of the indigenous West African population. In Europe, they had suffered anti-Semitic persecutions not only from European monarchs but from Europe's Christians and the majority of Europe's people. By contrast, and except in their religious practices, Ethiopia's Jews were indistinguishable in their physical appearance from the indigenous East African population. They suffered their own peculiar prejudices and persecution from their indigenous neighbors. Like their coreligionists in West Africa, Ethiopia's Jews were landless, but unlike the Sephardi Jews of West Africa, Ethiopian Jews occupied a lower status in East African society and were, in Ethiopia, the object of widespread prejudice and discrimination.

Besides the peculiar experiences of Ethiopian Jews, in West and East Africa European Jews found people who accepted and integrated them into existing indigenous communities. Here, Jews gained the hospitality and protection of African monarchs, acceptance from African Christians that they yearned for but did not receive in Europe. It is therefore safe to argue that, compared to the documented history of anti-Semitism (hatred of Jews) in North Africa and South Africa, one can speak of a philosemitic attitude toward Jews in wider areas of West Africa, although the situation was ambiguous in parts of East Africa. Nevertheless, in both regions, local attitudes toward Jews stood far from the destructive anti-Semitism that Jews suffered in Europe as a diasporic group. How, then, did people in East and West Africa view and think about the destructive anti-Jewish content of Nazi ideology and the persecution and physical annihilation of European Jews in the course of the Second World War?

Notes

1 For detailed discussions of this myth or legend, see Tudor Parfitt, *Black Jews in Africa and the Americas* (Cambridge, MA: Harvard University Press, 2013), 18; Hull, *Jews and Judaism in African History*, 192; Abebe Zegeye, *The Impossible Return: Struggles of Ethiopian Jews, The Beta Israel* (Trenton, NJ: Red Sea Press, 2018), chap. 1 (especially 13–39).
2 Hull, *Jews and Judaism in African History*, xv. See also xi–xii.
3 William F.S. Miles, *Jews of Nigeria: An Afro-Judaic Odyssey* (Princeton, NJ: Markus Wiener Publishers, 2013), xvii–xviii.
4 Labelle Prussin, "Judaic Threads in the West African Tapestry: No More Forever?" *Art Bulletin* 88, no. 2 (2006): 349.
5 Hull, *Jews and Judaism in African History*, 232.
6 Ibid., 16–17.
7 Ibid., 23.
8 Ibid., 25–26.
9 Ibid., 26–28.
10 Ibid., 29.
11 Ibid., 27–28. See also H.Z. (J.W.) Hirschberg, *A History of the Jews in North Africa: From Antiquity to the Sixteenth Century*, vol. 1, 2nd rev. ed. (Leiden: E.J. Brill, 1974), 21 [Translated from the Hebrew].
12 Hull, *Jews and Judaism in African History*, 30. For more detailed studies of the debate over the Berber heritage of some North African Jews, see Hirschberg, *A History of the Jews in North Africa*, 12–13; Paul Wexler, "Are the Sephardim Jews or Judaized Arabs, Berbers,

and Iberians?" in George K. Zucker, ed., *Sephardic Identity: Essays on a Vanishing Jewish Culture* (Jefferson, NC: McFarland & Co., 2005), 29–42.
13 Hirschberg, *A History of the Jews in North Africa*, 22–23.
14 Hull, *Jews and Judaism in African History*, 38–39. See also 42.
15 Ibid., 60–61, 70; Hirschberg, *A History of the Jews in North Africa*, 14. See also Jonathan Israel, "Jews and Crypto-Jews in the Atlantic World Systems," in Richard L. Kagan and Philip D. Morgan, eds., *Atlantic Diasporas: Jews, Conversos, and Crypto-Jews in the Age of Mercantilism, 1500–1800* (Baltimore, MD: Johns Hopkins University Press, 2009), 3, 5.
16 I thank my colleague Roger Ariew of the Department of Philosophy at the University of South Florida for offering me a blog write-up of his family history from which I obtained some of the ideas here about the two traditions in Judaism. For further information about the Sephardi and Ashkenazi traditions in Judaism, see Zucker, *Sephardic Identity*, chap. 2; Miles, *Jews of Nigeria*, xix–xx.
17 Hull, *Jews and Judaism in African History*, 61. See also Prussin, "Judaic Threads," 330.
18 Hull, *Jews and Judaism in African History*, 61–62.
19 Ibid., 50. See also 55 and 62.
20 Ibid., 209. See also 67–68; Abraham David, "Iberian Exiles in the Sixteenth-Century Ottoman Empire," in *Sephardic Identity*, 43–48.
21 Hull, *Jews and Judaism in African History*, 209.
22 Israel, "Jews and Crypto-Jews in the Atlantic World Systems," 5.
23 Hull, *Jews and Judaism in African History*, 209.
24 Ibid., xiii. See also 210.
25 Ibid. See also Hirschberg, *A History of the Jews in North Africa*, 19.
26 Hull, *Jews and Judaism in African History*, 210–211.
27 Ibid., 211.
28 Ibid., 212–213.
29 Ibid., 217–219.
30 Ibid., 219.
31 Ibid.
32 Ibid., 220.
33 For detailed analyses of this phenomenon of local agents of imperialism in Africa's colonial history, see Moses Ochonu, *Colonialism by Proxy: Hausa Imperial Agents and Middle Belt Consciousness in Nigeria* (Bloomington, IN: Indiana University Press, 2014), 2–4, 10, 11; Femi J. Kolapo and Kwabena O. Akurang-Parry, eds., *African Agency and European Colonialism: Latitudes of Negotiation and Containment* [Essays in Honor of A.S. Kanya-Forstner] (Lanham, MD: University Press of America, 2007).
34 Hull, *Jews and Judaism in African History*, 220–221.
35 Ibid., 221. See also British Foreign Office Research Department Confidential Report on "The Position of Jews in French North Africa," April 19, 1943, 1–3. Public Record Office [PRO], Foreign Office [FO] 660/167, *Jews in North Africa: Treatment of and Immigration into Palestine*.
36 Hull, *Jews and Judaism in African History*, 224–225.
37 Ibid., 226–227.
38 Ibid., 229.
39 Ibid., 173; Parfitt, *Black Jews in Africa and the Americas*, x.
40 Hull, *Jews and Judaism in African History*, 119–121.
41 Ibid., 123.
42 Shirli Gilbert, "Jews and the Racial State: Legacies of the Holocaust in Apartheid South Africa, 1945–60," *Jewish Social Studies: History, Culture, Society* 16, no. 3 (Spring/Summer 2010): 36, 38.
43 Hull, *Jews and Judaism in African History*, 123; Gilbert, "Jews and the Racial State," 34. See also Milton Shain, "South Africa," in *The World Reacts to the Holocaust*, 671.
44 Hull, *Jews and Judaism in African History*, 139.

45 Ibid., 140.
46 Gilbert, "Jews and the Racial State," 36.
47 Hull, *Jews and Judaism in African History*, 122, 139. See also Shain, "South Africa," 671.
48 Ibid.
49 Hull, *Jews and Judaism in African History*, 122.
50 Ibid. See also 140–141; Gilbert, "Jews and the Racial State," 38.
51 Hull, *Jews and Judaism in African History*, 146; Gilbert, "Jews and the Racial State," 36–38.
52 Shain, "South Africa," 673–674.
53 Gilbert, "Jews and the Racial State," 36–37.
54 Hull, *Jews and Judaism in African History*, 140–141; Gilbert, "Jews and the Racial State," 36; Shain, "South Africa," 674.
55 Hull, *Jews and Judaism in African History*, 141. See also Shain, "South Africa," 674.
56 For more information about the debate over the origins and Jewishness of the Ethiopian Jews, see Dawit Wolde Giorgis, *Red Tears: War, Famine and Revolution in Ethiopia* (Trenton, NJ: Red Sea Press, 1989), 317–320; Howard M. Lenhoff, *Black Jews, Jews and Other Heroes: How Grassroots Activism led to the Rescue of the Ethiopian Jews* (Jerusalem: Gefen Publishing House, 2007), chap. 6.
57 Zegeye, *The Impossible Return*, 16, 28–29, 31–32.
58 Hull, *Jews and Judaism in African History*, 185, 187.
59 Steven Kaplan, "Did Jewish Influence Reach Ethiopia via the Nile?" in Erlich Haggai and Israel Gershoni, eds., *The Nile: Histories, Cultures, Myths* (London: Lynne Rienner Publishers, 2000), 67.
60 Ibid., 67–68.
61 See Dena Freeman's chapters in Dena Freeman and Alula Pankhurst, eds., *Peripheral People: The Excluded Minorities of Ethiopia* (Lawrenceville, NJ: Red Sea Press, 2003), 314–316; Teshale Tibebu, *The Making of Modern Ethiopia, 1896–1974* (Lawrenceville, NJ: Red Sea Press, 1995), 67–69. See also Zegeye, *The Impossible Return*, 19, 85, 89–91.
62 See M. Avrum Ehrlich, ed., *Encyclopedia of the Jewish Diaspora: Origins, Experiences and Culture*, vol. 2 (Santa Barbara, CA: ABC-CLIO, 2009), 454.
63 See H.Z. (J.W.) Hirschberg, "The Problem of the Judaized Berbers," *Journal of African History* IV, no. 3 (1963): 320; Karen Primack, *Jews in Places You Never Thought Of* (Hoboken, NJ: KTAV Publishing House, 1998), 9–11.
64 See K.A. Dickson, "'Hebrewisms of West Africa'—The Old Testament and African Life and Thought," *Legon Journal of the Humanities* 1 (1974): 23–24. Dickson's article is an analytical discussion of Joseph J. Williams's classic book *Hebrewisms of West Africa* published in 1930. For more discussions of the claims of some West African groups to Jewish identity by allusion to their own Judaic beliefs and practices, see Hirschberg, "The Problem of the Judaized Berbers," 313–339; Aomar Boum, "Saharan Jewry: History, Memory and Imagined Identity," *The Journal of North African Studies* 16, no. 3 (September 2011): 325–341; Miles, *Jews of Nigeria*, 12, 15; Parfitt, *Black Jews in Africa and the Americas*, xi.
65 Boum, "Saharan Jewry," 326, 328–329, 335.
66 Ibid., 335–337. Miles refers in his book to the blunt dismissal by Ambassador Moshe Ram, a career diplomat at the Israeli Embassy in Nigeria, of people in Nigeria who claimed Jewish identity as a form of desperation for Israeli citizenship. Miles, *Jews of Nigeria*, 26. The Israeli diplomat's view is not unique. For more information about similar views expressed by Israeli politicians and Rabbis in the wake of Israel's consideration to airlift thousands of Ethiopian Jews to Israel in the 1980s and 1990s, see Lenhoff, *Black Jews, Jews and Other Heroes*.
67 Peter Mwangi Kagwanjia, "Unwanted in the 'White Highlands': The Politics of Civil Society and the Making of a Refugee in Kenya, 1902–2002." PhD dissertation, Department of History, University of Illinois, Urbana-Champaign, IL, 2003, 63–65, 74, 108. See also Julius Carlebach, *The Jews of Nairobi, 1903–1962* (Nairobi: Nairobi Hebrew Congregation, 1962), 16–20.

68 Naomi Musiker, "The Jews of Kenya," *Jewish Affairs*, vol. 59 (Winter 2004): 21. See also Carlebach, *The Jews of Nairobi*, 24–25.
69 Musiker, "The Jews of Kenya," 21.
70 Ibid., 22.
71 Prussin, "Judaic Threads," 345–346. See also 333–335, and Peter Mark and Jose da Silva Horta, *The Forgotten Diaspora: Jewish Communities in West Africa and the Making of the Atlantic World* (Cambridge: Cambridge University Press, 2011), 3, 8, 22.
72 Ibid., 1. See also Tobias Green, "Further Considerations of the Sephardim of the Petit Cote," *History in Africa* 32 (2005): 165–183.
73 Mark and Horta, *The Forgotten Diaspora*, 21; Prussin, "Judaic Threads," 345.
74 Mark and Horta, *The Forgotten Diaspora*, 16–17, 51.
75 Prussin, "Judaic Threads," 330–331.
76 Mark and Horta, *The Forgotten Diaspora*, 12. See also 8–9, 24, 27–29, 31, 37.
77 Prussin, "Judaic Threads," 329–330. Hull, *Jews and Judaism in African History*, 60, 65, 70. See also Miriam Bodian, *Hebrews of the Portuguese Nation: Conversos and Community in Early Modern Amsterdam* (Bloomington, IN: Indiana University Press, 1997), 6–7.
78 Prussin, "Judaic Threads," 330.
79 Ibid. See also Peter Mark and Jose da Silva Horta, "Catholics, Jews, and Muslims in Early Seventeenth-Century Guinea," in Kagan and Morgan, *Atlantic Diasporas*, 171, 173, 186.
80 See Note 11 of Prussin, "Jewish Threads," 350.
81 Ibid., 331.
82 Ibid., 328.
83 Ibid. See also 328, 342–344.
84 Mark and Horta, *The Forgotten Diaspora*, 34, 37.
85 Ibid., 18, 34–35, 37, 40–41, 44, 48, 50, 62, 67.
86 Mark and Horta, "Catholics, Jews, and Muslims," 174, 185. See also Mark and Horta, *The Forgotten Diaspora*, 4.
87 Mark and Horta, "Catholics, Jews, and Muslims," 173–174, 177, 185–186, 194.
88 Mark and Horta, *The Forgotten Diaspora*, 42–43, 45–47. See also Hull, *Jews and Judaism in African History*, 109–110.
89 See Hirschberg, "The Problem of the Judaized Berbers," 338–339. Hirschberg has argued that there is a "possibility" that some of the Berber traders of the trans-Saharan trade were Jews by descent or Berbers who had voluntarily converted to Judaism or had been converted to the faith by their Jewish associates, although this is "extremely questionable." Paul Wexler has also asserted, controversially, that Sephardi Jews may actually have Berber or Arab origins. See Paul Wexler, *The Non-Jewish Origins of the Sephardic Jews* (Albany: State University of New York Press, 1996), and Wexler, "Are the Sephardim Jews or Judaized Arabs, Berbers, and Iberians?" 31–32, 37–39. For more information on the trans-Saharan trade and its influence, see Ghislaine Lydon, *On Trans-Saharan Trails: Islamic Law, Trade Networks and Cross-Cultural Exchange in Nineteenth-Century Western Africa* (Cambridge: Cambridge University Press, 2009).
90 Prussin, "Jewish Threads," 332; Hull, *Jews and Judaism in African History*, 69. See also Primack, *Jews in Places You Never Thought Of*, 11.
91 Prussin, "Judaic Threads," 332.
92 Ibid., 348.
93 Ibid., 349.
94 Ibid., 338–339.
95 Ibid., 341.
96 Hull, *Jews and Judaism in African History*, 169. See also Musiker, "The Jews of Kenya," 21.
97 Prussin, "Judaic Threads," 332.
98 Ibid., 333.
99 Hull, *Jews and Judaism in African History*, 186.
100 Mark and Horta, "Catholics, Jews, and Muslims," 186.

101 Ibid., 175–176, 179, 184.
102 Carlebach, *The Jews of Nairobi*, 23.
103 Prussin, "Judaic Threads," 335.
104 Ibid.
105 Ibid., 336.
106 Carlebach, *The Jews of Nairobi*, 14.

2 Africans and Nazism

In his novel *No Longer at Ease*, Chinua Achebe presents a fictionalized story of the colonial burden of remaining loyal to the Empire while also wishing its downfall. At the precocious age of 11, the novel's protagonist Obi Okwonkwo had brought shame upon himself and the "mission school" he attended by "writing a letter to Adolf Hitler during the war." Achebe does not disclose the contents of Okwonkwo's letter to the *Fuehrer*, but the act drew the ire of the headmaster of the school, who deemed Okwonkwo a "disgrace to the British Empire." He received "six strokes of the cane on his buttocks" as corporal punishment for that brazen act of disloyalty and insubordination.[1]

What Achebe writes here is open to interpretation. However, it captures the aspirations and dilemmas of the colonial subject in the colonial encounter in West Africa. On one hand, dissatisfaction with the oppressions of the colonial state must have produced in Okwonkwo, as a subject of the British Empire in Africa, a measure of affection for the Empire's chief enemy in World War II, the Nazi state. If Okwonkwo professed admiration for Adolf Hitler's Germany, then his letter to the living embodiment of Nazism, at that time, captured the often unexamined aspect of the sentiment of the colonized. On the other hand, respect for the colonial order, whether sincere or induced, produced in the "obedient servants" of the Empire, typified in the headmaster's reaction, the type of loyalty to Great Britain and its Empire that made actions such as Okwonkwo's border on high treason. In the larger arena of Britain's empire building project in East and West Africa, these dual dilemmas of loyalty and disaffection coexisted.

Long before the Second World War began, people in Africa had formed various opinions about Nazi Germany, its leadership, and its nationalist ideology. Some of these views would later shape the broader African response to World War II. This chapter, however, looks at what colonial subjects and sovereign nations in East and West Africa knew and thought about Nazism as an ideology, about Hitler's published and rhetorical denunciations of Africans and Jews as groups of people, and about the rise of Adolf Hitler to the chancellorship of Germany. It pays particular attention to the role that a secret military assistance from Adolf Hitler to Haile Selassie's Ethiopia in 1934–1935 may have played in Ethiopia's silent reaction to Nazism compared to the open and clear critiques of that ideology from colonial subjects and the sovereign nation of Liberia. The chapter argues that there was initial admiration of Germany and German colonial rule in West and East Africa as a refreshing contrast to Britain's and France's colonial projects in the two regions. That admiration soon turned into anxiety and even fear, as more Africans became acquainted with Nazism as a governing philosophy and its genesis in Adolf Hitler's racist views of Africans and Jews and with his ideas about white supremacy, colonialism, and citizenship in his book *Mein Kampf.* Reports of a possible return of former German colonies in Africa to Nazi Germany and even the cession of Nigeria, the Gold Coast, and Liberia to the Nazi state complicated these anxieties and shaped the responses of colonial subjects and the two sovereign nations in West and East Africa (Liberia and Ethiopia) to the Second World War.

Africans and Jews in *Mein Kampf*

Hitler wrote about a wide range of issues in his *Mein Kampf* (My Struggle) from the prism of his own experiences and beliefs as well as the dominant social theories of his time.[2] In that autobiography completed in 1924, Hitler presents his diagnosis of why Germany lost the First World War (1914–1918) and what was needed to create a new German nation, as well as why he came to hate the Jewish people and despise "Negroes" (Africans and persons of African descent). He also offers his theory of human history; his view of the role that race, blood, and interracial copulation play in the fortunes of nations and should play in determining German citizenship; and the primacy of colonization and militarism in the birth of great nations.

In Hitler's view, Germany had lost the First World War not because of a lack of military might or the will of its soldiers, including Hitler as a corporal in the German army, to fight but due to a backstabbing campaign against the war in the German press to weaken the national resolve to forge ahead in a war that Germany could have won. In the mind of the founder and leader of the Nazi party—the National Socialist Democratic Labor Party (NSDAP in its German acronym) in the 1920s and future leader of Germany—in the 1930s, the November 1918 Armistice that ended the war was the work of a cowardly group of intellectuals in the German parliament influenced by Jewish bankers, journalists, and Marxists eager for the stability of global financial markets, which the continuation of war threatened. For this, Hitler branded the Jews, the press, the trade unions, and Marxists in Germany as "a gang of public pests" and "betrayers" of the German nation.[3] He considered their destruction as necessary for the revival of German nationhood. As he put it, "There is no such thing as coming to an understanding with the Jews. It must be the hard-and-fast 'Either-Or.'"[4]

Hitler's anti-Semitic prejudices, as he reveals them, had been shaped at an early age by the social environment in which he grew up in his native Austria. That environment was suffused with rabid anti-Jewish "sentiments" nurtured from "the activities of the Jews in certain branches of life" in Europe.[5] Among them were the participation of Jews in the publication of newspapers and books and their active roles in the arts, theater, finance, and the trade unions. It is these roles that some Jews played in the cultural and economic life of Austria that led Hitler to attribute to "the Jews" the full weight of society's problems. As publishers of newspapers, intellectuals at universities, and "public leaders of Marxism," Jews were—to Hitler, an avowed anti-intellectual—"artful" in their arguments, and he considered that a devious way of "dress[ing] up . . . falsehoods." On account of that, Hitler confesses he "gradually came to hate" the Jews.[6] Hitler's claim that he became "an out-and-out anti-Semite" because of the Jewish people's connections with "the Marxist teaching" is particularly revealing. He resented Marxism's repudiation of the privileges of aristocrats, its empowerment of the masses, emphasis on equality, and rejection of the idea that "nationhood and race have a primary significance" in human affairs. In Hitler's view, these liberal teachings of Marxism undermined "the very foundations of human existence and human civilization."[7]

As Hitler began to seek a political career in Germany after the end of the war, his assumptions about race became a key feature of his politics. He saw "race" as central to the "cultural, political, and moral" reasons why Germany had lost World War I and why the nation had fallen into deep "economic distress." For Hitler, the military defeat of Germany was "tragic" but not the main cause of the nation's postwar economic problems. Those problems were the "consequence" of the presence of "alien races" or non-German groups within Germany's borders.[8] Hitler saw the presence of Jews in German national life as the clearest example of how Germany had fallen prey to racial contamination. With this view, Hitler gave renewed strength to the prevailing idea in Germany that the Jewish people constitute "a race" based on their physical appearance and "inferior blood" and not a religious group based on its Judaic religious beliefs and practices as the Jews have long described themselves and have been known in their history. Hitler asks in his *Mein Kampf*, "Is not their very existence founded on one great lie, namely, that they are a religious community, whereas in reality they are a race? And what a race!"[9] In racializing a religious community to give force to his belief in the centrality of blood in defining the character of a group and a nation, Hitler branded the Jews as not only deceitful but as cunning, crafty, and devious in nature.[10] Hitler was not alone in upholding this view on race and blood. He wrote in the 1920s when the external physical characteristics of people were seen and accepted in Europe and North America as the measure of one's character and even intrinsic worth. Jews and Africans became the victims of these noxious racial theories.[11] In the 1930s, Hitler's *Mein Kampf* gave hatred of the Jewish people and prejudice against Africans a high propaganda value for those who took these aspects of Nazism seriously.

A corollary to the racial theories of the 1920s that Hitler appropriated was the belief in the hierarchy of human groups and the superiority and inferiority of some based on their physical appearance, place of origin, and assumed contributions to human history. Hitler identified "Aryans" as the superior people and "Jews" and "Negroes" as the inferior types. The "Aryans," he presumed, were "white" in physical appearance, pure in blood, creative in their culture, and descendants of the ancient Nordic and Teutonic peoples of Northern Europe.[12] To Hitler, the Aryans represented humanity's "best racial stock."[13] Hitler claimed that Germany's "security" and "existence" as a nation depended on the "maintenance" of its "racial stock unmixed" since "the highest aim of human existence is not the maintenance of a State or Government but rather the conservation of the race."[14] This view cast human history as a ruthless struggle for survival in which the fortunes of nations depended on their success in preserving a pure and homogeneous blood line or genetic pool. Hitler's conflation of blood and character bifurcated the diversity of the human experience into a strict dichotomy between people who have been creators of culture and therefore contributors to human civilization and those who have been mere consumers or parasites of what the creative races have produced. Since Hitler presumed that the "Aryan" and "Teutonic" races, represented by white Germans, have been the creators of human culture and civilization, that race of people needed to be preserved from contamination by the impure, inferior, and degenerate "Jews" and "Negroes" who have merely been consumers, in human history, of the progress, culture, and civilization that Aryans peoples have created.

To conserve the most creative of racial groups, Hitler believed that the State or Government should control the process of procreation by ensuring that only the "healthy and strong" and the racially pure are permitted to marry and reproduce.[15] For this greater purpose of preserving the purity of the German race and blood, not everyone, in Hitler's view, deserved to marry, reproduce, and even live. Jews, Africans, and people with physical disabilities and hereditary diseases were to be excluded from the process of procreation through state-sanctioned extermination or selective sterilization with the help of medical science.[16] It is in his chapter on "Race and People" that Hitler reveals his personal impressions about marriage and race and their implications for Jewish and African humanity. Here, Hitler contended that copulation between "two breeds which are not ... equal" or between superior beings and inferior types is a danger to society.[17] In his view, "whenever Aryans have mingled their blood with that of an inferior race, the result has been the downfall of the people who were the standard-bearers of a higher culture." Hitler sought empirical support for this theory in the history of North America. He saw the limited or "small degree" of interracial sexual contact between the Teutonic (European and Aryan) population of North America and the continent's non-European "inferior races" as responsible for the ability of white European settlers to maintain "a quality of mankind and civilization" that is "different from those in Central and South America." To Hitler, it is that success of keeping the European "racial stock pure" from any mixture with "other racial stock" that explains the domination of "the American Continent" by peoples of European heritage.[18]

Hitler acknowledged how futile it is to know the precise evolution of human history and which groups did what in that process.[19] Yet that admission did not deter him from seeking the simplest path to his own conclusion that the Aryans have been "the original standard-bearers of human culture." He arrived at that preferred conclusion by presuming that "it is much simpler" to discuss "the question as to what race or races were the original standard-bearers of human culture and . . . thereby the real founders of all that we understand by the word humanity" by looking at it from "the present time." By reading the long trajectory of the human experience backward to establish a historical connection between race and human accomplishment, from what he saw around him in the 1920s, Adolf Hitler found the "answer" he preferred. He concluded:

> Every manifestation of human culture, every product of art, science and technical skill which we see before our eyes today, is almost exclusively the product of the Aryan creative power. This very fact fully justifies the conclusion that it was the Aryan alone who founded a superior type of humanity, therefore he represents the architype [sic] of what we understand by the term: MAN.[20]

This is what Adolf Hitler regarded as his "short sketch" of the "universal history of civilization" and the perspective from which he wanted everyone "to investigate history."[21] By this simplistic historical methodology, Hitler assigned to European descendants of the "Aryan races" or "conquering Aryan tribes" the sole ownership of "progress" in human history.[22] From this theory of history, if the Aryans were the original humans and creators of all human civilization, then the rest of humanity is nothing but parasites who have merely attached themselves to what the Aryans have created.

The evidence of Jewish intellectual power in the Germany of Hitler's time was so overwhelming that Hitler could not overlook it. He sought, rather, to denigrate and diminish it through a caricature of the Jews as consumers and imitators of the culture of Aryans. By doing so, Hitler reinforced the view he intended his followers to have of the Jew as a "parasite" living off the creative product of the German "Aryan."[23] The many animal and biological metaphors by which Hitler sought to express his personal animosity toward the Jews betrayed his intent not only to dehumanize an entire group of people by denying them any creative ability or recognition as agents of human history but also to legitimize their persecution. To present the Jews of Germany as "foreign" in their ideas, spirit, attitude, and blood, Hitler also sought to question even their citizenship. He found Jews who regarded themselves as "Teuton," which Hitler associated with being "German," to be "impudent." Not even birth in Germany and knowledge of the German language established Jews as Germans in the eyes of Adolf Hitler. He put it bluntly that "[i]t is not . . . by the tie of language, but exclusively by the tie of blood that the members of a race are bound together."[24]

Not only did Hitler uphold the Darwinist and evolutionary ideas of the 1920s about the survival of the fittest species of nature, he also supported expansionist ideas about how the fittest could dominate. Hitler concluded that, as creators of human civilization, the White, European Aryan races were historically justified in conquering "inferior races" and in holding them as "slaves" for labor purposes.[25] He believed that "vast spaces still lie uncultivated all over the surface of the globe" and that those vast spaces cannot be left for the exclusive use of their inhabitants. "Such lands," Hitler argued, await "the people who have the strength to acquire [them] and the diligence to cultivate [them]."[26] Furthermore, militarism and colonialism seem justified because "[r]aces which are culturally superior but less ruthless would be forced to restrict their increase because of insufficient territory to support the[ir] population, while less civilized races could increase indefinitely owing to the vast territories at their disposal."[27] Hitler advocated Germany's colonial expansion in Europe, not in Africa. As he quipped, "Such a territorial policy . . . cannot find its fulfillment in the Cameroons but almost exclusively here in Europe."[28] Hitler's restriction of Germany's colonial interests to Europe was a product of his belief that colonization comes with the potential for sexual relations between the "superior" colonizers and the "inferior" colonized, leading to the mixing of blood. According to Hitler, it was when the Aryan "neglected to maintain his own racial stock unmixed" that he "lost his right to live in the Paradise which he himself had created."[29]

Adolf Hitler wrote more about Jews and Germany's decline in his *Mein Kampf* than he did about Africans. However, he was as contemptuous of Africans as he was of Jews in that book considered by some in Africa in the 1930s as "The Nazi Bible," or the primary source of Nazi ideology.[30] In a claim that is clearly inconsistent with known historical facts but useful for Nazi propaganda, Hitler blamed the Jews "for bringing negroes into the Rhineland, with the ultimate idea of bastardizing the white race . . . and thus lowering its cultural and political level."[31] Discerning readers of Hitler's autobiography must have wondered how the Jews could have been "responsible" for bringing Africans to the Rhineland, the industrial heartland of Germany, which France invaded and occupied in 1923, unless the French nation was led by Jews at the time, which was clearly not the case. For Adolf Hitler, Jews and France had become one and the same because of the "profound accord between the views of the stock-exchange, controlled by the Jews, and the chauvinistic policy pursued by French statesmen."[32]

By blaming the Jews for French foreign policy, Hitler ascribed to the Jewish people omnipotent abilities that exceeded their demographic makeup in Germany. But Hitler's intention to rally a nation and a movement against what he called "the Jewish danger" in the "downfall of the German people" was a reflection of his insatiable anti-Semitism.[33]

Hitler's blatant distortion of the history of the African presence on the Rhineland may not have mattered in the face of his key objective of railing against the adulteration of German blood by the introduction of "alien races" into Germany's borders. For someone who saw human beings in their natural and infinite diversity as a simple racial binary between superior Aryans and inferior foreign and non-Aryan races, Jews and "Negroes" became, in Hitler's thinking, quintessential non-Aryan aliens with inferior blood and indistinguishable in appearance and character. Hitler's interchangeable use of "Jews" and "Negroes" in his railings about race and blood morphed both groups together. His reference to Jews as "the negroid parasites in our national body" and the "black-haired Jewish youth" who corrupted "our innocent fair-haired girls" is a deliberate juxtaposition meant to link Africans and Jews in blood kinship as the mortal enemies of the German nation.[34]

Hitler counted France among his list of enemy states and people that posed an existential threat to the German nation. It was not only France's growing military might in the post–World War I period that accounted for Hitler's anti-French sentiments but also the large number of Africans in France's huge African empire and France's deployment of her African colonial subjects in World War I to fight against Germany. The French occupation of the German Rhineland and the use of West African soldiers from Senegal and other French colonies in North Africa to maintain that occupation, along with the subsequent sexual liaisons between German women and African troops on the Rhine, raised the hackles of Hitler and many Germans. Hitler's belief that "human culture and civilization are indissolubly bound up with the presence of the Aryan" made him even more concerned that "in a world which will be composed of mongrels and negroids all ideals of human beauty and nobility and all hopes of an idealized future for our humanity would be lost forever."[35] It was this "idealized future" threatened by the presence of Jews and Africans within Germany's borders that caused Hitler to harp persistently on the preservation of Germany's "racial stock." Hitler saw France's liberal assimilation policy that made Africans French citizens by cultural immersion and mastery of the French language as a dangerous contrast to the kind of citizenship and nationality based on race that he advocated for Germany. For its assimilationist cultural policy, combined with its foreign policy of "acquiring possession of the Rhine frontier," France became, in Hitler's view, "the implacable enemy of Germany."[36] In Hitler's mind, French statesmen and their Jewish financial partners had committed the ultimate sin against German blood and German soil, "[f]or the contamination caused by the influx of negroid blood on the Rhine, in the very heart of Europe ... and by infecting the white race with the blood of an inferior stock."[37]

Besides advocating for the preservation of German blood from contamination and infection by "hordes of African niggers" in the Rhineland, the father of Nazism did not see any useful purpose in the global efforts by white Christian Europeans to bring Christianity and European education to inferior and degenerate races. Hitler was especially critical of the role that the Church (Catholic and Protestant) had assumed in this social mission in European colonies in Africa. He scorned the efforts of European Christian missionaries "to convert the Hottentots and Zulus and the Kaffirs and to bestow on them the blessings of the Church." Rather than concentrating on the mission of saving "our European people," Hitler argued, "the pious missionary goes out to Central Africa and establishes missionary stations for negroes."[38]

It was not only the mission to convert Africans that angered Adolf Hitler but also the outcome of that process: the education of the African for intellectual and professional advancement. Hitler notes, with sarcasm and contempt, the periodic German newspaper reports "that in some quarter or other of the globe . . . a Negro has become a lawyer, a teacher, a pastor, even a grand opera tenor or something else of that kind." For Hitler, this "news" of the ability of "inferior races" to rise to the level of Europeans in intellectual and professional accomplishment could only confirm the "theory" propounded by "the cunning Jew" that "all men are equal." In Hitler's racist mindset, it is "a sin against reason" and "an act of criminal insanity to train a being [an African] who is only an anthropoid by birth . . . into a lawyer; while . . . millions [Europeans] who belong to the most civilized races have to remain in positions which are unworthy of their cultural level."[39]

Hitler's personal views and beliefs formed the bases of the type of fascism and white supremacy that came to characterize Nazism in the twentieth century. His metamorphosis from a simple soldier to a founder of a political party had been induced by his search for a "new Social Movement" to convince many Germans in their postwar mood of despair to support the creation of a new totalitarian and belligerent state to implement his ideas. His goal, as he revealed it in *Mein Kampf*, was to present a range of personal views and a set of ideas as propaganda tools for the new social movement—the Nazi party—for the creation of a new and "idealist Reich."[40] Hitler intended his National Socialist German Labor Party to be "the master of public opinion."[41] Doing so required "an agitator" and "a demagogue" capable of convincing and inspiring "great masses" of people about the "theory" underlying the Nazi party. Hitler assigned himself the responsibility of becoming the party's agitator and demagogue. He believed that the "majority of mankind is mentally lazy and timid." As a result, a propagandist or a demagogue can always secure a large group of "followers" for a doctrine. In Hitler's view, the "final triumph of a doctrine" depends on the ability of the propagandist to effectively convert "large bodies of men to the belief in that doctrine."[42] What became the foundational doctrine of Nazism in *Mein Kampf* was therefore a sensationalized and degrading portrait of Jews and Africans intended to incite the most virulent of anti-Semitic and anti-Black prejudices in Germany. Under that circumstance, if Hitler's view of a new German nation prevailed, there would be no such nationality as German Jew or Black German.

Visions of Germany in Africa before the Nazi Era

For those who study African history, the story of Germany's formal interactions with Africa begins with the infamous Berlin West Africa Conference of November 1884. It was from here, many Africanists contend, that Germany and the European nations attending the conference colluded to carve up the African continent into colonial spheres of influence. Prior to that conference (July 1884), Germany had already acquired, by subterfuge, the West African territory called Togoland as a protectorate. In that same month, and very typical of European strategies of colonial acquisitions in the nineteenth century, the German trading company C. Woermann and Jantzen and Thomaehlen concluded a "treaty" of trade and friendship with the political authorities in Cameroon to bring that West African land under German imperialism. The end of the Berlin Conference in February 1885 also marked the beginning of the integration of Tanganyika (present-day Tanzania) in East Africa into the German East Africa colonial empire. As the nineteenth century ended and the twentieth began, Germany's colonial empire in West and East Africa consisted of Togoland, Cameroon, and Tanganyika, areas in excess of 1 million square miles of land and containing an African population of nearly 14 million.[43] These German colonies existed in close proximity to Britain's colonies in the two regions of Africa. That offered Britain's colonial subjects a good sense of German rule by cross-border interactions, observations, and assumptions.

Historian Dennis Laumann has observed that three contrasting perspectives pervade the historiography of German colonial rule in Africa. First is a "pro-imperialist" viewpoint of high praise for the order, discipline, and economic infrastructure that German colonial administration brought its African subjects. This viewpoint is prevalent in the works of some German authors and non-German scholars of empire building. Second is an outright condemnation of Germany's brutal and even racist treatment of its colonial subjects in Africa. This "Marxist" and "anticolonial" perspective is evident in the writings of some British and American authors who try to contrast the "benevolence" of British and American imperialism with that of the Germans. Third is a "liberal" perspective that points to general admiration of the economic opportunities that German colonialism brought while also underscoring the forced labor and excessive taxation that accompanied it. This latter interpretation of German colonial administration is reflected in the works of African historians who have based their studies on oral histories of the former German colony of Togoland, which was split into British- and French-mandated territories after World War I.[44] The image that Germany evoked in its colonial subjects in East and West Africa inspired multiple perceptions of German rule even among the African subjects of the British and French colonies that shared boundaries with Germany's African colonies. The authoritarian rule of French and British administrators in the "mandated territories" (former German colonies), which Britain and France acquired under the Versailles Treaty at the end of the First World War, generated nostalgic feelings for German rule. In the British Gold Coast, closer to the neighboring French-mandated territory of Togoland (formerly a German colony), the popular perception was that colonial subjects would be better off if they were under the Germans.

On 30 January 1933, Adolf Hitler was appointed Chancellor of Germany by a German Reichstag (Parliament) that was too divided, unpopular, and weak to address the nation's mounting social and economic problems. Far from the expectation that as Chancellor with no prior political experience, Hitler would become an ineffectual head of state, his popularity actually soared, and his Nazi party increased its political standing in the eyes of the German electorate. In the March 1933 General Election, amid an ongoing economic depression, Hitler's National Socialist Party won a slim majority of the votes against several minor political parties. Hitler's political power was now effectively consolidated as leader of a coalition government. Many in Germany looked to him as the only one capable of restoring the grandeur of the German Reich.[45] The new Germany that Hitler yearned for in his *Mein Kampf*, in which there would be no place for Jews and "Negroes," was now on the brink of realization under his absolute leadership. People on the African continent—colonial administrators, colonial subjects, and citizens of sovereign nations—who followed global events took notice.

Reactions in colonial Africa

The rise of Adolf Hitler to power and the consolidation of Nazi ideology in Germany generated mixed feelings in West and East Africa. The *Gold Coast Spectator* newspaper in the British colony of the Gold Coast had published a 27 November 1937 article by a correspondent named "Anti-Nazi" (obviously a pseudonym) alleging the existence of "Nazi secret movements within the borders of [the] British Mandated territory" of Togoland. The author pointed to the clandestine activities of a society called Der Deutsch Togo Bund with headquarters in Accra and branches at Ho, Kpedze, Kpando, Hohoe, and Amedzove and a tour of the cells of that society by "a certain European, obviously holding a high office in the 'Bund' or a special secret service commissioner from Germany." According to this correspondent, the members of this Nazi secret cell included native Africans educated in German schools in the former German colony of Togoland who were previously employed as teachers and clerks in the German colonial civil service, and former African domestic servants of German missionaries and military officers who had knowledge of the German language. These nostalgic pro-Nazi Africans expected the Nazi regime to revive the economic and social conditions that they had enjoyed under German colonial rule. But from a contrary historical perspective, Anti-Nazi reminded these Nazi sympathizers of "Prussian autocracy in Togoland" in the colonial days, and its possible recrudescence in Nazi behavior, especially "the expulsion of Jews from Germany" and the Nazi regime's "deep-seated contempt for the Negro race."[46]

It was not only colonial subjects like that correspondent who was alarmed by Nazi activities within the African continent. Pro-German sympathies in East and West Africa were strong enough to aggravate colonial governments and Whitehall. In East Africa, similar fears abound about the appeal of Nazi Germany, according to a Colonial Office memorandum summarizing the views of the British governor in Tanganyika. The governor had already expressed to Whitehall his grave concern about the "penetration of Nazi ideology in [the] Tanganyika protectorate." He decried the open and "intensive Nazi propaganda to educate all Germans [in the East African protectorate] in Nazi ideology and thus keep them in closest relations possible with the Fatherland." In the governor's estimation, Nazi "propaganda" had been successful in the former German colony of Tanganyika "since the advent of the Nazi party."[47] From these reported Nazi activities in Togo and Tanganyika, it seems evident that the Nazi regime vigorously pursued the Weimar policy of infiltrating the former German colonies in West and East Africa to keep pro-German feelings alive and strong there.[48]

Similar favorable views of Nazi Germany existed in parts of the British colony of the Gold Coast, closer to the former German colony of Togoland. These pro-German feelings in the Gold Coast gave Governor Arnold Hodson "considerable cause for anxiety."[49] A Gold Coast newspaper, *Ashanti Pioneer*, shared the governor's anxieties. The paper had earlier claimed, as the *Gold Coast Spectator* newspaper had also done, that in certain parts of the Gold Coast, people clamored for German rule. However, the *Ashanti Pioneer* newspaper had a different and much broader reason for being apprehensive. It wanted people who harbored pro-German views in the British colony to be aware of the Nazi regime's treatment of Germany's Jewish population. The paper pointed to numerous foreign newspaper reports about the Nazi persecution of Jews as a warning to those who "clamor[ed] for Nazi Germany's rule." The paper noted the long history of the settlement of Jews in Germany and the participation of Jews in German national life, including wars Germany had fought before the Nazi era. In the view of the newspaper's editors, these contributions by Jews to Germany were sufficient reason for the Nazi state to treat its Jewish citizens in "the human way" and a sufficient warning sign of what could happen to Africans under Nazi rule. The paper put it bluntly:

> If Hitler and his bloodthirsty hounds have been able to treat their old friends in this ungodly manner, it would be sheer madness for any Gold Coast African to expect something better from the Germans.[50]

In the Colonial Office in London, the official reaction to pro-German attitudes in West and East Africa was that Nazism itself and the behavior of the Nazi state offered more effective anti-Nazi propaganda tools than anything colonial governments could devise. Harold Cooper, assistant colonial secretary in the Colonial Office, was confident that if enough people in Africa became aware of Nazism and Hitler's plan for Africans, that would change any pro-German feelings that may exist in any quarter of colonial Africa. That change, British colonial officials felt, could be initiated or led only by the educated and conscientious Africans in each colony who detested Adolf Hitler and "the savage racial doctrines for which he is known to stand."[51] In a letter that Cooper had prepared on behalf of the Colonial Office for publication in the *Times of London* in February 1940, the assistant colonial secretary pointed to what had happened "at a public meeting held in a village near Accra," the seat of government in the British colony of the Gold Coast. There, a local chief had reportedly argued that the affection of many people in the Gold Coast colony for Britain was "more than a natural expression of loyalty to the[ir] British rulers." Rather, it was the result of the knowledge that the Gold Coast's "fast-growing literate community" had about "world events" and the educated people's acquaintance with "the distasteful contents of *Mein Kampf*." Cooper concluded, in this official article for the *Times*, that Hitler's "brazenly outspoken book," particularly the contempt that the *Fuehrer* had expressed for the African, especially Hitler's reference to the African as a "semi-ape" upon whom it is a "sin against reason" to lavish Western education, was the best anti-Nazi argument that colonial governments have.[52] The *Times* agreed to publish this article. And the impact must have been immediate and keenly felt in Africa.

The view of a World War II veteran, Baby Sy, from the French colony of Upper Volta (now Burkina Faso), which shared a northern boundary with the Gold Coast, illustrates that impact. Sy remembered Hitler's particular dehumanization of Africans as "semi-ape" as his principal motivation for joining the Allied cause as a soldier against Nazi Germany. As he said in a July 2015 interview with the German broadcasting network *Deutsche Welle*:

> People didn't understand when they heard of talk about fascism. We were just told that the Germans had attacked us and considered us Africans to be apes. As soldiers we could prove that we were human beings, ... That was all the political explanation there was at the time.[53]

Another war veteran, John Henry Smythe, from the British colony of Sierra Leone, shared his own similar motivation for donning a military uniform to challenge Nazism in World War II with the British Broadcasting Corporation (BBC). In a November 2009 interview, Smythe recalled that he and his fellow recruits "read" about Hitler's attacks on "the British and the Americans for encouraging the blacks to become doctors and lawyers."[54]

One of the most unusual arenas in which colonized people also challenged and even ridiculed Nazi racial ideology was sports. Adolf Hitler had contended in his autobiography that boxing is one sport that "should be especially encouraged" in a new Germany because of its unmatched importance in "developing the militant spirit."[55] As Hans Massaquoi has recalled, the impending boxing match in June 1938 between Max Schmeling, the German, and Joe Louis, the American of African heritage, was presented by the "Nazi-controlled press" as the ultimate showdown that would affirm the superiority of the white Aryan race over the inferiority of the non-Aryan type, in the Nazi worldview. The Nazi state's propaganda chief Josef Goebbels had held up Schmeling as the symbol of Nazi Germany's "manly virtues of physical strength, precision reflexes, endurance, sportsmanship, [and] courage."[56] The eventual outcome of this boxing match exposed the contradictions of Nazi presumptions about race, blood, and ability, and the colonial African press did not hesitate to point them out.

The editorial page of the 2 July 1938 issue of the *Gold Coast Spectator* reminded its readers about how Adolf Hitler "has had his pride pricked" by the

Black boxer Joe Louis's defeat of the White German boxer Max Schmeling on 22 June 1938. As the paper put it:

> The result of the heavyweight world championship in boxing . . . proved the rank absurdity of the Nordic philosophy of superiority. . . . As if the Nordic defeats in the Olympic games were not enough to prove this, Louis has completely reasserted the Negro capability by a record-breaking blow—an eliminating smashing blow—to the man who thought himself superior even to others of his own race.[57]

The front page of the *Gold Coast Spectator* of 16 July 1938 featured a photograph of a fallen Max Schmeling and a standing Joe Louis, with no detailed write-up, except an evocative caption, "Aryan Blood Welters in Dust," and a brief description of the photograph itself. (See Figure 2.1.) For the editors of the newspaper, this particular victory of a boxer of African descent over an icon of the Nazi state was particularly comforting in its dual symbolism. First, it shattered the Nazi racial mythology of the supremacy of members of the Aryan white race over peoples of African descent and gave the "African his due"—recognition and respect. Second, it seemed a deserving payback for "the Nazi snobbery of the Negro athletes at the Olympic Games in Berlin" in 1936.[58]

The editors of the *West African Pilot* newspaper, in the nearby British colony of Nigeria, returned to Jesse Owens' Olympic performance and the Joe Louis–Max Schmeling bout to further ridicule Nazi theories on race and present a West African alternative concept on race and color. The *Pilot* contended, as did the *Gold Coast Spectator*, that the Louis and Owens victories have showed Nazi anti-Black racism to be "thoroughly ridiculous." The editors expected the well publicized performances of these two Black athletes to convince Adolf Hitler and the Germans "that the Negro is by no means inferior to them."[59] The *West African Pilot* newspaper spared no time in affirming the distinctive African belief in the equality of all people irrespective of their "degrees of pigmentation."[60]

The African-edited press not only attacked Nazism's central tenets (white supremacy and anti-African racism) that questioned the humanity of Africans. Editors and correspondents also assailed that ideology's associated bigotry: anti-Semitism, for moral solidarity with Jewish victims of Nazi persecution. The *West African Pilot* offered one of its strongest defenses of the humanity of Jews and a stern rebuke of Nazi-anti-Semitism, in its 10 January 1939 issue. A prominent front-page headline, "Jews Have Helped Modern Civilization," directed readers to Nnamdi Azikiwe's "Inside Stuff" column of that day. (See Figure 2.2.) The topic of discussion was "Anti-Semitism." The paper's editor Nnamdi Azikiwe debunked Hitler's claim that human progress and civilization, manifested in scientific discoveries and creative thought, are the exclusive accomplishments of the Aryan race. He recounted the many creative and original contributions of Jews to modern science and philosophical thought.[61] In remarks that were clearly intended as a critique of *Mein Kampf*, Azikiwe noted that as members of the human race, Jews, "[t]hroughout their history . . . have

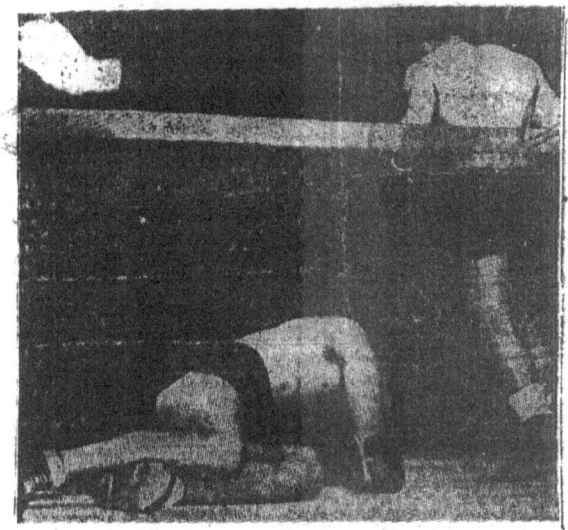

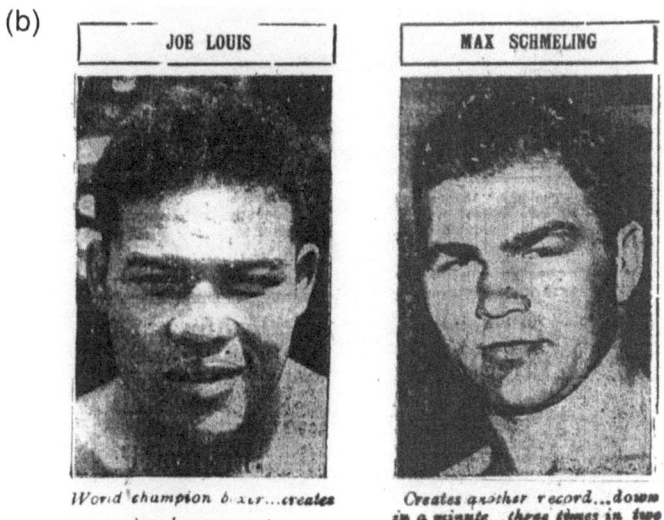

Figure 2.1 (a) *Gold Coast Spectator* photograph of the boxing match between Joe Louis and Max Schmeling; (b) photographs of Joe Louis and Max Schmeling in the *Gold Coast Spectator*, 16 July 1938

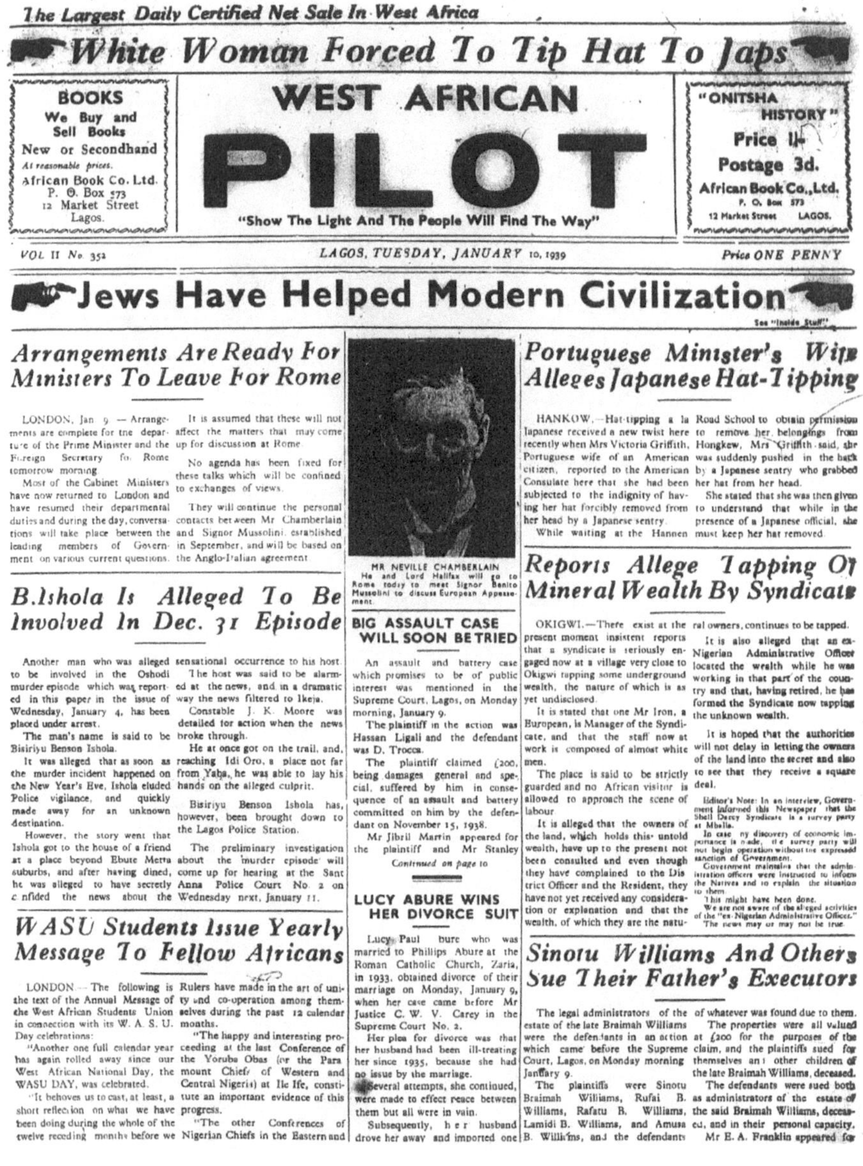

The Largest Daily Certified Net Sale In West Africa

White Woman Forced To Tip Hat To Japs

BOOKS
We Buy and Sell Books
New or Secondhand
At reasonable prices.
African Book Co. Ltd.
P. O. Box 573
12 Market Street
Lagos.

WEST AFRICAN PILOT

"Show The Light And The People Will Find The Way"

"ONITSHA HISTORY"
Price 1/-
Postage 3d.
African Book Co., Ltd.
P. O. Box 573
12 Market Street LAGOS.

VOL II No. 352 — LAGOS, TUESDAY, JANUARY 10, 1939 — Price ONE PENNY

Jews Have Helped Modern Civilization

See "Inside Stuff"

Arrangements Are Ready For Ministers To Leave For Rome

LONDON, Jan 9 — Arrangements are complete for the departure of the Prime Minister and the Foreign Secretary for Rome tomorrow morning.

Most of the Cabinet Ministers have now returned to London and have resumed their departmental duties and during the day, conversations will take place between the leading members of Government on various current questions.

It is assumed that these will not affect the matters that may come up for discussion at Rome.

No agenda has been fixed for these talks which will be confined to exchanges of views.

They will continue the personal contacts between Mr Chamberlain and Signor Mussolini, established in September, and will be based on the Anglo-Italian agreement.

MR NEVILLE CHAMBERLAIN
He and Lord Halifax will go to Rome today to meet Signor Benito Mussolini to discuss European Appeasement.

B. Ishola Is Alleged To Be Involved In Dec. 31 Episode

Another man who was alleged to be involved in the Oshodi murder episode which was reported in this paper in the issue of Wednesday, January 4, has been placed under arrest.

The man's name is said to be Bisiriyu Benson Ishola.

It was alleged that as soon as the murder incident happened on the New Year's Eve, Ishola eluded Police vigilance, and quickly made away for an unknown destination.

However, the story went that Ishola got to the house of a friend at a place beyond Ebute Metta suburbs, and after having dined, he was alleged to have secretly confided the news about the sensational occurrence to his host.

The host was said to be alarmed at the news, and in a dramatic way the news filtered to Ikeja.

Constable J. K. Moore was detailed for action when the news broke through.

He at once got on the trail, and, reaching Idi Oro, a place not far from Yaba, he was able to lay his hands on the alleged culprit.

Bisiriyu Benson Ishola has, however, been brought down to the Lagos Police Station.

The preliminary investigation about the murder episode will come up for hearing at the Sant Anna Police Court No. 2 on Wednesday next, January 11.

WASU Students Issue Yearly Message To Fellow Africans

LONDON — The following is the text of the Annual Message of the West African Students Union in connection with its W. A. S. U. Day celebrations:

"Another one full calendar year has again rolled away since our West African National Day, the WASU DAY, was celebrated.

"It behoves us to cast, at least, a short reflection on what we have been doing during the whole of the twelve receding months before we Rulers have made in the art of unity and co-operation among themselves during the past 12 calendar months.

"The happy and interesting proceeding at the last Conference of the Yoruba Obas (or the Paramount Chiefs of Western and Central Nigeria) at Ile Ife, constitute an important evidence of this progress.

"The other Conferences of Nigerian Chiefs in the Eastern and

BIG ASSAULT CASE WILL SOON BE TRIED

An assault and battery case which promises to be of public interest was mentioned in the Supreme Court, Lagos, on Monday morning, January 9.

The plaintiff in the action was Hassan Ligali and the defendant was D. Trocca.

The plaintiff claimed £200, being damages general and special, suffered by him in consequence of an assault and battery committed on him by the defendant on November 15, 1938.

Mr Jibril Martin appeared for the plaintiff and Mr Stanley

Continued on page 10

LUCY ABURE WINS HER DIVORCE SUIT

Lucy Paul Abure who was married to Phillips Abure at the Roman Catholic Church, Zaria, in 1933, obtained divorce of their marriage on Monday, January 9, when her case came before Mr Justice C. W. V. Carey in the Supreme Court No. 2.

Her plea for divorce was that her husband had been ill-treating her since 1935, because she had no issue by the marriage.

Several attempts, she continued, were made to effect peace between them but all were in vain.

Subsequently, her husband drove her away and imported one

Portuguese Minister's Wife Alleges Japanese Hat-Tipping

HANKOW. — Hat-tipping a la Japanese received a new twist here recently when Mrs Victoria Griffith, Portuguese wife of an American citizen, reported to the American Consulate here that she had been subjected to the indignity of having her hat forcibly removed from her head by a Japanese sentry.

While waiting at the Hannen Road School to obtain permission to remove her belongings from Hongkew, Mrs Griffith said, she was suddenly pushed in the back by a Japanese sentry who grabbed her hat from her head.

She stated that she was then given to understand that while in the presence of a Japanese official, she must keep her hat removed.

Reports Allege Tapping Of Mineral Wealth By Syndicate

OKIGWI. — There exist at the present moment insistent reports that a syndicate is seriously engaged now at a village very close to Okigwi tapping some underground wealth, the nature of which is as yet undisclosed.

It is stated that one Mr Iron, a European, is Manager of the Syndicate, and that the staff now at work is composed of almost white men.

The place is said to be strictly guarded and no African visitor is allowed to approach the scene of labour.

It is alleged that the owners of the land, which holds this untold wealth, have up to the present not been consulted and even though they have complained to the District Officer and the Resident, they have not yet received any consideration or explanation and that the wealth, of which they are the natural owners, continues to be tapped.

It is also alleged that an ex-Nigerian Administrative Officer located the wealth while he was working in that part of the country and that, having retired, he has formed the Syndicate now tapping the unknown wealth.

It is hoped that the authorities will not delay in letting the owners of the land into the secret and also to see that they receive a square deal.

Editor's Note: In an interview, Government informed this Newspaper that the Shell Darcy Syndicate is a survey party at Mballa.

In case any discovery of economic importance is made, the survey party will not begin operation without the expressed sanction of Government.

Government maintains that the administration officers were instructed to inform the Natives and to explain the situation to them.

This might have been done.

We are not aware of the alleged activities of the "ex-Nigerian Administrative Officer."

The news may or may not be true.

Sinotu Williams And Others Sue Their Father's Executors

The legal administrators of the estate of the late Braimah Williams were the defendants in an action which came before the Supreme Court, Lagos, on Monday morning January 9.

The plaintiffs were Sinotu Braimah Williams, Rufai B. Williams, Rafatu B. Williams, Lamidi B. Williams, and Amusa B. Williams, and the defendants of whatever was found due to them.

The properties were all valued at £200 for the purposes of the claim, and the plaintiffs sued for themselves and other children of the late Braimah Williams, deceased.

The defendants were sued both as administrators of the estate of the said Braimah Williams, deceased, and in their personal capacity.

Mr E. A. Franklin appeared for

Figure 2.2 Front-page headline, *West African Pilot*, 10 January 1939

distinguished themselves . . . by the individual contributions of their men and women to the stream of world culture and civilization, past and present."[62] Azikiwe exposed the folly in Nazi theories that ascribed negative characteristics to groups on the basis of race. He argued, "No trait is peculiar to the Jew" in the same way as no "Caucasoid," "Mongoloid," or "Negroid" can be associated with particular traits. Every human group, Azikiwe noted, has individuals who are greedy and those who are not; therefore the greed of some individual members of a group should not besmirch the integrity of all the members of the group. On account of that, "[T]here is no justification in singling out the Jew as particularly distinct from the human race, when it comes to certain vices."

In Azikiwe's view, the only redemption from a racist worldview that homogenizes a group is "Education," the type that trains humans to be "sympathetic and broad-minded in our outlook on the fate of mankind." That "education" should emphasize "the unity of the human race and attach more importance to individual (as distinct from racial) contributions to the advancement of humanity, irrespective of race, creed or colour." From this cognitive perspective, Azikiwe submitted that no one can dispute the fact that "the Jews have produced brilliant individuals who have made lasting contributions to our present day civilization." Drawing on an article purported to have been written by one John Beevers, in the *Sunday Referee*, published in London, Azikiwe reminded his readers that "Jesus, the founder of Christianity was a Jew." And so were Oskar Minkowsky, the Jewish scientist whose research on the pancreas in 1889 led ultimately to the discovery of insulin for the treatment of diabetes; Sir William Herschel, who discovered "infra-red rays"; Heinrich Hertz, whose original work on electromagnetic waves helped the Italian inventor Marconi to produce the modern radio; Casmir Funck, the biochemist "who discovered vitamins" in 1912; Sigmund Freud, "the great psychologist"; Albert Einstein, "the great mathematician-physicist"; and the philosopher Karl Marx, among others—"all great Jews who have contributed much to the stabilization of modern civilization." With these facts, Azikiwe ridiculed Hitler's caricature of Jews in his *Mein Kampf* and affirmed that peoples of Jewish descent have actually made their own original and creative discoveries that their fellow human beings have also used to advance human civilization.[63]

Colonial subjects who reacted to Nazism and its core belief in white supremacy articulated their own alternative African concept of humanity and civilization. In the 1930s, human civilization looked imperiled by the disturbing alarms of war and increasing reports about atrocities against Jews in the heart of Christian Europe. As Europeans who claimed to be on a "civilizing mission" to Africa drifted toward barbarism on their own continent, Azikiwe saw Africans as the world's only hope for moral and spiritual sanity. He advised that it was time Africans in particular "codified their Ethos" as a counterweight to "Christian Ethics" which Europeans have imposed on them and "proceed to educate Europe or other parts of the world on the moral and spiritual essence of man." Azikiwe noted that Africans will fail in their moral duty to "make the world a safe place to live in," if they overlooked or even justified "the barbarity committed against the Jews today."[64] To occupy a moral universe of their own in a "spiritually bankrupt world" and to serve as the guiding light for those who dismissed them as inferior beings, "Africans" needed to project their "respect [for] human rights" and their "humanitarian . . . philosophy of life" as a moral contrast to Nazism. Azikiwe viewed Nazism as "the German version of the doctrine of Nationalism" with its ultimate aim of "Germanifying the world with German 'kultur.'" Nazi racism, as a version of that "kultur" had so riled Azikiwe that he advised his fellow "Africans" to "study world politics objectively and then try to see what they could do to change the perverted ideas and notions of the so-called civilized world and preach to them the gospel of love."[65]

Nazi ideology and the conduct of the Third Reich caused some in Africa to reassess the essence and promise of Christianity and Western civilization as Europeans had presented them in the colonial encounter. Native African columnists and columnists of African heritage living outside Africa, who found space in the continent's influential African-edited newspapers to express their views, bemoaned the subversion of Christian morality and Western civilization in Germany by the Nazi leadership. J.O. Anyaduba's serialized three-part examination of "Christianity Today" in the *West African Pilot* in 20–22 of February 1939 mused that "conditions" in Germany since Hitler became Chancellor made Africans wonder whether Christianity "has ever been preached" in Germany. One of these conditions, the author revealed, was the "revolt against the Versailles treaty" and the conviction of the Nazi leadership that "Germany . . . never lost the war" but was simply "betrayed by Jews and Marxists." Anyaduba's article revealed that those in Africa who followed global affairs were aware of Hitler's autobiography *Mein Kampf*. For this particular correspondent, *Mein Kampf* exposed Hitler's quest for "hegemony over Europe," world domination, and "extermination of the Christian faith." Anyaduba's exasperation with the silence of Christian nations, in the face of the anti-Christian deeds of Nazi Germany, was palpable.[66] The editors of the *West African Pilot* exhorted readers of the newspaper to go to the "African Book Company, Ltd, 12 Market Street, Lagos" to buy and read the withering critique of Hitler's book by the Oxford philologist E. O. Lorimer entitled, "What Hitler Wants," to acquaint themselves further with Hitler's ambitions.[67] (See Figure 2.3.) On 15 July 1939, the newspaper ran a near-full-page advertisement of the availability of *Mein Kampf* at the African Book Company bookstore.

One of Azikiwe's most forthright critiques of Nazism and its threat to Africans came in a lecture on 4 November 1939. The Second World War had begun two months earlier in Europe. In that lecture entitled "German Nazism and the Destiny of Africans," given in Lagos, Azikiwe reportedly invoked the writings of top Nazi leaders and their pronouncements on Africa and Africans to underscore his central view that "the philosophical basis of Nazism, together with its principles and practice, tended to lead to one conclusion: That Africans are a doomed race, under the Nazi regime."[68] Azikiwe had referred to "pages 242, 243, 337, 359, 366 and 524" of Hurst and Blackett's 1939 issue of Hitler's *Mein Kampf* to support his view that "the Nazi regime looked upon African races as semi-apes whose blood contaminated the Aryans and who should be exterminated from the face of the earth either by sterilization or by oppression." In Azikiwe's view, nothing highlighted the common fate of Africans and

> "MEIN KAMPF"
>
> BY ADOLF HITLER
>
> Unexpurgated ... Uncensored ...
>
> "The first complete English translation of the most important book in the world."
>
> Price 8s 6d.   Postage 6d extra.
>
> **AFRICAN BOOK CO. LTD.**
> P. O. Box 573,   12 Market Street
> LAGOS, NIGERIA

Figure 2.3 Advertisement for Hitler's *Mein Kampf*, in the *West African Pilot*, 15 July 1939

Jews in the Nazi worldview more than the torture and killing of "many Jews" in Germany "for the simple reason that they were non-Aryan."[69]

On Nazi racism and colonial claims

It was not only the absurdity of Nazi racial ideas that rankled colonial subjects who knew much about them but also reports in foreign newspapers in the late 1930s that Nazi Germany intended to recover its colonies in Africa. These reports, reproduced in some of the African-edited newspapers, claimed that "Germany's future Colonial administration will be determined by the principles of National Socialism."[70] Even more perplexing were rumors, reported in the *Gold Coast Spectator*, of Poland's interest, with Germany's help, in obtaining Liberia as a colony because of the settlement of "many" Polish merchants and technicians in Liberia.[71] In 1937, the same newspaper reported on a speech made by Adolf Hitler to "a party of foreign journalists in Nuremberg" and at a Nazi party meeting that the peace of Europe depended on the return of Germany's colonies in Africa, now under the trusteeship of Britain and France, to the Nazi state. Hitler was reported to have claimed that:

> by having colonies and making the blacks work for us we will be able to provide much of the foodstuff we are now lacking. Without colonies,

especially India and Africa, England as well as France would be second rate Powers. No great nation today can do without colonies. Germany intends to be great and must have back her African possessions.[72]

A prominent newspaper, *East Africa and Rhodesia*, published in London but read widely in East Africa, also added to these anxieties with its own numerous reports about the planned cession of portions of Tanganyika, Togoland, Cameroons, Nigeria, and the Gold Coast to Nazi Germany for its raw material needs. These reports, the paper noted, were based on "active discussions in [the] British press."[73]

In West Africa, the influential *West African Pilot* bewailed the rumored "suggestion of the possibility of transferring Nigeria and other British colonies and mandates to Germany." While the newspaper acknowledged that this information obtained from the French newspaper *Le Jour* of 30 November 1938 and the *News Review* of London of 1 December 1938 may be mere "allegations," it still believed that they "could ultimately become 'fait accompli.'"[74] The rumors about the transfer of colonies or some negotiated agreement with Germany on this subject were known in West Africa as part of the Oswald Pirow plan. It was a plan purported to have been proposed by this pro-Nazi defense minister of South Africa featuring the cession of a portion of the large British colony of Nigeria to Germany as inducement for Germany to give up any thoughts of reclaiming her lost colony of Tanganyika and Southwest Africa (present day-Namibia) under British-mandated rule.[75] But, in its Saturday 7 January 1939 issue, the *Pilot* published a report from the Manchester *Daily Despatch* about Colonial Secretary Malcolm MacDonald's denial of prevailing rumors that Britain might hand over its colonies in Nigeria, Gambia, Gold Coast, and Sierra Leone to Germany in some political arrangement with Hitler's Germany.

Anxiety over the issue of Germany's colonial claims in Africa hinged on the fundamental moral question of the humanity of Africans in the worldview of the Nazi leadership. Colonial subjects in East and West Africa had read local and foreign press reports of the Nazi takeover of Austria and Czechoslovakia in 1938 and what these reports foretold about African distrust of European "appeasement" diplomacy, as well as the implications of these Nazi territorial annexations for Germany's claims to African territory. It was not only colonial subjects who had paid attention to what was happening in Europe. European settlers and colonial administrators did too. In the East African colonies of Kenya and Tanganyika, under British administration, colonial governors echoed the same feelings of uneasiness that colonial subjects and non-African residents felt about "Germany's colonial claims." In his confidential dispatch of 11 November 1938 on this subject to the Colonial Office, Governor Mark Young of the Tanganyika Territory (a former German colony now under British trusteeship) wrote:

> During the fortnight that has since elapsed the general sense of uneasiness over the future of the Territory has increased. The fear that the country

may once again pass into German possession is now widespread among the non-native community of Tanganyika and seems to be causing almost equal concern to the British settlers in Kenya. Mass meetings have been held in the Northern Province and on the Lupa Goldfields . . . and . . . resolutions passed.[76]

British settlers were not alone in opposing this potential transfer with meetings and protest resolutions. The "Indian community" and the "African community" did as well. As Governor Young reported, "the feeling of insecurity" within "the African population" in Tanganyika was "not confined to the educated native" although educated people in the colony envisioned their own distinctive protest. They were reportedly saving "every penny they earn" for the purpose of "migrating to adjoining territories" if Tanganyika were transferred to Nazi Germany.[77]

The insecurity that educated colonial subjects felt about Germany's colonial claims was self-preservationist. Nazism and the Holocaust provided the contexts for their reactions. Colonial subjects saw the ideology of the Nazi party and the attacks on Jewish intellectuals in the Third Reich as a premonition of what a "Germanified" Africa could experience. That was a widely shared fear in West and East Africa. In May 1938, a group that called itself the Left Book Club, Sierra Leone Branch, published a protest statement in the *New Times and Ethiopian News*, a newspaper edited by the pro-Ethiopia British activist Sylvia Pankhurst, affirming this latent fear.[78] The existential threat that Nazism posed to African intellectuals and African humanism was the subject of Azikiwe's "Inside Stuff" column in his newspaper on 20 January 1939. Azikiwe shared with his readers a statement that Rudolf Karlowa, a member of the Nazi regime's Foreign Political Staff, had made in the 1939 edition of the German Colonial Yearbook. Azikiwe claimed that Karlowa had made a detailed "nerve-tingling" admission about Nazi Germany's quest for a colonial space in Africa and Nazi intentions for Africans. Karlowa had reportedly argued:

> The principal problem of European nations in Africa is the restoration of the vanished trust of the coloured peoples in the leadership of the white nations. No other colonial nation is so suitable for the solution of this problem as Great Germany, because the principles of national Socialism, on the subject of the relations between the races are equally far removed from the false French civilization ideals, which are based on the creed of the French Revolution and the arrogant obscurity of Anglo-Saxon racial conceptions. . . . A spiritual crisis has been caused among the Native populations by the attitude of race pollution, adopted after the World war, by the Western democracies. The colonial task which lies before Germany is the struggle against African Bolshevism until its annihilation. . . . The day will come when the Fuehrer after peaceful discussions with the other Colonial powers, will call on the Youth of Great Germany to begin the march into the colonies.[79]

Azikiwe asked his "fellow Africans" to read Rudolf Karlowa's words and "weep." He described them as "a definite threat to African intellectuals."[80] Given what Hitler had inscribed in his *Mein Kampf* about educated Africans, Azikiwe's fears were not far-fetched.

Colonial subjects in Africa did not view these press reports about Germany's colonial claims as idle chatter. Educated Africans who had read *Mein Kampf* were aware of Hitler's stated interests in colonies in East Europe rather than in Africa. But the Weimar Republic had left Germany's colonial offices open, in the 1920s, indicating Germany's preparation for a future resumption of control over its former colonies.[81] As Adolf Ruger has noted, the Weimar Republic had also laid out strategies of keeping the colonial issue alive in the late 1920s. Part of that strategy, developed by the revived Colonial Department in the German Foreign Office, was to infiltrate the former German colonies in Africa in such a manner as to make their future return to Germany inevitable. The "first targets" of this infiltration strategy were Tanganyika in East Africa and Togoland and Cameroon in West Africa.[82] Jolanda Ballhaus has added that the Weimar interest in Germany's former colonies in Africa did not dissipate in the Nazi period. That notwithstanding Hitler's written and rhetorical preferences for a colonial Empire in Europe, the cautious approach of the Nazi regime to the colonial question in Africa did not signify an abandonment of or disinterest in the revival of Germany's colonial Empire in Africa.[83] Colonized people in Africa were also aware of the presence of strident advocates for colonial territories in Africa such as Hermann Goring, Frantz Ritter von Epp, Werner von Blomberg, and Konstantin von Neurath, among others, within the Nazi government. Nazi officials spoke about the acquisition of an even greater empire in Central Africa. In the 1930s, the Nazi regime revived the dormant infrastructure for overseas colonization and began training a new cadre of Germans for service in a future German colonial empire in Africa.[84]

While Azikiwe asked thoughtful colonial subjects to "weep" over what Nazi Germany had planned for them, he also wanted them to "resist this challenge by collaborating with the Mother Country [Great Britain]."[85] What is revealing here is that for Africans like Azikiwe, the prospect of a Nazi-controlled West Africa created an ironic sense of kinship between British colonial liberalism and African self-preservation. Overt Nazi racism made overt British racial paternalism tolerable in Africa. Equally ironic was the fact that the Nazi state's horrendous treatment of German Jews appeared to have reassured colonial subjects in Africa that Britain will not allow Germany, under Adolf Hitler, to regain control of its former African colonies and perpetrate that type of pogrom in Africa. That optimistic feeling was apparent in a news item featured in the *African Morning Post* of 27 January 1939. In this daily newspaper, published in the Gold Coast and also edited by Azikiwe, the leader of the British Labor Party Sir Archibald Sinclair was reported to have pointed to the "public indignation" in Britain against "the unprecedented attacks on the Jews in Germany by the Nazi dictatorship" and the negative effects that will have on any British "policy of appeasing Hitler with ever-growing concessions."[86]

There is no doubt that for colonial subjects who were attuned to global affairs in the late 1930s, the treatment of German Jews at the hands of the Nazi state foreshadowed what could happen to Africans in an Africa under German control. The backdrop to this conviction were the well-known Nazi beliefs and actions. As Azikiwe discussed in his 3 February 1939 "Inside Stuff" column, aptly titled "Loose Thinking," by their treatment of European Jews and their "pronouncements [and] writings," the leaders of Nazi Germany had proven themselves incapable of ruling Africans too. Azikiwe did not mince his words:

> I would say that the Nazi Germans should, on no account, be allowed to regain their former foothold on the African continent as rulers of Africans. The racial theory of Nazism is definitely anti-African and that destroys any argument of goodwill on the part of the Germans.[87]

If the antipathy towards Nazism was so deep and widespread in colonial East and West Africa, how was the situation in the two sovereign nations (Liberia and Ethiopia) in the same regions of Africa, where Nazi Germany already had a foothold through established diplomatic relations?

Views of sovereign governments: Liberia

While the apprehensions of colonial subjects and administrators about Nazism are revealed through colonial documents and the pages of some of the African-edited press, the people of the sovereign West African nation of Liberia spoke, unfiltered, about Nazism through their government and in the pages of their nation's influential newspapers. Contrary to the common view that the United States controlled Liberia as its informal colony, it was rather Germany that dominated Liberia's economy, prior to World War II, with America's interest focused mainly on "maritime and missionary activities."[88] The Germanic States had been the first among a few states, in 1848, to recognize Liberia as an independent and sovereign nation. As a result, Liberia's cordial diplomatic relations with Germany, in the early twentieth century, was a reciprocal political act. Germany's loss of its African colonies at the end of World War I and before the ascension of Adolf Hitler to the chancellorship of Germany had come with the forfeiture of essential tropical products and agricultural commodities. Africa's only two sovereign nations, Liberia and Ethiopia, therefore, became the only conduits for German access to needed natural products on the African continent. From Liberia, in particular, Germany obtained rubber, cocoa, palm-oil, piassava and pepper.[89] In the 1920s, German merchant ships brought Liberia's natural products to Europe. In June 1922, Liberia and Germany established diplomatic relations, at the consular level, primarily for this commercial purpose. Therefore, in diplomatic terms, Liberia's consul-general in Germany at this time, Momolu Massaquoi, became "the first official representative" of a sovereign African nation to Germany since World War I.[90] Until the outbreak of World War II, when Liberia broke diplomatic relations with Germany, the majority of the West African nation's medical doctors were German in nationality.[91]

Liberia's relations with Germany soured as the Nazi party came to power. From 1933 onward, Nazi Germany's open commitment to the "destruction of all non-Aryans" led the Nazi state to target Africans and Jews for persecution.[92] As Hans Massaquoi, the grandson of the Liberian consul-general in Germany and a Black German witness to Nazism, has observed, "so few" Black Africans lived in Germany, unlike Jews. As such, Black Africans were "relegated to low priority status" among the so-called non-Aryan people the Nazi state intended to destroy.[93] That was not the thought in much of colonial West and East Africa. Even that "low-priority status" of Africans in the Nazi ideology of racial purification by extermination did not exempt Africans, the quintessential non-Aryans in the Nazi worldview, from particular Nazi-inspired indignities. Hans Massaquoi has written about his visit to a "spectacular exhibit" in Nazi Germany in the 1930s. It was a bizarre "display of [dark-skinned] human beings in a zoo behind fences" alongside an exhibit of "monkeys, giraffes, lions, elephants, and other African wildlife." The human beings on display in this exhibit, side by side with animals from Africa, were "barefoot and dressed in tattered rags."[94] The meaning and symbolism of this so-called cultural show of Africa and Africans were unmistakable for the Germans who went to see it. It demonstrated that in Nazi ideology, Africans did not weigh much or stand very high on the scale of humans with value.

The racist doctrines of the Nazi state, which deemed Africans as racially inferior and no better than the lowest primates, did not make relations with the sovereign African nation of Liberia, born out of the history of slavery and racism, any easier. Although Liberia had maintained diplomatic relations with Germany throughout the Nazi years, official Liberian discomfort with Nazism was a subdued undercurrent in that relationship. Exposure of that discomfort came very late, but when it did, it was categorical and unambiguous. Liberia's President William V.S. Tubman spoke for many in his nation and throughout Africa when he stated, categorically, in January 1944:

> I am opposed to Nazism not because it is of German origin, but because I have believed, and am convinced, that it was contrived to be, and is being used as, a subtle but potent instrument to effect the dissolution and destruction by treachery of everything that stands for morality, humanity, justice, righteousness and even common decency.[95]

Although the official Liberian view of Nazism came late, Liberia's influential newspapers had much earlier provided the national sentiment on the rise of Hitler, the essence of Nazism, and the implications of both for the humanity of Africans. C. Frederick Taylor's *The African Nationalist*, in Liberia, like Nnamdi Azikiwe's *West African Pilot* in Nigeria, saturated the West African region with detailed information about Nazism and the contents of Hitler's *Mein Kampf*. In a detailed analyses of what he called "The Nazi Plan for Negroes," Hand Habe, a writer or correspondent for Liberia's *African Nationalist*, outlined in serialized articles in June 1941 five clear implications of Nazism for Africans. One, the colored peoples are an inferior race whose place must be filled by the White "master race." Two, intermarriage between Whites and Blacks or half-breeds and Whites is forbidden. Here the correspondent invoked the Nuremberg racial laws of November 1935, which the Third Reich had passed to forbid interracial marriages. Three, persons belonging to a race other than the White Aryan race will have no electoral rights in the German colonial empire. Four, Negroes are forbidden access to railways, streetcars, restaurants, motion pictures, and all public establishments. Special transportation and public services will be created for them both in Germany and in the occupied territories. Five, members of inferior races are not allowed to join the Nazi party or its subsidiary organizations or serve in the German army. They could, however, serve in labor battalions. Habe asked readers to imagine "the fate of colored people in a German colonial empire" with these Nazi beliefs. The writer drew "one essential difference between Hitler's Negro policy and his Jewish policy." According to this author, while Hitler intended to drive all Jews out of Germany, he reserved enslavement for Negroes. The imagery of "slavery" and "enslavement" is interlaced with how part of the Liberian press viewed Nazism.[96] Given Liberia's history as a settlement for freed slaves from the United States, that prism of discussion must have resonated with the paper's readers.

Not everyone in Liberia spurned the Nazi state or even impugned Nazi racial policies. *The Liberian Crisis* monthly magazine, edited by Z.B.H. Roberts, bewailed the gradual erosion of Liberia's racial identity as a Black nation and the gradual disappearance of pride in blackness in Liberia through interracial marriages between Liberians and Germans living in the African country. In a May 1934 editorial entitled "Black No More," the magazine had referred, with some interest, to "[a] Bill passed by the Reichstag of Germany" prohibiting "marriages by Germans with Negroes, Jews, or any other race of Color under the penalty of 'Treason.'" The editor of the magazine asked rhetorically whether the Nazi government believed that the passage of that bill in Germany also required German citizens in Liberia to obey it. The paper quipped, ironically, that while it appreciated "the patriotism and race-pride of the [German] promoter of the Bill," it wished Africans and "Liberians in particular" would emulate this Nazi policy forbidding interracial marriages.[97]

Ethiopia

The reactions of Africa's other sovereign nation, Ethiopia, to Nazism and the Nazi state are not as clear and as well documented as Liberia's. In fact, Ethiopia's difficult-to-find position on Hitler's Germany disguises as much as it reveals. While diplomatic relations between Ethiopia and Germany have received some limited investigation, the official position of the Ethiopian government on Nazism has yet to be fully documented. The works of Bairu Tafla and Wolbert Smidt are the most prominent of the very limited studies of the relations between Ethiopia and Germany through the Nazi years.[98] A review of these two works and other literature reveals that Haile Selassie's Ethiopia was the recipient of secret military assistance from Hitler's Germany in 1935, to deal with Benito Mussolini's invasion of Ethiopia in that year, a fact that the Ethiopian emperor admitted in an interview with the French newspaper *Le Figaro* in 1950. This secret deal had been negotiated by David Hall, "a descendant of an Austrian Polish Jew from Cracow" who had served as Haile Selassie's private advisor. With the emperor's permission, this Jewish advisor to the emperor had traveled to Nazi Germany to obtain Hitler's consent for the delivery of German military assistance to the embattled African kingdom following Mussolini's attack on Ethiopia in 1935.[99] That this secret assistance from Nazi Germany could have accounted for Ethiopia's reticence on Nazism, compared to Liberia's forthright condemnation of Nazism and open denunciations of the Nazi state by colonial subjects in West Africa, cannot be discounted. Neither can that be held as the primary reason for Ethiopia's absence of opinion on what many in the rest of Africa saw as a racist and pernicious anti-Black and anti-African ideology. Perhaps a look at Ethiopia's peculiar relations with Germany might offer some additional contexts, and it is to Bairu Tafla's book that one can turn for that historical context.

Between 1871 and 1873, Ethiopia sought German diplomatic assistance and moral support to counter Egyptian aggression and to ward off European protestant Christian missionary activities in Ethiopia. But Germany did not enthusiastically offer the help Addis Ababa wanted.[100] Ethiopian officials had explained their persistent flirtations with European nations against Ethiopia's Muslim neighbors as necessary "on grounds of common religion [Christianity]." Monarchs and diplomats in the Prussian court never had much regard for Ethiopian Orthodox Christianity.[101] The first German diplomatic mission to Ethiopia came toward the end of 1880. As the nineteenth century gathered to a close, much of Africa had been partitioned into colonies controlled by Britain, France, and Portugal. Germany had four colonies sparsely populated and with poor natural resources to satisfy Germany's growing industrial and commercial needs. The rise of British power in the Red Sea area and the Nile valley threatened German interests in East Africa. A friendly Ethiopia could offer a useful defense perimeter to protect German colonial possessions in East Africa. Ethiopia's Emperor Menelik had contacted Kaiser Wilhelm II of Germany in 1901 and sought German recognition of Ethiopia's sovereignty while also encouraging German economic interest in Ethiopia.[102]

In 1907, an Ethiopian delegation visited Germany as a reciprocal gesture for the visit of a German envoy to Ethiopia in the same year. Even in these early years of Ethio-German diplomacy, as in later years, Ethiopia's paramount objective was the acquisition of weapons for national defense from whoever could provide them. As Bairu Tafla has noted, Nazi Germany was among the countries Emperor Haile Selassie approached for weapons for Ethiopia's defense.[103] And Germany's new Chancellor did not rebuff that approach despite his well-known contempt for Africans. It is important to emphasize that Adolf

Hitler had already laid out his strategic framework for military alliances that converged neatly with Ethiopia's needs. He reviled Germany's prewar idealistic military alliances that sought to protect smaller and vulnerable nations in the name of collective security. After the humiliating experiences in the First World War, Hitler wanted Germany's postwar political and military alliances to advance only Germany's interests. As he wrote in his *Mein Kampf*, "anyone who expects to form alliances with foreign nations on the basis of a pro-German feeling among the statesmen of other countries is either an ass or a deceiver." To him, "The necessary condition for linking together the destinies of nations is never mutual esteem or mutual sympathy, but rather the prospect of advantages accruing to the contracting parties."[104] And as we will see in the next chapter, Ethiopia and Nazi Germany found mutually advantageous reasons for a secret military alliance.

Nazi Germany's dalliance with Ethiopia appears to have been reciprocal in nature. Pro-Nazi attitudes in Ethiopia had been stronger throughout the 1930s than they were in parts of West Africa. As Wolbert Smidt has revealed in a correspondence with this author, until 1935 the Nazi German press was "overwhelmingly positive about Ethiopia."[105] That certainly was unusual, given the prevailing Nazi attitude towards "Africans" as has been documented in the memoir of Hans Massaquoi. According to Smidt, following the Italian invasion and occupation of Ethiopia in 1935, some German immigrants who were close to the fascist Italians arrived in Ethiopia. These "new" Germans formed a Nazi party group in Addis Ababa, the Ethiopian capital, and became "close to the Ethiopian leadership." Smidt reveals that pro-Nazi sympathies in Ethiopia were openly expressed in the sale of Hitler's portraits in the Ethiopian capital in the 1930s. But, as Smidt acknowledges, the extent to which this open marketing of the Fuehrer's portraits suggested any deep admiration of Hitler and Nazism in Ethiopia is "difficult to say." However, "scattered [German] data" exist, according to Smidt, that reveal Germany's sympathies toward Ethiopia, even among "important personalities in the Nazi leadership (including Hitler himself)." While Smidt is uncertain about similar pro-German sympathies among the Ethiopian leadership, his "guess" is that "based on the sympathy of many Ethiopians for Germany in the First World War," it is possible that some of Ethiopia's leaders "shared some of the Nazi spirit and looked at Germany's attempts of regaining old splendor with sympathy."[106]

Conclusion

Adolf Hitler's catalogue of prejudices against Jews and Africans became the cornerstone of Nazism and can be summarized as follows. As publishers of major newspapers, the Jews of Germany had swayed public opinion against the First World War and thus "betrayed the greatest sacrifice which a human being can make for his country."[107] Through their activism in the trade unions, Jews had inspired workers in munition factories to embark on strikes that denied the German army the needed materiel to win the war, thus costing "the lives of thousands of German soldiers."[108] As purveyors of Marxist ideology and advocates of the "equality" of all people, "no matter what their race or colour may be," Jews had instigated ordinary people and inferior races to revolt against aristocratic privileges and the supremacy of Aryan races.[109] As leading bankers and therefore presumed to have real economic power, Jews, in Hitler's view, have been responsible for the fluctuations in the global stock exchange and thus complicit in Germany's postwar economic hardships.[110] But, above all, as members of the inferior races themselves, Jews, through their marriages with Germans, have contributed to the contamination of the purity of the German blood and have thereby undermined the health and moral character of the German nation.[111] With the press under their control, their status as intellectuals, and Marxism as their analytical tool, only the Jews presumably had the capacity to mobilize the inferior races of the world against the survival of Germany as the standard-bearer of Nordic, Aryan, Teutonic, White, European civilization. What became the ideology of the Nazi party comprised nothing more than Hitler's personal anger and assumptions about prevailing conditions in postwar Germany dressed up in some of the dominant theories of race, evolution, and Social Darwinism of the nineteenth and twentieth centuries. That Germany's postwar circumstances shaped many of Hitler's assumptions about human history is perhaps the most disturbing and dangerous feature of Hitler's *Mein Kampf.*

Hitler, the artist and soldier, hated intellectuals and complicated arguments. His interest in commands and simple narratives made him see anyone—intellectuals and parliamentarians—who offered complex analysis of social and political issues as deliberately cunning and crafty. That anti-intellectual proclivity shaped his implacable hatred of Jews, many of whom were intellectuals in Germany. In his *Mein Kampf,* he took that disdain for complexity and intellection to a very simplistic, ahistorical, and prejudicial level of understanding human history. It is in that reading of history and conclusions about race that Nazism acquired its most enduring and poisonous legacy.

That there was admiration for Germany and even for German colonization in Africa was not surprising, given the need some colonial subjects had to find contrasts to the British and French colonialism they knew and detested, and the German control they imagined and even romanticized. Pro-German sympathies in Britain's colonies in East and West Africa may therefore have been understandable anticolonial feelings. As more colonized and sovereign peoples in these parts of Africa became acquainted with Nazism and with the writings and speeches of Adolf Hitler, their initial pro-German feelings turned into determined opposition to Nazi Germany in statements and sentiments and later in armed combat. Of all the concerns that colonized and sovereign peoples in Africa had about the absurdities of Nazism, it was the persistent press reports about the "transfer" of former German colonies in Africa and of additional territories on the continent to Nazi Germany that raised the hackles of many Africans. Colonial subjects in Africa who looked at Nazism in its dual toxicity as a threat to the survival of Jews and Africans saw themselves as having a common history of persecution with all Jews. And that made them pay particular attention to the Nazi treatment of European Jews and to join forces with Britain and its allies to fight against Nazi Germany in the Second World War.

Notes

1 Chinua Achebe, *No Longer at Ease* (London: Heinemann Educational Books, 1960), 8. I thank my University of Ghana classmate Robert Akrong for drawing my attention to this anecdote in Achebe's novel.
2 Hitler, *Mein Kampf*. See also Massaquoi, *Destined to Witness*, 52–54, and Baranowski, *Nazi Empire*, 25–27, 139, 152.
3 Hitler, *Mein Kampf*, 160–161, 181–182, 189, 212–213.
4 Ibid., 191.
5 Ibid., 61, 63, 124.
6 Ibid., 64–67, 222–223.
7 Ibid., 69, 150–151.
8 Ibid., 208–209, 210–213.
9 Ibid., 213.
10 Ibid., 223.
11 For more information on the dominant ideas on race in Europe and North America in the 1920s, see Benoit Massin, "The Science of Race," in United States Holocaust Memorial Museum, *Deadly Medicine: Creating the Master Race* (Washington, DC: United States Holocaust Memorial Museum, 2004), 91–93, 96, 100, and also Baranowski, *Nazi Empire*, 25, 27, 47, 54–55.
12 Scholars differ in their views on who the "Aryans" are and where they came from. Some believe that the term *Aryan* actually refers to "the language spoken by Indo-Germanic settlers from Persia and India who migrated over centuries into Europe." Clearly, Hitler and the Nazi movement "perverted" the meaning of *Aryan* to advance their racist aims. See United States Holocaust Memorial Museum, *Nazi Ideology and the Holocaust* (Washington, DC: United States Holocaust Memorial Museum, 2007), 13.
13 Hitler, *Mein Kampf*, 23.
14 Ibid., 97, 198.
15 Ibid., 130. See also 229.
16 Ibid., 367.
17 Ibid., 257.
18 Ibid., 259.
19 Ibid., 262.
20 Ibid.
21 Ibid., 265.
22 Ibid., 264, 266.
23 Ibid., 276–277.
24 Ibid., 283.
25 Ibid., 268.
26 Ibid., 132.
27 Ibid.
28 Ibid., 135–137.
29 Ibid., 268. For more analyses of the long history of German thoughts about colonialism and "racial contamination," see Baranowski, *Nazi Empire*, 55–57, 59–60, 141.
30 For this description of Hitler's *Mein Kampf*, see *The West African Pilot*, Editorial page on "The Nazi Bible," Thursday March 2, 1939, 4. For a similar description of Hitler's book, as the "Nazi Gospel," see *The West African Pilot*, Editorial page, "Stop Hitler!" Thursday April 18, 1939.
31 Hitler, *Mein Kampf*, 296.

32 Ibid., 557.
33 Ibid., 297.
34 Ibid., 502. See also 296.
35 Ibid., 348. For more information about the deployment of French troops from West Africa for the French occupation of the German Rhineland, see Baranowski, *Nazi Empire*, 113–115, and Echenberg, *Colonial Conscripts*, 94.
36 Hitler, *Mein Kampf*, 397, 553.
37 Ibid., 557. See also 561.
38 Ibid., 366.
39 Ibid., 389–390.
40 Ibid., 396.
41 Ibid., 421.
42 Ibid., 518–520.
43 Albert F. Calvert, *German East Africa* (New York: Negro Universities Press, 1970), ix. This book was first printed in 1917; Baranowski, *Nazi Empire*, 29–32; Paulette Reed-Anderson, *Rewriting the Footnotes: Berlin and the African Diaspora* (Berlin: Die Ausanderbeauftragte des Senats, 2000), 16, 24.
44 Dennis Laumann, "A Historiography of German Togoland, or the Rise and Fall of a 'Model Colony,'" *History in Africa* 30 (2003): 199–200, 203–207. See also Amenumey, "German Administration in Southern Togo," 625, 628.
45 Robert Gellately, *Backing Hitler: Consent and Coercion in Nazi Germany* (Oxford: Oxford University Press, 2001), 3, 9, 12.
46 Anti-Nazi, "Nazi Agent Tours Togoland, But Natives Are Wide-Awake: Will Have Nothing of Nazism," *The Gold Coast Spectator*, November 27, 1937, 1794.
47 Internal Colonial Office Memorandum, "Permanency of Mandate: Assistance to Non-German Planters," n.d. (but possibly written in November 1938). PRO, CO 691/160/13/1938.
48 For more information about the Weimar Republic's policy of keeping pro-German sentiments alive in former German colonies in Africa through strategic infiltrations, see Stoecker, *German Imperialism in Africa*, 314.
49 Governor Arnold Hodson to the Lord Lloyd of Dolobran, P.C., July 30, 1940, "Public Opinion in the Gold Coast Towards the War." Public Records and Archives Administration Department (PRAAD), Ghana National Archives (GNA). File: CSO 23/5/32.
50 "German Propaganda" [Editorial], *The Ashanti Pioneer*, vol. 1, no. 167, Saturday May 25, 1940, PRAAD, GNA. File: CSO 23/1/75, No. S.0066/SECRET, 1939–1941.
51 Harold Cooper, Assistant Colonial Secretary, to Under-Secretary of State for the Colonies, Colonial Office, February 6, 1940, *Despatches from Secretary of State to Governor, 1940*, vol. III, PRAAD, GNA. File: ADM 1/1/523.
52 Ibid.
53 *Deutsche Welle*, "Africa in World War II: The Forgotten Veterans," https://www.dw.com/en/africa-in-world-war-ii-the-forgotten-veterans/a-18437531.
54 BBC News, "The Africans Who Fought in World War II," http://news.bbc.co.uk/2/hi/africa/8344170.stm.
55 Hitler, *Mein Kampf*, 372.
56 Massaquoi, *Destined to Witness*, 115.
57 Editorial page, "Hitler's Dilemma," *The Gold Coast Spectator*, July 2, 1938, 852. The reference here to the 1936 Berlin Olympic Games may have reminded the paper's readers of the exploits of two American athletes of African descent Jesse Owens and Cornelius Johnson. Owen had won four gold medals in his track and field sporting activity, Cornelius Johnson one gold medal in the high-jump field event. Both men were refused the congratulatory handshake they deserved by the German Chancellor who had previously extended that respect and courtesy to German medal-winning athletes. Hitler, reportedly, left the Olympic Stadium before Cornelius received his medal. See Massaquoi, *Destined to Witness*, 122–123.
58 "Hitler's Dilemma."

59 "Inferiority Complex" [Editorial], *The West African Pilot*, vol. 1, no. 216, Thursday August 9, 1938, 4.
60 Ibid.
61 Zik, "Jews Have Helped Modern Civilization: Inside Stuff: Anti-Semitism," *The West African Pilot*, vol. II, no. 352, Tuesday January 10, 1939, 4.
62 Ibid.
63 Ibid.
64 Ibid.
65 Zik, "Inside Stuff: Ask Me Another," *The West African Pilot*, Thursday January 12, 1939, 4.
66 J.O. Anyaduba, "Christianity Today (1)," *The West African Pilot* [WAP], February 20, 1939, vol. II, no. 386, 5; "Christianity Today (2)," *WAP*, February 21, 1939, vol. II, no. 387, 8.
67 "Our Literary Alcove: What Hitler Wants," *The West African Pilot*, vol. II, no. 389, February 23, 1939.
68 "Nazism & Fate of Africans," Front-Page report in the *West African Pilot*, vol. II, no. 604, Lagos, Saturday November 4, 1939.
69 Ibid., 4–5.
70 "Nazis Confirm Plans for Colonial Drive in Africa." Front-page article—reproduced from a foreign newspaper—in *West African Pilot*, vol. II, no. 509, Tuesday July 18, 1939, 1.
71 Front-page article: "Cabinet Ministers Have No Peaceful Ends, Declares Hitler's Dr. Goebbels. Reason: International Affairs, Germany Wants Her Colonies Back. Poland Too Wants Her Share of Colonies, Organizes 'Colonial Days,'" *The Gold Coast Spectator*, May 28, 1938, 667.
72 "White Europe Squabbles over Blacks in Africa," *The Gold Coast Spectator*, no. 1570, October 16, 1937.
73 "German Claims to Colonies: Active Discussions in British Press," *East Africa and Rhodesia*, 13, no. 643, January 14, 1937, 570; "Colonies: The German Case Stated by General von Epp," 13, no. 644, Thursday January 21, 1937, 602; "German Colonial Claims: 'Ever and Again,'" February 4, 1937, 666.
74 Zik, "Inside Stuff: That Volte-Face," *West African Pilot*, Monday January 9, 1939, 6.
75 "Mr. Pirow's Mission" [Editorial], *West African Pilot*, vol. 1, no. 312, Saturday November 19, 1938, 4. See also Our Correspondent Special to the West African Pilot, "Mr. O. Pirow Plans to Placate Germany and Prevent War," *The West African Pilot*, vol. 1, no. 311 Friday November 18, 1938.
76 Confidential dispatch from Governor [Mark Young], Dar es Salaam, Tanganyika Territory, to Malcolm MacDonald, Secretary of State for the Colonies, Downing Street, London, November 11, 1938, PRO, CO 691/160, File: "Tanganyika 1938, Permanency of Mandate. German Aspirations: Nazi Activities."
77 Ibid.
78 Letters to the Editor, "Protest: Return of African Colonies to Germany," *New Times and Ethiopian News*, May 28, 1938, 8.
79 Zik, "Inside Stuff: African Bolshevism," *The West African Pilot*, 11, no. 361, Friday January 20, 1939, 4.
80 Ibid.
81 Baranowski, *Nazi Empire*, 140, 147–148, 175.
82 Adolf Ruger, "The Colonial Aims of the Weimar Republic," in *German Imperialism in Africa*, 314. See also 298, 300, 303, 309, 313.
83 Jolanda Ballhaus, "The Colonial Aims and Preparations of the Hitler Regime 1933–1939," in *German Imperialism in Africa*, 337, 340.
84 Ibid., 347; Baranowski, *Nazi Empire*, 140, 147–148, 175.
85 Zik, "Inside Stuff: African Bolshevism," 4.
86 Anonymous "Correspondent," "London Public Is Indignant Against Unprecedented Attacks on German Jews: Liberal Party Leader Declares That Nazi Attacks on Jews Make It Dishonourable for Britain to Give over People of Africa to Germany," *The African Morning Post*, vol. V, no. 24, Friday January 27, 1939, 4.

87 Azikiwe, "Inside Stuff: Loose Thinking," *West African Pilot*, vol. II, no. 372, Friday February 3, 1939, 4.
88 Harrison Akingbade, "U.S. Liberian Relations During World War II," *Phylon* 46, no. 1 (1985): 25–26; Kenneth Y. Best, "My Odyssey in Pursuit of a German/Austrian Visa: A Personal Testimony to God's Miraculous Love and Power," *Daily Observer*, Tuesday September 28, 2010, 4.
89 Massaquoi, *Destined to Witness*, 4.
90 Ibid., 9.
91 Best, "My Odyssey in Pursuit of a German/Austrian Visa," 4.
92 Massaquoi, *Destined to Witness*, xii.
93 Ibid., xvi.
94 Ibid., 25.
95 E. Reginald Townsend, ed., *President William V.S. Tubman of Liberia Speaks. Major Addresses, Messages, Speeches and Statements, 1944–1959* (Monrovia: Department of Information and Cultural Affairs, 1959), 18. See also Nathaniel R. Richardson, *Liberia's Past and Present* (London: Diplomatic Press and Publishing Company, 1959), 183.
96 Hand Habe. "The Nazi Plan for Negroes," *The African Nationalist*, vol. 3, no. 52, Monrovia, Liberia, Saturday June 7, 1941, 2. Hand Habe's article could have been a reprint of one published elsewhere by the Hungarian-born author and journalist Hans Habe, who fought with the French army in World War II and also wrote a novel about his experiences at the Evian Conference of Summer 1938. See Hans Habe, *The Mission*, a novel translated from the German by Michael Bullock (New York: Coward-McCann, 1966).
97 *The Liberian Crisis*–a monthly Publication, Lower Buchanan, Grand Bassa, Liberia, vol. 2, May 1934, 1. Found in the *Collections of the Honorable Louis Arthur Grimes*, 1883–1948. Uncatalogued, Africana Room, University of Liberia, Main Library.
98 Bairu, *Ethiopia and Germany*; Wolbert Smidt, *Ethiopia and Germany: 100 Years of Diplomatic Relations* (Addis Ababa: Goethe-Institut, 2005).
99 I thank Professor Rudolf Agstner, Austria, for sharing this information with me in an e-mail correspondence on November 2, 2012, and also for directing me to Professor Wolbert Smidt's book from which Professor Agstner obtained these details.
100 Bairu, *Ethiopia and Germany*, 75.
101 Ibid., 76, 80.
102 Ibid., 99–100.
103 Ibid., 141.
104 Hitler, *Mein Kampf*, 552.
105 Author's e-mail correspondence with Professor Wolbert Smidt, University of Mekelle, Ethiopia, October 17, 2013.
106 Correspondence with Wolbert Smidt. I thank Toni Weiss, then candidate for DPhil in politics at University of Oxford, for introducing me and my research on this book to Wolbert Smidt. While conducting research in Ethiopia in 2013 for this book, I visited the Ethiopian Ministry of Foreign Affairs with Hirut Abebe-Jiri, an Ethiopian human rights activist resident in Canada, who was interested in the subject matter of this book, to seek primary documents on Ethiopia's relations with Nazi Germany and on Addis Ababa's official position on Nazism and the Holocaust. After contacting top officials of the Ministry and discussing the importance of this research for understanding the broader African perspective on Nazism and the Holocaust, I did not receive the information I needed to corroborate the contents of both Bairu Tafla's and Wolbert Smidt's books, as well as my private correspondence with Professor Smidt that I have outlined here.
107 Hitler, *Mein Kampf*, 190.
108 Ibid., 185.
109 Ibid., 287. See also 401.
110 Ibid., 285.
111 Ibid., 286.

3   Africans and World War II

It is now part of conventional knowledge that the "history" of warfare is more than the story of the soldiers who actually fought on battlefields. It is also the story of the perceptions of war, war propaganda, and the use of war by people who did not fight in it as a conduit for moral conversation.[1] The published accounts of the involvement of colonial subjects from Africa in World II are vast. Those that directly relate to the subject of this book have already been reviewed in the introduction. Much of that literature and more beyond it examines the recruitment and deployment of colonial subjects for military service at various theaters of the war, the various war charities set up in the colonies to gather monetary and material contributions to the war effort, the courageous exploits of African soldiers in the service of the Allied Powers, and the disappointments that these soldiers faced when they returned home after the war.[2]

This chapter takes a different angle of analyses from the orthodox approaches in the existing Africanist historiography on the war. It looks at the gathering clouds of war in the 1930s and how Africans understood and interpreted them, how colonial regimes explained the origins and the purpose of war against Nazi Germany and its allies, and how the colonized and sovereign peoples of Africa viewed the Allied explanations and what was at stake for them. The chapter shifts the story of Africans and World War II from the historiography's dominant focus on how colonial subjects fought the war, or contributed money and materials to it, to an alternative analysis of how Africans, both subject and sovereign, thought about the war, assessed its meaning, and used it as a framework for challenging colonialism and also articulating their own concepts of civilized and ethical conduct in human interactions. Understanding the views and reactions of colonial subjects in Africa and the continent's two sovereign nations (Ethiopia and Liberia) to World War II requires a new analytical approach: an intellectual and diplomatic history of the Second World War from an African perspective. This chapter provides that. It reaffirms an acknowledged fact in the historiography of the Second World War, as it relates to Africa, that for many people on the continent what became known as "World War II" began much earlier in Africa than it did in Europe with the Italian invasion of Ethiopia in 1935.[3] What this chapter adds to that historiography, however, is a study of how British colonial administrators used Hitler's views of Black Africans and the

Nazi treatment of European Jews to induce a sympathetic interest in the war in West Africa in particular and how colonial subjects in the region used the official explanations of why war against Nazi Germany was necessary to initiate their own conversation about colonialism, racial equality, economic justice, civilization, and human decency.

Gathering clouds of war in Europe

The foreboding signals of war in Europe and anticipation that war might also engulf colonial subjects in Africa were clear to those in Africa who had access to newspapers and radio at the beginning of 1939. In an observation that now looks prescient, Nnamdi Azikiwe had written in his "Inside Stuff" column in the *West African Pilot* newspaper on 26 January 1939 that "the history of the world [was] moving at such a rapidity that a crisis might develop at any moment in which case it will be necessary for us [Africans] to play our part." He appealed to "those who hold dominion over us [colonial governments]" to trust the readiness of British colonial subjects in West Africa to prove their "friendship at a critical moment."[4] For colonial subjects who made their voices heard in newspaper columns, war, provoked by Nazi Germany, was inevitable in the 1930s. Two factors appear to have induced this dire expectation. First was distrust among this group of Africans of European appeasement diplomacy. Second was their widespread knowledge of the content and ideological agenda of Adolf Hitler's *Mein Kampf*, which one columnist in a major newspaper in West Africa called "that Nazi Gospel."[5] Germany's annexation of Czechoslovakia in 1938 and the inability of Britain and the other European nations to stop that militaristic territorial grab appeared to key opinion leaders in Africa that the groundwork for one of Hitler's major ideological objectives had already been laid. A columnist in the *West African Pilot* newspaper described it in a declarative column entitled "Stop Hitler!" "In that Nazi Gospel [*Mein Kampf*], the Fuehrer sets Germany not one, but two tasks. The first, was inclusion of all Germans in the Reich, the second, was foreign conquest by the shedding of blood."[6] It was this second Nazi task, a war of domination "by any means," that some informed people in Africa viewed as bearing deadly implications for the peace of a continent (Africa) and the humanity of its resident and dispersed populations (Africans).

The editors and some columnists of the *West African Pilot* may have seen Nazi territorial expansionism in global terms, but its peculiar threat to West Africa loomed large in their analyses of Nazi perfidy. For them, Nazi Germany's annexations of Austria and Czechoslovakia in 1938 to reunite German-speaking peoples in that part of Central Europe to mainland Germany signaled the seriousness of the Nazi regime in its reported interest in regaining lost colonies in Africa. Another columnist asked evocatively, "What Next! Colonies?"[7] Nazi territorial annexations in Europe made Africans on the west coast of Africa more vigilant about what the Nazi regime could do in the Cameroon where Germans nationals lived and about the danger that such annexation could pose to Africans in the nearby British colony of Nigeria. The editors of the *Pilot* reminded their readers that "coming events cast their shadows" and that, in view of Nazi Germany's behavior in Europe and the acquiescence of European diplomats to it, colonial subjects needed to "pause and consider what is in store for them, in the light of current world affairs." The paper's editorial page of 23 March 1939 declared rather ominously that "[t]o be forewarned is to be forearmed."[8] By Monday 28 August 1939, the editors of the *West African Pilot* had concluded that "WAR seems inevitable."[9] This foreboding conclusion was based on "the usual frontier incidents which are preparatory to the invasion of one country by another" and requests made of German citizens by their government to "evacuate certain countries which are beyond the Rome-Berlin axis." The *Pilot's* editorial page of that day entitled "The Signs of the Times" sounded a somber note:

> We wish that we could interpret the signs of the times more optimistically but the factors outlined above are so portentous that unless wiser counsel prevails and reason is substituted for emotions, on both sides of the fence, then it would be necessary to repeat the carnage of 1914, and prove once more that the allegation of man's superiority to the lower animals of creation is nothing but a sham.[10]

Two fascist invasions, one world war

Nazi Germany attacked and occupied Poland on 1 September 1939. Two days later—3 September—France and Britain, the European nations with the largest colonial empire in Africa, declared war on Germany and thus took their colonial subjects along with them into the Second World War (1939–1945). David Killingray and Martin Plaut have noted that of the estimated 1 million people recruited from the African continent to fight in this war, West Africa alone provided "more than 200,000 soldiers and labourers for military service" in East and North Africa between 1940 and 1943. From the British colonies of Uganda, Tanganyika, Nyasaland, and Northern Rhodesia, in the then East and Central African territories, came another "324,000 men" recruited between September 1939 and October 1945. Most of these men served in the Ethiopian campaign against Italian forces.[11]

The Italian invasion of Abyssinia (the sovereign nation of Ethiopia) in East Africa in October 1935, which had preceded the Nazi invasion of Poland in September 1939, made the African nation one of the first victims of the type of fascist aggression that triggered World War II. Thus, for colonial subjects in Africa, the "Second World War" had some of its roots in the Italian invasion of Ethiopia, and therefore that war began much earlier on their continent than it did in parts of Europe. Andrew Stewart has documented and analyzed this "first phase" of World War II and the "first victory" that resulted from it on African soil. This so-called East Africa campaign led to the defeat of 300,000 Italian forces in July 1941. They included Italy's colonial subjects from North and

East Africa, equipped with 325 aircraft and 23 ships. The "British and Commonwealth forces" who defeated them included Britain's colonial subjects from India, South Africa, Nigeria, the Gold Coast, Kenya, and Uganda, together with Ethiopian fighters, and a handful of soldiers and sailors from France, Belgium, and Australia. The British and Commonwealth forces constituted "just one quarter" of the size of the Italian force in the field. The defeat and subsequent clearance of Italian forces from areas in Ethiopia, Kenya, and Somaliland in East Africa, which they had occupied since October 1935, marked the "first [Allied] victory in this vital strategic theater" of the Second World War.[12]

The initial lukewarm reaction of those who held dominion over Africans to the attack on a sovereign African nation by a European nation-state reveals two perplexing elements in the history of the Second World War from the African perspective. First, it consolidated one of the core grievances of the more discerning colonial subjects against European colonialism—the privileging of White European interests over those of Black Africans. That fact is well-known and adequately documented. As the editors of the *Gold Coast Spectator* newspaper saw it, that fascist aggression in Africa in 1935 was ignored by the major European powers and later confronted with inadequate war materials and preparation set the stage for the series of German invasions of sovereign nations in Europe between 1937 and 1939 that ultimately led to the outbreak of World War II.[13] Second, the international politics of the 1930s produced some very unusual compromises and secret alliances. Here, the role that possible pro-Nazi feelings in Addis Ababa and secret military transactions between Ethiopia and Nazi Germany played in shaping the attitudes of Britain, France, and the United States toward that fascist Italian aggression in Africa remains to be fully documented. Only a brief outline of that inadequately studied history and its possible role in shaping the contours of World War II is attempted here.

Tensions between Hitler and Mussolini over Austria and the outbreak of hostilities between Ethiopia and Fascist Italy in 1935 created the type of historical instance that often leads to peculiar and absurd relationships. As already noted in the previous chapter, Bairu Tafla and Wolbert Smidt have partially documented, in separate publications, the secrecy and intricacy of Ethiopia's relations with Nazi Germany.[14] As Bairu has noted, Nazi Germany's "general political scheme" in the 1930s was sabotaging "Italian plans in Ethiopia."[15] To that end, the Nazi German foreign ministry sent Major Hans Steffen, a retired German officer "who also acted as a double agent" for the Nazi government to discuss "strategic questions" with Ethiopian Emperor Haile Selassie at the end of 1934. Steffen reportedly promised the delivery of German weapons, in addition to a proposal to equip three divisions of the Ethiopian army at the cost of 33 million Reichsmarks, to be repaid in Ethiopian agricultural products over a period of ten years. As this plan leaked to the Italian mission in Addis Ababa and was lambasted by the Italian press, the German foreign ministry issued a vehement denial. Yet, as Bairu argues, "six months later, Hitler secretly provided Ethiopia with some weapons and medicaments."[16] In July 1935, Haile

Selassie sent his "councilor [sic]" David Hall to negotiate the procurement of German weapons for Ethiopia. Hitler, reportedly, approved this deal totaling 350,000 Reichsmarks. From this official Nazi government fund, Germany shipped "about ten thousand Mauser rifles, ten million cartridges, as well as machine guns, automatic pistols, hand grenades, a few cannons, munitions and medicaments" to Ethiopia.[17]

Given Adolf Hitler's well documented contempt for Africans and Jews, it is hard to imagine his motives for secretly assisting an African monarch who claimed Jewish descent in his war against Germany's ally, Italy, through a Jewish emissary, David Hall. Equally startling is the "amazingly quick" manner in which the German response came, as Bairu describes it. It is possible that what Wolbert Smidt has observed as a very positive pro-Nazi attitude among Ethiopia's leaders may have endeared Ethiopia to Adolf Hitler. However, Bairu sees the Nazi German secret military aid to Ethiopia as a "stratagem" rather than as Hitler's love for an African monarch or his interest in helping an African kingdom to defeat a European nation-state. To Bairu, "the question of Austria and a few other matters" had complicated the relationship between the *Fuehrer* and the *Duce*.[18] It appears that the rift between Hitler and Mussolini over the ownership and control of the German-Austrian-Italian-speaking territory of South Tyrol, in the Aegean mountains, played some role in Hitler's calculations. Hitler had already written about his preferences for beneficial military alliances and strategies for the "restoration of lost districts . . . which were formerly parts of the State, both ethnically and politically" in *Mein Kampf*.[19]

Adolf Hitler had made his reasons for contracting international military alliances clear in his autobiography.[20] Hitler was especially bitter about the loss of South Tyrol as a "German province" at the end of the First World War in the Armistice that concluded the war in 1918. He saw the "reconquest of South Tyrol" only through "the force of arms" and the beneficial military alliances required to accomplish that objective.[21] Hitler was blunt about the latter in his view that:

> if [Germany] cannot form an alliance with England because she has robbed us of our colonies, or with Italy because she has taken possession of South Tyrol, . . . then there remains no other possibility of an alliance in Europe except with France which, *inter alia*, has robbed us of Alsace and Lorraine.[22]

Mussolini had already declared his intention to defend the South Tyroleans against any Nazi annexation attempt. Therefore, assisting Haile Selassie with German military hardware to tie Mussolini's army down in a protracted war of attrition in Abyssinia was in Hitler's military interest if the Nazi state contemplated a possible *Anschluss* of South Tyrol.[23] It is possible that Ethiopia's silence over Nazism must have been a strategic by-product of this secret alliance—a type of Faustian bargain. As Richard Pankhurst has noted, Nazi Germany's secret military aid to Ethiopia "was not known to the Ethiopian public" until the emperor "disclosed it (long after the war)."[24]

War and the official colonial explanation

Certainly, the fascist Italian invasion of Ethiopia had ultimately led to a successful military campaign in that part of Africa by a hurriedly assembled group of multinational fighters. Some characterize it as the first Allied victory in World War II. However, it was the Nazi invasion of a European nation (Poland) that aroused the anger of Britain, France, and the United States and that led them to mobilize their citizens, as well as the subjects of Britain's and France's colonial empire in Africa, to confront this Nazi version of fascism in Europe. News of that confrontation in Europe had trickled into the colonies through a variety of sources. They included newspaper articles, radio broadcasts, mobile cinema film clips, official propaganda pamphlets, statements by key colonial administrators and their pliant supporters, and official resolutions induced by the colonial state, among others. News bulletins and commentaries in English and local languages and a weekly publication *Empire at War* kept colonial subjects informed about the war and their wartime duties. On 5 September 1939, four days after the Nazi attack on Poland, and two days after the British declaration of war, the colonial government of the Gold Coast prevailed upon members of the colony's Legislative Council, an informal advisory body that included local chiefs and some educated Africans, to pass a resolution pledging their "unwavering loyalty and tenacious support in the strenuous and difficult times that lie before the Empire."[25]

This unwavering loyalty came first from pronouncements of traditional chiefs who sat in the Legislative Council. The most prominent of them was Nana Ofori Atta, paramount chief of Akyem Abuakwa and member of the Council for the Eastern Province of the Gold Coast colony. Ofori Atta spoke for many of his compatriots when he assured the British government "that if the time comes and we are called up we shall to the best of our ability discharge our duty to the Empire of which we are happy to be a part." Nana Tsibu Darko IX, *Omanhene* (paramount chief) of Assin Atandaso and member for the Central Province of the colony, added that "we are determined now as in 1914 to stand by the Empire and to follow the leadership of its great Ministers in defence of this Empire."[26] For chiefs such as Ofori Atta and Tsibu Darko who could be described as extensions of the colonial state, declarations of support for the war and Great Britain were nothing more than the customary loyalty and duty expected of subjects in a traditional political culture. Not every colonial subject, however, was so determined to be an unwavering loyalist to the Allied cause. To understand the complexities of the African attitude, one has to examine how the clouds of the approaching war were explained by colonial administrators and how other colonial subjects besides the traditional chiefs interpreted the meaning of the war they were called upon to fight with unwavering loyalty.

On 12 March 1940, six months after the outbreak of the Second World War, the Governor of the Gold Coast Sir Arnold Hodson addressed the colony's Legislative Council. He characterized the proceeding war as the result of the "aggression," "oppression," and "lust for domination" by the Nazi leadership and its "constant interference with fundamental liberties and decencies." For him, the war was being fought for the "preservation of our essential freedom and democracy."[27] Governor Hodson applauded the "unity" that the Gold Coast colony had shown against "the intolerable bankruptcy, and the onslaught on religions and ideals ... by the leaders of Nazi Germany." The "unity" the Governor alluded to had been expressed in the "rush" of many men, some of whom had reportedly given up "profitable employment," to recruiting offices in the West African colony to enlist as soldiers. Some chiefs and farmers had also shown their support for the war's objectives by providing "timber, fuel, and foodstuffs free to the military authorities." Some educated Africans had also shown their support by "giving lectures in English and in local vernaculars ... and organizing functions in aid of war charities."[28] The African press lent its support by carrying advertisements encouraging many to join the colonial army. (see Figure 3.1)

African attitudes

Despite these outward demonstrations of loyalty to the Empire, some colonial subjects in West Africa continued to debate what German aggression and domination in Europe, as well as the explanation of the war by colonial administrators as a struggle for liberation, freedom, and civilization, actually meant for the subjects of British colonialism who lived far away from the location of that German aggression. British colonial officials in West Africa acknowledged in many confidential dispatches to London that there were "distinct, if muted signs of disaffected persons" in the region. The Gold Coast colonial government had blamed this disaffection on effective Nazi propaganda and a widespread view in the colony that the British are "greedy." Many colonial subjects believed that the prevailing high prices of consumer goods in the colony, even as colonial recruits pledged their lives to Great Britain in the war, constituted a supreme economic injustice that had been deliberately "engineered by Britain to keep the African poor and fill the pockets of the Englishman." Disaffected colonial subjects pointed to other unjust colonial laws, "which some Africans found irksome." They included the banning of locally brewed gin, which some Africans saw as another act to "favor" the more expensive English brands of alcohol.[29]

The *Ashanti Pioneer* newspaper, published in the heartland of the cocoa-producing and Twi-speaking Akan people of the Gold Coast, catalogued what it considered to be the core "grievances against the colonial government." Top of the list was the declining purchasing price of cocoa, the primary cash crop in the colony. The editors of the paper, however, deemed this grievance as less important than the implications for Africans of a German victory in the ongoing war. In its editorial of 25 May 1940, the paper made it:

> plain to all her readers who in their nightmare clamour for Nazi Germany's rule, and are trying to infuse such maniacal thoughts into the minds of poor illiterate men and women that it is not long ago when Hitler and his

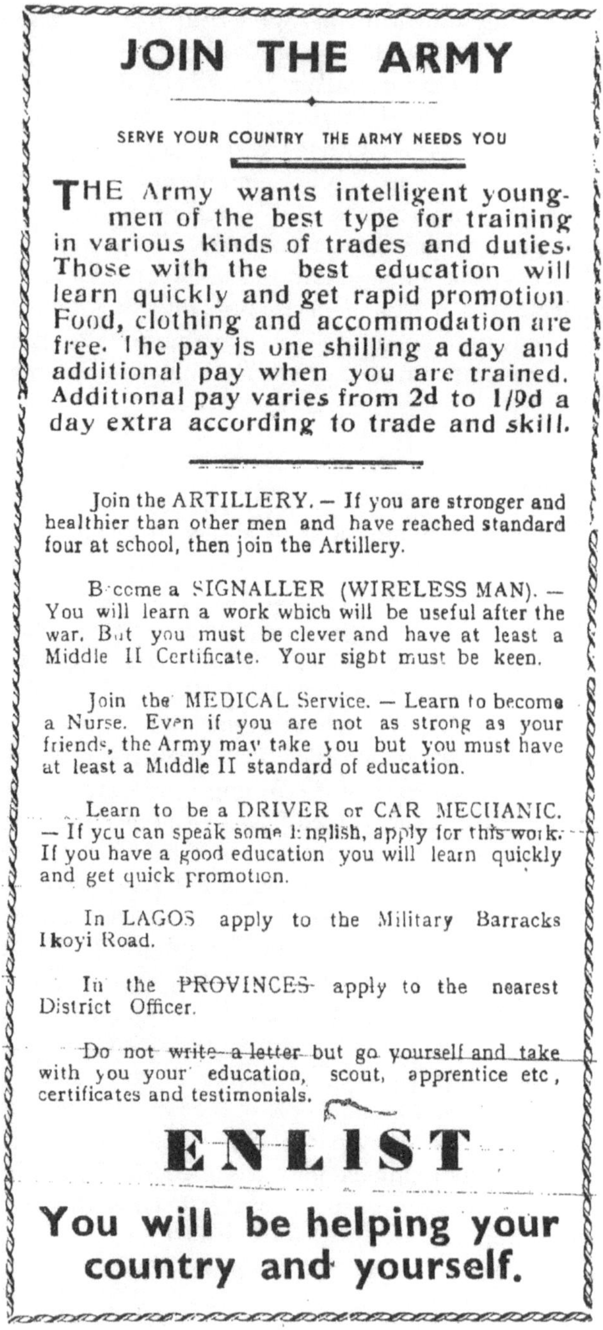

JOIN THE ARMY

SERVE YOUR COUNTRY THE ARMY NEEDS YOU

THE Army wants intelligent young-men of the best type for training in various kinds of trades and duties. Those with the best education will learn quickly and get rapid promotion. Food, clothing and accommodation are free. The pay is one shilling a day and additional pay when you are trained. Additional pay varies from 2d to 1/9d a day extra according to trade and skill.

Join the ARTILLERY. — If you are stronger and healthier than other men and have reached standard four at school, then join the Artillery.

Become a SIGNALLER (WIRELESS MAN). — You will learn a work which will be useful after the war. But you must be clever and have at least a Middle II Certificate. Your sight must be keen.

Join the MEDICAL Service. — Learn to become a Nurse. Even if you are not as strong as your friends, the Army may take you but you must have at least a Middle II standard of education.

Learn to be a DRIVER or CAR MECHANIC. — If you can speak some English, apply for this work. If you have a good education you will learn quickly and get quick promotion.

In LAGOS apply to the Military Barracks Ikoyi Road.

In the PROVINCES apply to the nearest District Officer.

Do not write a letter but go yourself and take with you your education, scout, apprentice etc, certificates and testimonials.

ENLIST

You will be helping your country and yourself.

Figure 3.1 Enlistment advertisement in the *West African Pilot*, 13 October 1941

gang of lunatics mercilessly persecuted the Jews for the simple reason that these poor people had money which the Reichstag needed.[30]

The editors offered a range of "suggestions" that the British colonial government could take against "Nazi sympathizers" in the Gold Coast. They urged the British to seize the "private wireless sets" of people who appear to have been won over by German propaganda or their own self-serving admiration of Nazi Germany and keep those radio sets until the end of the war. On 30 May 1940, the Gold Coast Executive Council, an advisory body consisting of the governor and other European officials, discussed, at its meeting, the suggestion made by the *Ashanti Pioneer*. The Council advised the governor to authorize the colonial police to confiscate the private radio sets of all "persons considered untrustworthy" and also to initiate prosecutions in the colony for the spread of German propaganda "as an example to the Community." And if these deterrent measures failed to stop growing pro-German attitudes in the colony, a request should be sent to the Colonial Office in London for "telecommunication equipment" to begin a "counter-propaganda" broadcast.[31]

Despite these worrying trends, the British government remained confident that a favorable African attitude to the war could be cultivated through chiefs and pro-British educated Africans. In the end, the colonial administration sought comfort in the opinions of "the large and fast-growing literate community" in the Gold Coast that kept "in eager touch with world events and long ago acquainted itself with the distasteful contents of *Mein Kampf*."[32] Thus, the African interest in World War II was to be whipped up through emphasis on two principal themes: Hitler's view of Africans and the Nazi treatment of Jewish men, women, and children and the implications of that for Africans and their cherished institution of the family. Colonial administrators in Britain's West African colonies, therefore, subordinated any discussions of the origins of the war with Nazi Germany as a consequence of European appeasement diplomacy toward the Nazi state to a new narrative on Hitler's megalomania that if not addressed with African involvement would consume not only Europeans but Africans especially. In this narrative, colonial subjects did not have to look far into European diplomacy for explanations but merely to the contents of Hitler's autobiography, the pronouncements of the Nazi leadership, and the implications of a Nazi victory for Africans and Jews as a group.

Official British anxiety about the mixed attitude to the war in West Africa was captured in a confidential report from a conference of information officers in the region held in Accra in February 1942. Those who attended included British officers from the Gold Coast, Nigeria, and Sierra Leone. The outcome document of this conference affirmed that:

> [t]he war [has] left a vast majority of Africans in rural areas untouched. To them it was a "white man's war." The African in the "bush" found a degree of security in the war which he had not found in peace. So long as the

Germans did not come to upset that security, the waging of the war could be safely left to the White man. The African could do little to help him.[33]

It was not only in rural West Africa that the view of the war as a European problem prevailed. Among some of the region's educated voices, doubts about the African obligations in the war persisted too. One of the prominent educated African voices in the war period was that of Mr. Robert Gardiner, a research student from the Gold Coast studying in London. A speech he delivered in London in March 1942, entitled "West Africa and the War," echoed some of the observations colonial officials had made about the ambivalent attitudes to the war in West Africa in the previous month. Gardiner's speech was deemed significant enough to merit a dispatch of it in a confidential mail by the Colonial Office in London to Sir Alan Burns, the then governor of the Gold Coast, on 11 June 1942. In this speech, Robert Gardiner noted that educated Africans have discussed and studied the British press since the war broke out. He asked a set of pertinent questions that many educated Africans asked: Is the Empire worth dying for? Does the African feel a sense of danger, when he sees that the security of the Empire is threatened? Gardiner defined a "sense of danger" as "consciousness of belonging together." He saw the fundamental question in the war conversation as whether "the African realize[s] that in the long run his true interests are bound up with the fate of the British Empire and the Allied cause." Gardiner noted "some hindrances to Empire patriotism" that were "peculiar to the West African colonies." He identified one of those hindrances as the widespread view in West Africa that "this is a White man's war." He underscored the efforts that "educated Africans" in the region have made to convince "their fellow citizens" about "the great principles for which the war is being fought." These "great principles," Gardner acknowledged, were not so much "the atrocities which Hitler's hordes may or may not commit against Africans," as the colonial government often emphasized, but rather "fighting for a chance to live as human beings." Fighting for "a common conception of life" was, to Gardiner, "the undefined attitude of West Africans to the second world war."[34]

The lax attitude of many educated Africans in West Africa to World War II prevailed against the background of grievances over economic inequalities in the colony and the penchant of the European members of the Gold Coast Legislative Council to vote in unison against every economic and social justice issue the African members of the Council supported. Even as he made the strongest case for a pro-war West African attitude, Gardiner could not obscure his concern that "the clash of the economic interests of white and black [in the Gold Coast colony] is beginning to dawn on us ... [especially the] suspicion that the Government will always protect and support white interest." Gardiner noted that "these are some of the facts which damp down our loyalty." While Gardiner did not subscribe to the dominant view that the Second World War was "a White man's war"—a type of European-on-European violence –he saw in that war a "racial element." He described that racial element as "the struggle against the forces attempting to uphold the idea of racial domination."

Gardiner's hope was that the Second World War "will solve one of the most critical problems of our age, namely, the racial and colour problem" whose existence represented "a weakness in the British Empire."[35]

It was not only the colonial subjects in the British Empire who had passionate reservations about becoming involved in a war triggered by aggression in Europe. The sovereign nation of Liberia had its own reservations. On 19 September 1939, the government of Edwin J. Barclay had proclaimed Liberia's "neutrality" in the war. Two historical factors may have conditioned what President Barclay considered as the "realities" that Liberia faced. First, Liberia had suffered an intense German bombardment for participating in World War I and that historical memory lingered in Liberia. Second, the country had suffered near economic collapse when its major trading partner Germany broke its trade relations with the sovereign West African nation in the course of that war. However, in early 1944 when V.S. Tubman became president, the world had changed so dramatically that Liberia could not ignore the new realities of the time. The Allied powers were winning the war, and the Axis powers very close to defeat. That reality of the 1940s now made impolitic Liberia's policy of neutrality. Monrovia had entered into a defense agreement with the United States in late 1942, and American forces were already stationed in Liberia.[36] That sovereign African nation became an important strategic ally in the Allied war effort following the Japanese control of the major sources of natural rubber in Malaya and Singapore in the Far East (Southeast Asia) in the 1940s. With these sources of natural rubber lost to the Allied Powers, Liberia became the only source of natural rubber accessible to the Allied nations for the production of tires for their war planes and oxygen masks, among other military needs. Liberia had declared its neutrality as the war began and, given the fact that Nazi Germany was Liberia's major trading partner with a significant number of German doctors and merchants living in Monrovia, the capital city, the visit to Liberia in January 1943 by the American President Franklin D. Roosevelt was significant in many respects. Franklin Roosevelt used the special historical relationship the United States had with Liberia to convince the sovereign West African nation's government to break diplomatic relations with Germany, put Liberia's rubber at the disposal of the Allied nations, and make Liberia available for the storage of Allied war supplies. As a major military base for about 5,000 American troops, after 1942, Liberia became a key transit point for Allied military aircraft between South America and North Africa. Liberia's Robertsfield airport featured prominently in Allied bombing raids in Morocco, Tunisia, and Algeria in North Africa.[37]

On 27 January 1944, Liberia officially declared war on Nazi Germany and the Japanese Government.[38] In explaining his government's position to the 40th Liberian Legislature, in its first sitting, President William V.S. Tubman declared Liberia's opposition to "Nazism" as well as "Fascism and Japanese militarism" as the nation's new foreign policy.[39] Liberia's president spoke for his nation and for many colonial subjects in Africa who looked at Nazism with great anxiety even as they viewed the ongoing war with ambivalence. With the passage of a war resolution by the Liberian Legislature on 27 January 1944, Liberia became a sovereign African ally of the Allied Powers.[40] As it became evident in the course of the 1940s, Africans, subject and sovereign, came around to fighting on the Allied side. Nazism and what the Nazi leadership stood for, in the eyes of Africans, made this turn-around possible.

Notwithstanding the initial mixed opinions about African involvement in the "White Man's War," colonial authorities were right to anticipate that the "Nazi attitude to the negro" would be a sufficient reason for Africans to come along and fight on the side of the British against the Germans.[41] In the British colony of the Gold Coast, closer in location to the sovereign nation of Liberia, that anticipation bore fruit in the open expressions of loyalty from prominent chiefs who represented aspects of rural opinion. For some of these chiefs, their loyalty to the Allied war effort was triggered in part by the violations of the "ethics of war" and basic human decency by Nazi Germany. In October 1940, Nana Ofori Atta had urged the Gold Coast Legislative Council to approve an amount of £4,000 from available public funds as humanitarian aid for victims of Nazi bombing raids in London.[42] The chief's proposal was motivated by "news of the many hundreds of women and children and also of the aged and infirm, who have been rendered homeless and made to suffer . . . by the indiscriminate bombing of London by Nazi raiders." This, the chief noted, has "come to us with great shock."[43]

The manner in which the Nazi regime pursued war caused Ofori Atta to offer some key lessons to the Nazi leadership from African martial history and humanitarian laws:

> We in the Gold Coast are not ignorant of the ethics of war nor the necessities of it. Some time ago some of us were actually engaged in conflict with others and the creed of war as we believed it to be was "death to the enemy." By that we mean the combatants or warriors in the field or the able-bodied men who are in a position to return blow for blow. Even to us, we never understood war to mean war on women and children as we see it being done today.[44]

For Ofori Atta and those who thought like him, what was at stake for the African in World War II was not blind loyalty to Empire but a moral defense of human decency and civilized conduct. As the chief put it, "[T]he aged and infirm, women and children are being murdered by the Nazis and we feel that it is our duty to express not only our sympathy in words but to show a tangible mark of it."[45] Ofori Atta's motion for African relief aid to the suffering in Europe was carried with the backing of another chief, who also viewed the ongoing war as a "great war to secure the future of civilization," as prominent chiefs of the Gold Coast understood it.[46] Nana Amanfi III expressed his "gratification" with the "success of our men the 'Green Caps' in East Africa." For him:

the enemy against whom we are fighting can be likened to a venomous snake of the python class [Nanka]. The head of this snake is Hitler and the tail is Mussolini; we are cutting the tail all right in Africa but the head still remains to be cut in order to kill it completely (that is victory). It is therefore essential that there should be no relaxation in our war efforts.[47]

He also assured the Gold Coast colonial government that the Provincial Council of Chiefs would ensure that "there will be considerable rapid inflow of recruits" for the war through conscription.[48]

It is very clear that the persecution of Jews in Germany, as an undercurrent of the war, also served as a powerful reason for rallying support in West Africa for a war that some colonial subjects, understandably, viewed as a tribal conflict between white people in Britain and Germany. Colonial subjects saw the fate of the Jews as intricately tied to their own in a postwar world likely to be regulated by Nazism. While traditional chiefs may have seen their role in the war as recruiters of their subjects to fight for a larger moral cause—duty to humanity and civilization—some educated Africans saw the war differently. For them, the war and sacrifice in it were a social and material transaction between colonial subjects and the colonial state. G.E. Moore, municipal member for Cape Coast in the Gold Coast Legislative Council, pointed to colonialism's authoritarian ethnocentrism that allowed preferential treatment of Europeans in the Gold Coast colony. Moore echoed much of the concerns of the educated African elite as opposed to those of the chiefs:

> We are all, Africans and Europeans, fighting in this war side by side, as members of an Empire; we are fighting Hitler because he thinks the other members of the human race are not human or at most not as equally human as the Germans and therefore he must dominate them and keep them down. If this is why we are fighting Hitler then why should we allow the same feeling or the same treatment to go on among ourselves in our empire?[49]

G.E. Moore's view that "Africans should be admitted into the higher grades of the colonial service" as district commissioners, magistrates, and law officers of the colony was a major sticking point for the educated colonial subjects who were implored by the colonial state to convince their fellow African war skeptics about the necessity of fighting and dying in a war raging far from their homes.[50] For educated Africans, as opposed to the views of the traditional chiefs, duty and loyalty to authority were not enough to induce sacrifice. Shedding blood needed a tangible material outcome in the improvement of colonial conditions if the war was to be seen beyond the racial construction of it by some Africans as a White Man's War.

While the issue of racial and economic justice was discussed in the decorous atmosphere of the Gold Coast Legislative Council, in the nearby British colony of Nigeria, that same grievance was handled in the brisk pages of the

African press. Nnamdi Azikiwe's *West Africa Pilot* had been a leading voice on this matter. Colonial authorities in Nigeria saw Azikiwe's newspaper as the "sole offender" in the publication of "undesirable articles" on the ongoing war and its meaning for colonial conditions. The newspaper's publications on "the conditions of service of African Government servants" in the colonial civil service, war bonuses for enlisted men, and the "terms of service of the lower paid African public servant" were viewed by the colonial administration in Nigeria as "likely to incite disaffection" and "encourage discontent" against the colonial administration.[51] Governor John Evelyn Shuckburgh sought authorization from London in November 1941 to limit publication of certain articles in the colony or subject such publications to "certain conditions." The governor bewailed the fact that editors of various African newspapers in Nigeria, including Azikiwe's paper, had rejected the colonial administration's efforts to control press reports about the war with "a weekly Press Conference in the office of the Information Officer," similar to what the Gold Coast administration had succeeded in doing. As the governor noted, "The Editors made it clear that they were not particularly interested in obtaining an enlightened and authoritative interpretation of the War news and that they had no desire whatever to seek any advice from the Information Officer."[52] In short, the African press in colonial Nigeria sought an independent discussion of the war and what it meant to the African.

Promoting a healthy African interest in the war

Against the disturbing backdrop of mixed African interest in the raging war, British officials in the West African colony of the Gold Coast desperately looked for the best means of "promoting a healthy [African] interest in the war."[53] Doing so required a three-pronged strategy. The first was information control through press censorship or official press releases. The second was continuing the exposure of Hitler's anti-African racism. The third was making Africans aware of the continuing Nazi persecution of European Jews. Since colonial subjects did not make any color or racial distinction between the British and the Germans or between European Jews and White Europeans, the colonial government anticipated that these strategies would convince many Africans that their own survival as Black people was at stake if the anti-African Nazi leaders who treated White Europeans, who happened to be Jews, in that horrendous manner, won the war. This British strategy was aimed at the majority Akan population of the Gold Coast and its dominant cocoa producers. The British had been particularly concerned about the Akan obsession with cocoa, guns, and gin. In a colonial propaganda pamphlet *Empire at War: Britain's Might Forbids the Slavery of Africa*, published on 2 August 1940 by the Department of Information of the Gold Coast colony, the colonial government expressed the following thoughts with little diplomatic nicety:

> There are a few stupid people in this country who say that it doesn't matter very much whether Britain or Germany wins the war because they say

that the Gold Coast people will be as well off under Hitler as under King George. There are others more stupid still, who say that the people of the Gold Coast will be better off under the Germans because there will be a better price for cocoa, everyone will get land free, there will be no restrictions on guns and illicit gin.[54]

In this pamphlet, also submitted to the prominent Akan lawyer in the Gold Coast Dr. J.B. Danquah, the Gold Coast colonial administration intended to amplify its strategies of combatting growing pro-German feelings among the Akan, which, in many ways, were deeply anti-British sentiments. The new strategy was to mix history and emotion in focusing Akan attention on Nazism. John Wilson, the information officer in the governor's office, had suggested that the best way to contain pro-German feelings among the Akans in particular was to get Dr. Danquah and influential Akans, especially teachers, to make specific public statements. They should contrast Nazi Germany's separation of Jewish families and the transportation of Jewish parents to concentration camps for slave labor with Akan reverence for the idea of "family" and show how a similar German conduct in the Gold Coast could end the institution of family as the Akans of the Gold Coast have known it. The colonial propaganda pamphlet *Empire at War* conveyed this message in stark terms:

> Here are some facts about what the Germans have done to Poles, Czechs and Jews. A common sight in Germany is train-loads and lorry-loads of slave-labourers arriving from Poland and Czechoslovakia. These Poles, Czechs and Jews are compelled to labour on the farms of their German masters. The Germans themselves have stated that 1,000,000 Poles, 750,000 Czechs, and 220,000 Jews are so enslaved. These slaves include men, women, and children over 14 years of age. Like prison convicts, they are made to wear marks on their clothes so that they can be recognized for what they are. Poles wear a red cross on a white background. The Jews wear a white double triangle against a yellow background. These modern slave gangs work in groups of 20 and are guarded by armed Germans.

Besides drawing the attention of the Akans in particular to what Nazi Germany could potentially do to "their whole family system" and to the institutions governing property and inheritance, the Gold Coast colonial Information Office thought another "useful type of propaganda" would be to invoke the trans-Atlantic Slave Trade as a framework for discussing the implications of German rule in the Gold Coast. Again, *Empire at War* was blunt in its race-coded narrative:

> As these people are transferred from their homes, Germans are sent to take their place. Often the Germans take over the houses and possessions of the people they have forced into slavery.... This state of affairs is no better than the slavery of the Middle Ages and it is little better than the slavery

to which former generations of Gold Coast Africans were subjected in the bad old days.... Such is the German treatment of white people, some of them people of their own German race. We have heard of, and some of us have read in *Mein Kampf*, the disgraceful things Hitler has said of African people. Can Africans expect any better treatment from Germany than Europeans? The answer is a clear "No". Who then are these stupid people in our midst who in their ignorance or treachery would once again sell Africa into slavery?[55]

Clearly, the British colonial administration in the Gold Coast intended to stir up painful African historical memories for strategic gain. A propaganda tool that painted the searing image, and its associated symbolism, of Jewish mothers stretching their arms out in anguish to hold onto their children as they were torn from their arms by SS soldiers was certain to revive in the minds of the people of the Gold Coast similar memories of slave traders tearing families apart in their capture of children from their mothers for sale on waiting slave ships on the coasts of West Africa.

These strategic narratives appear to have had their anticipated effects. In his correspondence with the acting secretary of Native Affairs of the Gold Coast colony, John Wilson, the chief information officer of the colony, reported the positive effects of the contents of the pamphlet *Empire at War* on "several Africans." He claimed that many of them had spoken approvingly of the pamphlet and that Dr. Danquah, especially, had "considered it of such importance that he has asked permission to translate it into Twi," the language of the Akan people of the Gold Coast.[56] The governor's office as well as the offices of district commissioners also received numerous requests from "local teachers" seeking permission to translate the speeches of the governor and "other prominent Africans and Europeans" about Nazi Germany into the Twi language of the majority Akan people of the Gold Coast.[57] In another correspondence with the conservative British politician Lord Lloyd of Dolobran, John Wilson reaffirmed the successful impact on colonial subjects of British war narratives about Nazi behavior and persecution of European Jews. He reported that "the strong family feeling which exists in the Gold Coast has been outraged by German disruption of the family, both the Nazi system of youth training within Germany itself and by the taking of Poles and Czechs to Germany to work in conditions that are little better than slavery."[58] To the extent that prominent chiefs and custodians of native customs, such as Ofori Atta, Amanfi III, and Tsibu Darko, invoked the Nazi treatment of Jews in their own war exhortations to their subjects, the colonial strategy of using the Nazi persecution of Jews to induce a sympathetic African interest in World War II appears to have been successful.

Colonial subjects fought in World War II, but they did not march enthusiastically into the war. The passage of war conscription bills by colonial administrations and the repeated exhortations of chiefs, the Empire's most obedient servants, point to popular resistance to recruitment despite the economic enticements of military service. Chiefs found it difficult to fill their conscription quotas requested by the colonial state. As obedient a servant of the British Empire as he appeared to be, Nana Amanfi III of Asebu, and a member of the Gold Coast Legislative Council, conceded that there must be reasons for the reluctant response of colonial subjects to the call for military duty. As he put it, "I do not think it will be wise on my part as the representative of the people to hide this secret. There are grievances in the hearts of the people."[59] These grievances included the failure of the colonial government to employ or rehabilitate ex-soldiers who had fought in the First World War, thus leaving many of them in desperate economic and social straits. For the colonial subject exhorted to die in defense of the racial equality and democracy he had been denied under colonialism, conscription came with great irony and death in battle with supreme contradictions. So while many were won over by official explanations of the war and voluntarily enlisted for military service, some reluctant others were "picked up" and forcibly enlisted on the orders of their local chief or seized for enlistment on a trip to the local market. For others, conscription or volunteering to fight in the war was inspired by a self-preservationist purpose. They had lived through the Italian occupation of Ethiopia and had also read Hitler's *Mein Kampf* and seen the stark realities of Fascism and what a German victory could mean for Black Africans. John Henry Smythe, an ex-soldier from Sierra Leone in West Africa, who had read Hitler's book and other commentaries on Nazism, summed up his own self-preservationist motivation for enlisting: "We read what this man [Hitler] was going to do to the blacks if he gets into power.... It was a book which would put any black man's back up and it put mine up."[60]

For the British government, the power of the voice of "the intelligent African" in the colony was the greatest concern as much as the greatest comfort. Official colonial propaganda was therefore aimed at channeling the mind of that kind of African toward official interpretations of the war. A propaganda article drafted mainly to sway public opinion about the ongoing war in the Gold Coast in particular and accommodating various comments offered on the draft within key offices of the Colonial Office in Whitehall reveals the thoughts that shaped British official strategies of extracting the patriotism of educated and conscientious Africans. On 14 July 1942, Sir Donald Cameron, director of the Broadcasting Division of the Ministry of Information in the Colonial Office, drafted a long letter entitled "Hitler's New Order" to be sent "for use on the Gold Coast" after various departments of the Colonial Office commented on it.[61] In this letter, Donald Cameron referred to Adolf Hitler as "that enemy of mankind" who believed that "Germans are a chosen race ... and ... as such they alone are entitled to all the best conditions of life." He reiterated the dominant war information theme that "Germans," including "Hitler himself—despise non-Europeans even more than they profess to despise the rest of Europe." Therefore, "it is abundantly clear that Africans would not be justified in thinking that they would receive any more favourable treatment than meted out by Germans to Europeans not belonging to the German 'chosen race.'" To those in Africa who had concluded that the raging war in Europe seemed "remote" to them, Donald Cameron asked them to think about this:

> It emerges from German writings that when Germany wins the war and the spoils are handed out, her share of Africa is to include not only the Cameroons and the Congo, but also Nigeria, Kenya, Tanganyika, Uganda and the Rhodesias. It is certain that if she could win the war by breaking the power of the British Empire, she could, and would, seize a large slice of tropical Africa.... How would that affect you; how would it affect your cocoa? ... Now it is well known that before the war the world's supply of cocoa had so largely increased—mainly on account of the increased output from West Africa.... If Hitler held a subjugated Europe of impoverished millions, many of whom consumed your cocoa before this war ... the demand would naturally decline more steeply, with a further steep decline in the price.... What would happen to your cocoa—and to you—if Hitler could obtain his ambition and become master of the world, is too hideous to contemplate.[62]

This initial line of argument that sought to play on the fears of cocoa producers did not generate the type of consummate support Donald Cameron had hoped for. The circulated comments, both typewritten and handwritten, highlight intrasectional politics in Whitehall that pervaded British interest in producing the type of war information that could persuade intelligent Africans. From the Economics Department of the Colonial Office, one Mr. Caine argued that it was "dangerous to labour too much the disadvantages to a country of being a primary producer without industrial development." Since the Gold Coast was "likely to be for a considerable time" a primary producer without industrial development, "if we point out how the wicked Germans are going to prevent other countries from continuing or developing industrial production, the intelligent African might well ask just what the British propose to do to promote desirable industrial production in West Africa."[63] He suggested, "The better thing is to concentrate on saying that the Germans would fix the terms of trade entirely without consultation with the subject states and entirely in their own interest." But, even this argument, Mr. Caine feared, "might expose us to something of a come back in that our intelligent African might point out that since the outbreak of war the price of cocoa has been fixed by the British Government without any obvious consultation with the cocoa producers." He suggested that the claim that what would happen to Gold Coast cocoa in the event of a German victory will be "too hideous to contemplate" be discarded since it borders on "journalistic exaggeration."[64] Mr. Carstairs of the same department agreed with Mr. Caine's comment and added that:

> the more we try to describe the probable activities of Germany in West Africa, the more this description will resemble a widespread conception of

the existing policies adopted in West Africa by the United Africa Company. I think that for propaganda purposes, it would be better to stick to the "half-apes" [a reference to Hitler's description of Africans in his *Mein Kampf*].[65]

A handwritten comment from one Mr. F.J. Pedler reinforced Mr. Carstairs's comments and reiterated that "the 'half-apes' argument ... is the really good one" over the economic argument preferred by the Ministry of Information. Mr. Pedler argued that "Africans on the Gold Coast attribute to the United Africa Company and its associates exactly the kind of wickedness which Sir Donald Cameron attributes to Hitler."[66]

By 4 August 1942, the consensus view within the Colonial Office over Donald Cameron's propaganda piece for the Gold Coast was that it needed to be given a "damper." The final official response to Donald Cameron's draft article was delivered in a confidential note signed by Noel Sabine of the Colonial Office on 6 August 1942. While Sabine considered Cameron's article "interesting," he echoed the views of key sections of the Colonial Office that intelligent Africans on the Gold Coast would not appreciate it "in view of the present unpopularity and suspicion attached to the United African Company whose policies are in some quarters represented as not much different from the Nazi New Order" about which Cameron had written. Sabine suggested that "it would be wiser, for the time being at least, to avoid the lines applied in your article to the cocoa theme in West Africa."[67] While the argument about economic domination by a victorious Germany was discarded, the social argument about Hitler's racist insult of Africans as "apes" was maintained as the dominant colonial propaganda theme. That ex-soldiers, such as Baby Sy, and John Henry Smythe remember this particular trope in British military recruitment drives in West Africa 70 years after the war, as already noted in Chapter 2, indicates that this strategy of using Hitler's dehumanization of Africans as a military tool had its desired impact on some colonial subjects.

War and the conversation about social justice and human decency

The debates in West Africa over the necessity and even morality of war with Nazi Germany transcended African critiques of Nazism, the distaste for Nazi persecution of German Jews, and condemnation of Nazi war crimes. Discussions about the war also created room for other conversations about social and racial justice in the colonies. There was much that separated colonial subjects from colonial administrators in conceptions of the morality of African involvement in the war. However, Nazi racial attitudes and the daily reports of Nazi anti-Jewish pogroms, along with echoes of Germany's interest in repossessing its former colonies in Africa, produced a discernible lull in the anticolonial attitudes of colonial subjects. Nana Ofori Atta's speech in the Gold Coast

Legislative Council meeting of 18 February 1941 captured the thoughts of many in colonial West Africa:

> Let every responsible man in this country do his duty, particularly at this time to make the people understand that it is . . . for our liberty and freedom that this war is being fought. It must be remembered that Africa and Africans were among the aims which Hitler had in waging this war. Before the war broke out Hitler claimed that the former German colonies should be returned to Germany. Well we all know what sort of man he is. If this had been agreed to and a place like Togoland had been given to him, what would have happened to us in the Gold Coast? We all know that at one time his only claim was Danzig but what happened? He simply walked into Czechoslovakia and took the Czechs who bear no relation to German as slaves.[68]

One of the subjects of the Legislative Council's debates on that day was racial equality and the humanity of Africans. Ofori Atta had concluded his statement in the Council by arguing that he was "sure that after the war, we shall have a better Gold Coast; equal rights and opportunities will be conceded to us."[69] But Governor Arnold Hodson had a different view. He had to inject a startling but forthright dose of imperial realism into Ofori Atta's expectations. After suggesting that he had listened to the speeches of the African representatives in the Council "with great interest," the British governor warned:

> There is no doubt that there is an impression abroad that after the war this muddled and distracted world will be changed into something resembling, as far as is possible, a human paradise. I must warn Honourable Members against this impression because, in my own view, the years immediately after the war will be more difficult and trying than the war itself. It, therefore, behooves us, one and all, not to cast our hopes too high. . . . Now to turn to the burning question which is agitating your minds so much namely, higher European posts for Africans. My view, given to you on so many occasions, are well known to you all. Certain colonies have stated that it is their policy, in the course of time, to give *all* European posts to Africans. This is not my policy, and I am quite convinced that it is not the wish of the Africans themselves. After all, Africans are very fair and generous-hearted in their views and I feel certain they realize the immense debt of gratitude they owe to Europeans for the work they have done, and are doing in the Gold Coast, and they also realize that without the Imperial Government they would not be able to retain the independence of the Gold Coast against foreign Powers who covet its riches. It would, therefore, be ungenerous to return the debt of gratitude you owe to Europeans by turning them out of their employment when you have passed through the bad and difficult periods of your history largely owing to their help, and have reached your present high state of culture and civilization owing to

their activities. I feel sure you will agree with me that the [civil] service is infinitely stronger with Europeans serving in it than without them.⁷⁰

Governor Hodson's private feelings, made public on that day, about racial equality and social and economic justice were clear. He did not anticipate any rapid transformation of the status quo in the colony after the war. His view of an African ascension to civilization and high culture under European tutelage was consistent with the dominant British view of colonialism and also mirrored the perspectives of British settlers in colonial Kenya. For Arnold Hodson, the persistent demands by the European-educated people of the Gold Coast for high positions in the colonial service, on their own land, amounted to a lack of an African appreciation for the "civilizing mission" that European colonialism represented. Hodson saw a "fifty-fifty" sharing between Europeans and Africans of the "senior posts" in the colonial state, not a total takeover by Africans, as the "right" public policy.⁷¹ That policy position contradicted the cause for which colonial subjects had been summoned to fight in World War II to combat domination of one racial group by another in Europe and in the world.

As the war wound to a close, this simmering grievance of educated Africans against British colonialism resurfaced. The Gold Coast Legislative Council Municipal member for Accra, Mr. Akilagpa Sawyerr, revived this simmering concern in an evocative address in March 1945, in the Legislative Council to the new Governor Sir Alan Burns:

> Your Excellency, . . . An African child is born into the world. Gradually he grows up. The moment he becomes conscious of his existence as a human being in his own native country—in the land of his birth, what does he find? Everywhere, at the top of every service—the European, the Englishman—at the bottom—the African. He feels greatly dissatisfied; and from that moment he begins to ask himself the reason why. It is not possible for Your Excellency to appreciate to the full this feeling of innate dissatisfaction I am trying to portray. And however much some Africans in the Senior Service of the Government may smile and try to dissemble their feelings in the presence of their European Heads of Departments, the fact remains that there is not a single African in the whole country holding the post of a Head of Department after more than a century of our connection with Great Britain. And that feeling of dissatisfaction grows and increases day by day.⁷²

While Sawyerr's sentiment may not have been representative of opinions of every colonial subject in West Africa, it captured a central grievance of some colonial subjects about racial inequality akin to Nazi racism. The approaching victory against Nazi ethnonationalism and its other racist manifestations therefore empowered more colonial subjects to openly and fearlessly discuss the contradictions of white supremacy in the colonies and the persistent exhortations of colonial subjects by the British to help defeat Nazi racism in Europe. In short, Africans did not necessarily "fight for Britain" in the Second World War. They fought for themselves, given what a large number of Africans perceived could be the implications for them if the Axis Powers won the war.

Conclusion

The reality of Nazi territorial annexations in Central Europe and rumors of the transfer of Nigeria and the Gold Coast to Nazi Germany created palpable anxieties in both colonies in West Africa. Nazi racial antipathy towards Africans and Jews fueled that anxiety. Thus, fighting against Hitler, from the perspective of African concerns about dignity and survival, became, in the minds of colonial subjects, a fight for self-preservation. The success of that foremost objective came to depend, however, on fighting in the Second World War with their British colonial overlords. Fear of Nazism ironically tied the humanity of Africans to an uncomfortable and even paradoxical embrace of British colonialism. Nonetheless, persuading colonial subjects to fight and even die in a war they were ambivalent about took many years of experimental British propaganda tactics. Three years into the war, the Colonial Office was still searching for the most persuasive argument to rally support in West Africa for war against Germany and one that would not trigger embarrassing comparisons between Nazism and colonialism. Initially, the British tried a narrative that emphasized the economic implications of a German victory for raw-material-producing colonies in Africa. That line of argument was abandoned because it was viewed as likely to generate a counterargument from intelligent Africans about the domineering and discriminatory economic actions of colonial governments and European trading companies. The consensus official preference was therefore a narrative that emphasized Hitler's racism and grand designs for global conquest. In that simple narrative, intelligent colonial subjects were not expected to look far to see World War II as a war to save them and human civilization. They could relate to it by looking at the contents of Hitler's book and the Fuehrer's intentions for Jews and Africans, what the Nazi regime had actually done to Jews in Europe, and what it could potentially do to Africans in Africa.

For the intelligent African whom colonial war propaganda was designed to sway, the shift by Whitehall to a social and racial narrative—Hitler's contempt for the African—was equally counterproductive. It allowed colonial subjects to make the kind of comparisons between the supremacist worldviews of the Nazis and the entrenched privileges of Europeans in colonial society similar to the economic counterarguments the Colonial Office sought to avoid. Ultimately, it was neither the economic argument nor the racial one that generated the healthy interest in the Second World War the British sought among the most conscientious of colonial society. Rather, it was the broader moral lesson in the Nazi treatment of European Jews that intrigued the most insightful of colonial subjects. Africans like Namdi Azikiwe, G.E. Moore, Robert Gardiner, and Akilagpa Sawyerr, who articulated the thoughts of the discerning colonial subject, saw the fate of Europe's Jews in the hands of the Nazis as a reflection of their own condition under colonial rule and potential fate in an uncertain future. Thus, African support for World War II was far from a supine demonstration of loyalty to Great Britain and its colonial empire. Access to reports about the condition of Jews in Nazi Germany created in the minds of colonized Africans a veritable bond of kinship with European Jews anchored in a visible and concurrent shared history of persecution. They saw the fate of Europe's Jews as intricately tied to their own in a world that could potentially be governed by Nazi racial dogmas. That intellectual framework for understanding the meaning of the Second World War allowed colonial subjects to invoke the atrocities of the Nazi regime against Europe's Jewish population to challenge colonialism's intrinsic Nazism and its authoritarian ethnonationalism.

Clearly, colonial subjects in Africa were not oblivious to reports of Nazi persecution of German and other European Jews before and during World War II and Nazi violations of the ethical boundaries of warfare. Colonial subjects distilled that knowledge from various press reports and the limited reports colonial administrators shared about the horrendous details of the Holocaust. What better explanation could exist beyond the possibility that the British must have found the details of the Holocaust too embarrassing an evidence of European savagery to share with their colonial subjects, mindful that the most discerning among them would use that evidence to undercut the orthodox narrative of colonialism as a civilizing mission to save the African from savagery and barbarism. Undoubtedly, the Nazi persecution of Jews was one of the moral catastrophes that lurked in the background of World War II. Colonial subjects in Africa were not oblivious to that undercurrent of the global war. How they viewed and discussed what has been described as one of the "seminal catastrophes" of the first half of the twentieth century is a salient but often silent theme in African and Holocaust historiographies.[73] It is to this salient subject matter—African reactions to the Holocaust—that we now turn.

Notes

1 Heike Liebau, Katrin Bomber, Katharina Lange, Dyala Hamzah, and Ravi Ahuja, eds., *The World in World Wars: Experiences, Perceptions and Perspectives from Africa and Asia* (Leiden and Boston: Brill, 2010), 2.
2 For additional studies of Africa and World War II, including more recent work on the subject, see Byfield and Brown, *Africa and World War II*. Earlier publications on the subject include Gregory Mann, *Native Sons: West African Veterans and France in the Twentieth Century* (Durham, NC: Duke University Press, 2006); Richard Osbourne, *World War II in Colonial Africa: The Death Knell of Colonialism* (Indianapolis, IN: Riebel-Roque, 2001); David Killingray and Richard Rathbone, eds., *Africa and the Second World War* (New York: St. Martin's Press, 1986).
3 Stewart, *The First Victory*, 49. See also Meshack Owino, "Africa and the Second World War," in Martin S. Shanguhyia and Toyin Falola, eds., *The Palgrave Handbook of African Colonial and Postcolonial History*, vol. 1 (New York: Palgrave Macmillan, 2018), 356–357, 367.
4 Zik, "Inside Stuff: Trust Us," *West African Pilot*, 11, no. 368, Saturday January 26, 1939, 4.
5 Anonymous, "Stop Hitler!" [Editorial], *West African Pilot*, 11, no. 432, Thursday April 11, 1939.

6 Ibid.
7 Anonymous, "What Next! Colonies?" *West African Pilot*, vol. II, no. 438, Thursday April 25, 1939.
8 Editorial page, "Ominous Shadows," *West African Pilot*, vol. II, no. 413, Thursday March 23, 1939.
9 Editorial page, "The Signs of the Times," *West African Pilot*, vol. III, no. 543, Monday August 28, 1939, 4.
10 Ibid.
11 Killingray and Plaut, *Fighting for Britain*, 8, 46, 58.
12 Stewart, *The First Victory*, 49, 51, 72–73, 233, 241.
13 Editorial page, "When Friends Desert," *Gold Coast Spectator*, Saturday September 24, 1938. See also a reprint, in the *Spectator*, of an article by Chatwood Hall entitled "Fascism Now Threatens Czechoslovakia: Fruits of Concessions to Aggressors Beginning with Abyssinia," July 2, 1938.
14 Bairu, *Ethiopia and Germany*; Smidt, *Ethiopia and Germany: 100 Years of Diplomatic Relations*. Also Wolbert Smidt, "Germany, Relations with [Ethiopia]," in Siegbert Uhlig, ed., *Encyclopaedia Aethiopica*, vol. 2 (D-Ha) (Wiesbaden: Harrassowitz Verlag, 2005).
15 Bairu, *Ethiopia and Germany*, 141.
16 Ibid., 142. See also Smidt, "Germany, Relations with [Ethiopia]," 770.
17 Bairu, *Ethiopia and Germany*, 142.
18 Ibid., 141. Bairu's point about the role that Mussolini's and Hitler's row over Austria must have played in Nazi Germany's secret military aid to Ethiopia was confirmed to the author in his e-mail correspondence with Richard Pankhurst on October 29, 2007. Pankhurst is a well-known writer on Ethiopian history, a naturalized Ethiopian who had good access to Haile Selassie's palace and Ethiopia's ruling elite, and someone in a good position to know aspects of this peculiar relationship.
19 Hitler, *Mein Kampf*, 545.
20 Ibid., 552.
21 Ibid., 558–559, 561, 567.
22 Ibid., 567.
23 Wolbert Smidt, in his e-mail correspondence with this author on October 17, 2013, also acknowledges Hitler's strategy of weakening Mussolini by offering secret military assistance to Ethiopia. For a brief reference to Hitler's and Mussolini's "rivalry over Austria and the German-speaking territories in Italy," see Richard Pankhurst, *Sylvia Pankhurst, Counsel for Ethiopia: A Biographical Essay on Ethiopian, Anti-Fascist and Anti-Colonialist History, 1934–1960* (Hollywood, CA: Tsehai Publishers and Distributors, 2003), 26.
24 Author's e-mail correspondence with Richard Pankhurst, October 29, 2007.
25 Gold Coast Government, *Proceedings of the Meetings of the Legislative Council Held in the Colonial Secretary's Office, Accra, at 10:00 am, on Tuesday September 5, 1939*. PRAAD, GNA. File: ADM 14/2/31.
26 Ibid.
27 Gold Coast Government, *Proceedings of the Meetings of the Legislative Council held in the Supreme Court, Accra, at 10:00 am, on Thursday March 12, 1940*. PRAAD, GNA. File: ADM 14/2/34, 2–4.
28 Ibid.
29 John Wilson, Information Officer, Gold Coast colony, to the Colonial Office, "Further Report on Public Opinion in the Gold Coast," November 1, 1940, PRAAD, GNA. File: CSO 23/5/32.
30 "German Propaganda" [Editorial].
31 Minutes of the Executive Council, 6-6-40, PRAAD, GNA. File: CSO 23/1/75, No. S.0066, "Secret" 1939–41.
32 Cooper, *Despatches from Secretary of State to Governor*.
33 Confidential Report of Conference of Information Officers held at Accra in February 1942, PRAAD, GNA. File: CSO, vol. 1, no. 2420. Conference attended by Mr. T.

Barton, Gold Coast (Chair), Mr. H.C.B. Denton, Nigeria, Mr. A.B. Matthews, Sierra Leone. Information Officer from Gambia unable to attend.
34 "West Africa and the War," Address given by Mr. R. [Robert] Gardiner, from the Gold Coast colony, at a meeting at Chatham House on Tuesday March 24, 1942. PRAAD, GNA. File: CSO 23/5/168, *West Africa and the War*. Robert Gardiner was conducting special research on the Gold Coast colony under the Nuffield College Colonial Research Scheme sponsored by the Royal Institute of International Affairs, Chatham House, London.
35 Ibid.
36 D. Elwood Dunn, *The Foreign Policy of Liberia During the Tubman Era, 1944–1971* (London: Hutchinson Benham, 1979), 55.
37 "American Liberia Relations During World War II," unpublished material obtained from the Africana Library of the University of Liberia. See also Judith Byfield, "Producing for the War," in Byfield and Brown, *Africa and World War II*, 27, 30, and Akingbade, "U.S. Liberian Relations During World War II," 27, 30.
38 Richardson, *Liberia's Past and Present*, 183.
39 Townsend, *President William V.S. Tubman of Liberia Speaks*, 18.
40 Dunn, *The Foreign Policy of Liberia During the Tubman Era*, 55.
41 Cooper, *Despatches of Secretary of State to Governor*.
42 Legislative Council, Gold Coast Colony, *Debate Session 1940*. Issue 2, PRAAD, GNA, October 2, 1940, 13–14. File: ADM 14/2/35.
43 Ibid.
44 Ibid.
45 Ibid.
46 Gold Coast Colony, *Legislative Council Debates*. Session 1942, Issue 1. February 26, 1942, PRAAD, GNA. File: ADM 14/2/38.
47 Gold Coast Government, *Proceedings of the Meeting of the Legislative Council Held in the Supreme Court (Court C), Accra, at 10:00 am, on Tuesday February 18, 1941*. PRAAD, GNA. File: ADM 14/2/36, 86.
48 Ibid.
49 Gold Coast Colony, *Legislative Council Debates*.
50 Ibid.
51 Secret dispatch from the Governor to Lord Moyne, Secretary of State for the Colonies, London, November 20, 1941, British National Archives [PRO]. File: CO 875/13/5, *Press Censorship, Nigeria*.
52 Ibid.
53 Governor Arnold Hodson to the Lord Lloyd of Dolobran, P.C., "Public Opinion in the Gold Coast Towards the War."
54 John Wilson, Information Officer, Department of Information, Gold Coast Colony, to the Honorable Acting Secretary of Native Affairs, Accra, "Empire at War," no. 45, August 13, 1940, PRAAD, GNA. File: CSO/23/5/32.
55 Gold Coast Colonial Government, Department of Information, *Empire at War: Britain's Might Forbids the Slavery of Africa*, no. 45, August 2, 1940, PRAAD, GNA. File: CSO 23/5/32.
56 John Wilson to Acting Secretary of Native Affairs, August 13, 1940, PRAAD, GNA. File: CSO 23/5/32.
57 One of these many requests came from one local teacher T.K. Kyei. See T.K. Kyei, to the News Officer, Kumasi, April 29, 1940, PRAAD, GNA. File: CSO/23/5/19. File: "Speeches and Addresses Relating to the War Delivered by H.E. the Governor and Other Prominent People." Permission was granted to T.K. Kyei by the Chief Commissioner's Office in Kumasi.
58 Wilson to Lord Lloyd of Dolobran, PC, November 1, 1940, PRAAD, GNA. File: CSO 23/5/19.
59 *Proceedings of the Meeting of the Legislative Council Held in the Supreme Court (Court C), Accra, at 9 am on Wednesday June 11, 1941*. PRAAD, GNA. File: ADM 14/2/37.

60 BBC News, "The Africans Who Fought in WW II," by Martin Plaut, BBC Africa Analyst, August 28, 2014, http://news.bbc.co.uk/2/hi/africa/8344170.stm
61 "Hitler's New Order," by Sir Donald Cameron, Ministry of Information, Colonial Section. Public Relations File ab 628/14 C, *Propaganda: Gold Coast, 1942–43*. PRO. CO 875/6/9.
62 Ibid.
63 "Mr. Caine to Sir Donald Cameron, July 21, 1942," in *Propaganda: Gold Coast, 1942–43*.
64 Ibid.
65 "Mr. Carstairs to Sir Donald Cameron, July 22, 1942," *Propaganda: Gold Coast, 1942–43*.
66 "Mr. F.J. Pedler to Mr. Carstairs, July 27, 1942," *Propaganda: Gold Coast, 1942–43*.
67 "Noel Sabine to Sir Donald Cameron, August 6, 1942," *Propaganda: Gold Coast, 1942–43*.
68 Gold Coast Colony, *Proceedings of the Meeting of the Legislative Council held in the Supreme Court (Court C), Accra, at 10:00 am on Tuesday February 18, 1941*, 96–97. PRAAD, GNA. File: ADM 14/2/36.
69 Ibid.
70 Ibid., 114–116.
71 Ibid.
72 Gold Coast Colony, *Proceedings of the Meeting of the Legislative Council Held in the Supreme Court (Court C), Accra, at 9:30 am on Monday the March 19, 1945*. Legislative Council Debates. Session 1945, Issue 1, 105, PRAAD, GNA. File: ADM 14/2/44.
73 Liebau et al., *The World in World Wars*, 8.

4   Africans and the Holocaust

There is no persuasive dispute among scholars about the historical reality and also significance of the Holocaust. In his contribution entitled "The Holocaust: Where We Are, Where We Need to Go" to the book *The Holocaust and History: The Known, the Unknown, the Disputed and the Re-examined*, Eberhard Jackel counted the Holocaust among "historical events of central importance."[1] As Heike Liebau and others have also reaffirmed, the Holocaust was one of the "seminal catastrophes" of the first half of the twentieth century.[2] Some scholars, including Jackel and Wyman, acknowledge that the Holocaust was a major war aim of Nazi Germany during the Second World War. As such, the Holocaust generated "reactions in Germany, the country of the perpetrators" as well as perceptions and responses from "those in the rest of the world" who either witnessed the Holocaust in close proximity or read about it from a distance.[3] What remains in contention, however, is how the Holocaust is defined. What is also "unknown" among the "known" facts of the Holocaust is how people in sub-Saharan Africa, as part of the rest of the world, responded to this global catastrophe while it was going on. This chapter takes the study of the Holocaust to that unknown terrain of investigating the reactions, in East and West Africa, to this historical event of central importance.

What is "the Holocaust"?

Holocaust comes from an ancient Greek word *holocaustos* meaning "the burnt sacrificial offering dedicated *exclusively* to God" or "that which is completely burnt."[4] In the thirteenth century, the lower-case English derivative *holocaust* was used in some English versions of the Bible to refer "specifically to a religious sacrifice" in the form of a burnt offering.[5] Until the outbreak of World War II, some scholars and writers used the word *holocaust* to describe a wide range of situations including the complete destruction of cities by fire, the massacre of large numbers of people in violent political processes, or the callous disregard of dominant nations for the welfare of their subject populations. For instance, in June 1939 the *West African Pilot* newspaper published an article by one E.C.T. Herman on the prevailing allegations that Britain intended to transfer parts of its West African colony of Nigeria to Nazi Germany. Herman asked that "Abyssinia has been crucified: will Nigeria now be offered as a holocaust for the peace of Europe?"[6] In all these earlier usages, the word *holocaust* retained its original religious connotation as a divinely ordained act or a bad thing that had to happen for a greater good to emerge. In the course of World War II, particularly the early 1940s, the word *holocaust* acquired new meaning and raised new concerns. When some newspapers and scholars characterized the war in Europe, especially the deliberate destruction of Polish Jews and other groups of people in gas chambers by the Nazi regime, as a holocaust, the implied explanation of that atrocity as an obligatory religious ritual (a form of burnt offering) raised serious and legitimate concerns. From the late 1940s onward, the phrase "the Holocaust," in its upper-case form, gained a new secular and didactic meaning as a rare horrible event or the ultimate evil act. It came to represent the mass murder of European Jews by the Nazi regime in the works of some writers, including those who had survived the horrors of the Nazi death camps.[7] Again, misgivings remained about whether that is an appropriate use of the phrase or even the term *Holocaust*.

There are scholars who argue in their work that "the Holocaust" should be used exclusively to describe the Nazi persecution and attempted destruction of European Jews because the Nazi regime targeted them as Germany's primary enemies. Of this group of scholars, the works of historians Saul Friedlander, Donald Bloxham and Tony Kushner, and Steven Katz are perhaps the most notable. Friedlander puts his understanding of the Holocaust in italics for emphasis in his book *Nazi Germany and the Jews, 1939–1945: The Years of Extermination*. He sees the Holocaust as the "*persecution and extermination of the Jews of Europe*."[8] Friedlander's view is similar to Bloxham's and Kushner's. Although they see the term *Holocaust* as an "unscientific" description of what happened to the Jewish people in Nazi Germany and point to alternative and more applicable terms such as "final solution" or "Nazi Jewish policy," Bloxham and Kushner accept the use of the term *Holocaust* "as [a] shorthand for the Jewish experience during the Second World War and/or the Nazi period."[9] Historian Steven Katz is not that nuanced in his conception of the *Holocaust* or *Shoah*, which he uses interchangeably. He sees "the Holocaust" as both "the immolation of European Jewry and the intended extinction of world Jewry." Katz is unapologetic in his view that the Holocaust is "phenomenologically unique" in the long history of state-organized mass murders.[10] He argues that until the Holocaust occurred, "never before ha[d] a state set out, as a matter of intentional principle and actualized policy, to annihilate physically every man, woman, and child belonging to a specific people."[11] In the view of Steven Katz, "it is this unmediated, intended, complete *physical* eradication of every Jewish man, woman, and child that defines the particular, singular nature of this event that we call the Holocaust."[12]

Other scholars contend that the Holocaust should not be viewed exclusively as a Nazi genocide against only the Jewish people but rather broadly to include other victims of the Nazi regime. These scholars point to the persecution and also destruction of the Roma and Sinti people (Gypsies), people with physical and genetic disabilities, members of the Jehovah's Witnesses religion, Black Germans, and homosexuals, among other groups, by the Nazi regime as equally targeted and similarly unique. A few scholars in this group go as far as to argue that the word *Holocaust* should be applied more loosely as a descriptor of intentional mass killing of people committed by governments or settler groups. Of this opposing school of thought on the Holocaust as a concept, the works of author Ina R. Friedman and historian David E. Stannard are among the most prominent.

Writing in 1995, in her article "The Holocaust: The Other Victims of the Nazis," Ina R. Friedman noted that 50 years after the end of the Second World War, "few people are aware that Jews were not the only victims of the Nazis."[13] She emphasizes that "in addition to six million Jews, more than five million non-Jews were murdered under the Nazi regime." The non-Jewish victims of the Nazi regime were "Gypsies, Jehovah's Witnesses, homosexuals, Blacks, the physically and mentally disabled, political opponents of the Nazis, including Communists and Social Democrats, dissenting clergy, resistance fighters, prisoners of war, Slavic peoples, and many individuals from the artistic community whose opinions and works Hitler condemned." Like the Jews, these people were also considered by the Nazi regime as "racially, socially, and physically defective" for the pure and perfect society it wanted to create.[14] Therefore, by applying the term *Holocaust* solely or exclusively to the Jewish victims of the Nazi regime, scholars dismiss deliberately or overlook inadvertently other important aspects of the complex structure of Nazi crimes.

David E. Stannard's views on how the Holocaust should be defined and studied mirror those of Ina Friedman's. As Stannard argues, "within the framework of the Holocaust itself," there was another "unique . . . campaign of genocide conducted by the Nazis against Europe's Romani (Gypsy) people, which resulted in the mass murder of perhaps 1,500,000 men, women, and children."[15] Stannard points out that at Auschwitz, the Holocaust's emblematic site of mass murder, the Nazi regime "systematically" exterminated "many . . . of Europe's Jews, [and] Gypsies" as well as other human beings the Nazi regime characterized as "useless."[16] Like Bloxham and Kushner, Stannard finds alternative terminologies as more applicable and descriptive of the Jewish experience in Nazi Germany than the word *Holocaust*. He prefers "Jewish Holocaust" or "Judeocide," as a better definition of the "inhuman destruction of 6,000,000 [Jewish] people" in Europe by the Nazi regime.[17] David E. Stannard is the most revolutionary in his understanding and use of the term *Holocaust*. He contends that it was the same racist theories that the Nazis used to classify people in Europe as "worthy" and "unworthy" before the "Jewish Holocaust" that European settlers also used to categorize "the natives of the Americas" and perpetrate against them "an even more massive genocide" for "four grisly centuries" after 1492.[18] Stannard implies that the term *Holocaust* should not be reserved for the exclusive description of the Jewish experience in Nazi Germany. Rather, it should be used to describe massive campaigns of murder and extermination of dehumanized groups by governments or settlers in colonial or empire-building ventures.

From that conceptual threshold, Stannard sees the term *Holocaust* as also applicable to the Native American experience and regards the "Jewish Holocaust" as similar to the "American Holocaust" in its historical origins.

Perhaps the most striking definitions of the Holocaust that acknowledge the validity of the positions of both schools of thought are the conceptions adopted by the United States Holocaust Memorial Museum (USHMM) and Israel's Yad Vashem Holocaust Resource Center as the global repositories of Holocaust historical documents, as well as the United Nations. The USHMM defines the Holocaust as "the systematic, bureaucratic, state-sponsored persecution and murder of six million Jews by the Nazi regime and its collaborators."[19] However, the Museum concedes that "[d]uring the era of the Holocaust, German authorities also targeted other groups because of their perceived 'racial inferiority.'" These groups are listed as the "Roma (Gypsies), the disabled, and some of the Slavic peoples (Poles, Russians and others)." The Museum adds that the Nazi regime and its collaborators also persecuted "Communists, Socialists, Jehovah's Witnesses, and homosexuals" on "political, ideological, and behavioral grounds."[20] This is also the definition of the Holocaust adopted by the United Nations, although the global organization views the Holocaust in terms of its outcome and universal lessons. The UN's agency for education, UNESCO, takes a view of the Holocaust that is identical to the definition adopted by the United States Holocaust Memorial Museum. UNESCO's 2017 global policy guide on *Education About the Holocaust and Preventing Genocide* states that "[t]he term "Holocaust" (or *Shoah*, meaning "catastrophe" in the Hebrew language) is used to refer to the systematic, bureaucratic, state-sponsored persecution and murder of six million Jews by Nazi Germany and its collaborators." Additionally:

> During the era of the Holocaust, German authorities also targeted other groups because of their perceived 'racial inferiority'; among them were Roma (Gypsies), people with disabilities, and some of the Slavic peoples (Poles, Russians and others). Other groups were persecuted on political, ideological and behavioural grounds, among them Communists, Socialists, Jehovah's Witnesses and homosexuals.[21]

In its Resolution establishing a *Holocaust Remembrance Day* as an international day for honoring the memory of the victims of the Holocaust, the United Nations reaffirmed that "the Holocaust which resulted in the murder of one third of the Jewish people, along with countless numbers of other minorities, will forever be a warning to all people of the dangers of hatred, bigotry, racism and prejudice."[22]

Yad Vashem takes a similar view but with a forthright divergence. It defines the Holocaust as "the sum total of all anti-Jewish actions carried out by the Nazi regime between 1933 and 1945: from stripping the German Jews of their legal and economic status in the 1930s; segregating and starv[ing them] in the various occupied countries; [leading to] the murder of close to six million Jews in Europe by the Nazis." Like its institutional counterpart in the United States,

Israel's Yad Vashem sees the Holocaust as "part of a broader aggregate of acts of oppression and murder of various ethnic and political groups in Europe by the Nazis." For Yad Vashem, the Holocaust has "special significance" for Jews because of "the exceptional attitude with which its perpetrators—the Nazis— regarded their Jewish victims."[23] The Holocaust resource center in Israel acknowledges that, in the 1950s *Holocaust*, a word "which originally meant a sacrifice burnt entirely on the altar," supplanted the biblical word *Shoah*, which had been used in the "early 1940s" as "the standard Hebrew term" for describing "the murder of European Jewry." Unlike the Museum, Yad Vashem prefers to use the Hebrew term *Shoah* instead of *Holocaust* to describe "the murder of and persecution of European Jewry."[24] It is noteworthy that even in these hybrid institutional definitions, the primacy of the Jewish experience in understanding the Holocaust remains dominant.

From the internationally recognized (UN) conception of the Holocaust, we can now assert that people in sub-Saharan Africa (West and East Africa, in particular) had substantial knowledge about the Holocaust, while it was happening, and reflected in diverse ways on its meaning and implications. This chapter focuses on what people in the two regions of Africa knew and thought about the persecution and murder of European Jews by the Nazi regime as a principal feature of the Holocaust from the beginning of the Third Reich in 1933 to its end in 1945. It also examines the sources and depth of that knowledge, the contexts in which people in the two regions of Africa assessed what they knew, how they used their knowledge and assessments of the Holocaust to challenge some of the conditions under which they lived, and some of the immediate impact that the Holocaust had on race-based colonial policies in colonial Africa. The chapter fills some major gaps in African and Holocaust historiographies. It reinforces the thesis of this book that colonial subjects and sovereign peoples in Africa knew much more about the Holocaust, as an undercurrent of World War II, and reflected on it in various ways than scholars who study African history and the history of the Holocaust have hitherto acknowledged it. It provides an African perspective on a major catastrophe that took place in the course of a global war in which people in Africa participated as combatants, commentators, philanthropists, and pacifists. While this chapter is not about how *Holocaust* or *Shoah* should be defined, it adds some important evidence, from the African perspective, to how this conceptual controversy can be satisfactorily resolved.

Sources and scope of knowledge

The Holocaust, as it is now understood internationally, was very well publicized in the colonial African press. From the rise of the Third Reich in 1933 to its demise in 1945, various newspapers in East and West Africa chronicled the particular treatment of Jews by the Nazi regime. These newspapers obtained their information from a wide range of foreign news sources, as well as official British diplomatic correspondence. In the front pages, editorial spaces, feature articles and sidebars, as well as in the regular and letters columns, interested readers learned about the horrid details of the persecution of Jews and the imposition of legal restrictions on them in Germany in particular. A careful examination of newspapers in the two regions of Africa, along with information that colonial administrators shared with their subjects, reveals that colonial subjects and sovereign peoples in West and East Africa were fully aware of the major phases and transitions in the history of the Holocaust. In the 1930s, African press reports and colonial documents captured the widespread anti-Jewish persecutions in Germany and East Africa. These reports took a new and ominous turn in the 1940s toward the documentation and analyses of the actual physical annihilation of Jews in Continental Europe by the Nazi regime.

As early as September 1933, nine months after the Nazi party assumed power, the *Uganda Herald* newspaper in East Africa, edited by Indian emigres, published a long feature article by "an outside contributor" on what that anonymous correspondent described as "Germany's present extraordinary treatment of the Jews."[25] The article, based on information from "Reuters cables from Europe," contained detailed accounts of growing and systematic harassment of "naturalized German citizens" who happened to be Jewish. What must have shocked colonial subjects who read it were the astonishing reports that "8000 Jewish doctors, 4000 lawyers, 2000 dentists, and thousands of other Jews have been deprived of their living, and thousands of them are fleeing" Germany and "becoming refugees in the surrounding nations." The contributor did not miss the perplexing irony of this Nazi assault on one of Germany's accomplished professional groups. As the anonymous author wondered "[a] nation that suddenly wakes up ... and begins to ... destroy the very cream and essence of its citizenship—that element of its life that has done such a lot to make the nation what it is—is apparently cutting its own throat." Colonial subjects in West Africa shared that sentiment. The irrational nature of this Nazi conduct, as the author pointed out, was that for the Nazi regime it was the Jewish identity of these doctors, lawyers, and dentists that marked them for singular harassment even if their disappearance cost Germany vital national talent. However, the editors of the *Herald* took pains to dissociate themselves and their newspaper from the anonymous contributor's explanation of this evolving Nazi genocide against the Jews as the unfolding of ancient Judaic prophecy or "part of the Divine purpose."[26] In the typical style of newspapers that do not wish to endorse controversial opinions, the editor wrote that "[w]hile welcoming views on this all important and engrossing subject, the views expressed in this article are those of an outside contributor, not those of '*The Uganda Herald*.'"[27] Despite that editorial caveat, by giving space to this article, the editors of the *Herald* showed interest in the accelerating pace of Nazi persecution of Germany's Jews.

People in Africa were also not oblivious to another major feature of the Holocaust when it happened in Germany: the Nuremberg Laws of 1935. The *Daily Guardian* newspaper in Freetown, Sierra Leone, edited by the Krio intellectual Thomas Decker, reported in September 1935, based on a Reuters news source, that the Nazi regime had banned intermarriages between Jews and

Germans as well as the employment of German household servants by Jews.²⁸ The *Liberian Crisis* monthly newspaper in Monrovia had expressed its own dissatisfaction with interracial marriages between Africans and Germans in that sovereign African nation several months before the Nazi prohibition of interracial marriages in Germany.²⁹ That position aligned the Liberian newspaper with the tenor of the Nazi marriage laws. To the degree that only newspapers in the British colony of Sierra Leone and the sovereign nation of Liberia appear to have taken interest in the Nuremberg laws, this is very significant. For these African societies—one colonized and the other independent, but both with a common history as nations of people freed from slavery in the British West Indies and in the United States, respectively, many of whom were children of interracial marriages—the issue of interracial relationships struck a key chord in ways that were different from the rest of Africa.

Notwithstanding this peculiar fact in the West Africa region, it was the Nazi regime's efforts to enforce the Nuremberg Laws in East Africa that made this aspect of Holocaust history noteworthy in the African context. By doing so, the Nazi regime gave its anti-Jewish persecutions a trans-European character. Governor Mark Young of the Tanganyika territory, under British mandate, had transmitted a translated version of a "notice," originally written in German and addressed to German Jews in East Africa, to the Foreign Office in May 1939. The notice, which the governor indicated was contained in an original letter written in September 1935 and signed by the German Consul in Nairobi, had been sent to one Franz Gutmann, a German Jew resident in Nairobi in the British colony of Kenya. That notice reminded all Jews "living in East Africa" of a German law that required them to give their "newly born children . . . Christian names" with effect from the beginning of January 1939.³⁰ The directive also outlined who the Nazi regime considered a Jew under German law. A Jew was defined as one who is:

> descended from at least three pure Jewish grandparents or a person who is half Jew as a result of descent from two pure Jewish grandparents. Also whoever on the 15 September 1935 belonged to a Jewish religious Community or was thereafter absorbed into one, or whoever on or after 15 September 1935 was married to a Jew, and whoever is born from a marriage concluded after 15 September 1935, and whoever as a result of illegitimate intercourse with a Jew . . . is born illegitimately after the 31 July 1936.³¹

The British governor in Tanganyika must have sent this translated German document to both the Foreign Office and the Colonial Office in May 1939 by special request. In responding to Parliamentary questions in April 1939 about German activities in East Africa, Secretary of State for the Colonies Malcolm MacDonald had disclosed that about 1,290 German nationals lived in Kenya. He also informed the House of Commons that British subjects of Jewish descent who lived in Kenya had also received letters from official German sources addressed to *Deutsch Ost Afrika* (German East Africa), asking them to pay their share of a collective fine the Nazi regime had "recently" imposed on Jews in Germany for the assassination of Ernst vom Rath, a German diplomat in Paris, by a Polish-Jewish student.[32] These disclosures suggest that the Nazi regime never gave up its post–World War I interest in regaining control of former German colonies in East Africa. Extending Nazi anti-Jewish laws passed in Germany to East Africa was the most concrete expression of that lingering interest amid the perception also that what used to be German East Africa was still a de facto part of the Third Reich.

From persecution to imprisonment in concentration camps

Besides the Nuremberg laws, the events of *Kristallnacht*, another feature of the Holocaust, received extensive coverage and instructive analyses in the African press thanks to official British sources. Perhaps the most extensive information that British officials had on the persecution of Jews in Germany, prior to the war and soon after the Nazi-authorized assaults on Jews in November 1938, was a confidential British document entitled *Papers Concerning the Treatment of German Nationals in Germany, 1938–1939*.[33] (See Figure 4.1.) This document (hereafter *Papers*) was "presented by the Secretary of State for Foreign Affairs to Parliament by the Command of His Majesty" and shared with British colonial administrators in Africa as a special enclosure to an official circular on 3 November 1939.[34] Examination of the contents of some newspapers in East and West Africa during the 1930s and 1940s suggests that details of this document became available to Africans and helped to shape their perspectives on the Holocaust.

The *Papers* is a collection of highly confidential letters, testimonies, and memoranda sent by British diplomats in various missions and consulates in Germany and Austria to the Foreign Office in London between 3 March 1938 and 18 February 1939. Accompanying these diplomatic dispatches were many confidential letters and memoranda from Jews and other prisoners who had recently been released from the Nazi-operated concentration camps at Buchenwald and Dachau. The letters offer eyewitness accounts of the systematic and wide-ranging atrocities and indignities the prisoners had endured. The British government did not intend to make these eyewitness accounts of Nazi atrocities at Buchenwald and Dachau public. It did so nevertheless and even shared them with colonial administrators in Africa, with the knowledge that colonial subjects might have access to them, in response to the German government's "propaganda" accusing Great Britain of "atrocities committed by the British in the Boer War" in South Africa between 1899 and 1902. According to the British government, the Nazi regime intended to use that propaganda to motivate White Afrikaners in South Africa to revolt against British colonialism. Not only that, but the British decision to share these highly secret details of anti-Jewish atrocities inside Germany and Austria for public judgment in Britain and Africa had also been triggered by the circulation of "stories . . . of brutal treatment of Germans by the Allies in the present war."[35]

Figure 4.1 Confidential British document detailing Nazi persecution of Jews prior to the war, also sent to British colonies in Africa

Source: Found in the Ghana National Archives, Accra.

It is clear from the *Papers* that the Nazi regime intensified its arrest, detention, torture, killing, and forced emigration of Jews in Germany after the assassination, in Paris, of Ernst vom Rath, Secretary of the German Embassy in that city, by a Polish-Jewish student Herschel Grynszpan on 7 November 1938. The assassination was immediately followed by two days of intense anti-Jewish demonstrations that also resulted in the mass arrests of Jews in Germany and Austria in what has become known in the history of the Holocaust as *Kristallnacht*, or the Night of Broken Glass. The ninth and tenth of November 1938 were the most fateful days in the postassassination anti-Jewish pogroms and atrocities. Large numbers of shops and houses owned by Jews as well as synagogues were set on fire or their glass windows smashed with instruments. On 9 November, about "nineteen synagogues" were deliberately burned by rampaging mobs in Vienna. The Nazi-controlled press applauded these acts of vandalism and arson.[36] Many of the Jews who were arrested on these fateful days and in the weeks afterward ended up at Buchenwald and Dachau detention centers. Heads of British Consulates in Germany and Austria kept the Foreign Office in London informed about the observations of Jews who survived to recount their ordeals to Jewish Refugee agencies and British diplomats.

Undoubtedly, the public disclosure of the *Papers* by the British government was done as a tit-for-tat game of diplomatic poker.[37] That, however, should not detract from the disturbing details the document offers about five horrifying features of the persecution of Jews in Germany and Austria between March 1938 and February 1939. One, when individual Jews were arrested and why. Two, the concentration camp to which they were sent and the prisoners they met there. Three, how prisoners were identified. Four, the nature of the work in the camps and the treatment Jewish prisoners in particular received. Five, the length of time the imprisoned spent at a camp and the conditions under which they were released. The consistency of the eye-witness accounts of torture, starvation and murder lend credibility to the experiences of the informants, many of whose identity British diplomats protected under pseudonyms.

The story of one "Herr X, a well to do Jewish business man" in his "sixties," and imprisoned in the Buchenwald concentration camp for "six weeks" in 1938 is particularly revealing.[38] He recounts excruciating "sixteen"- hour-per-day working hours in the Buchenwald camp during which prisoners were "forbidden to drink even in the hottest weather." While the food "was not bad," it was "insufficient." During his six-week ordeal, "the work of Jewish prisoners was doubled, and their rations halved." Their work consisted of "moving heavy stones, often far beyond the strength" of prisoners. It also included "standing at attention for many hours" and frequent "flogging" for "such small offences as drinking water during working hours." The "usual punishment" of "twenty-five strokes" of public flogging often made many prisoners unconscious. Jews in particular were told by the guards who administered these brutal treatment "that the Fuhrer had himself given orders that the Jews might receive up to sixty strokes."[39] At the time of Herr X's imprisonment at Buchenwald in 1938, the camp had "8000" prisoners. Of that number "1,500" were Jews, 800 were

"Ernste Bibelforscher [International Bible Students]." The remainder were "politicals" and "so-called criminals and gypsies." On identification of prisoners, Herr X recalls that everyone held at the camp "wore a badge." Jews wore "yellow with the Star of David," and the "Bible Students" (possibly members of the Jehovah's Witnesses religion) "violet." While "Jewish prisoners wrote and received letters twice a month," the Bible students "were allowed no communication" at all. Their "courage and religious faith" earned them Herr X's "highest respect" because "they professed themselves ready to suffer to the uttermost what they felt God had ordained for them." Death was a daily occurrence at Buchenwald. Relatives of prisoners who died at the camp were informed by an official to collect their "ashes on payment of 8 marks." When he was finally released, Herr X spent "three weeks in bed." The Charity Organization that took Herr X's testimony and communicated it to the British Foreign Office "confirmed" his statement with similar accounts it received from released prisoners. One of the consistent patterns is that "no Jewish prisoner is ever released unless he can produce evidence that he is able to leave Germany."[40]

The story of Herr Z is similar. He owned "a small business in Germany" and was "arrested in June 1938" in a police roundup of people on a Berlin street.[41] He was first taken to the Alexanderplatz prison cell. Without being charged with any specific offense, he was forced to sign a form approving his remand in "protective custody." He was put on one of several "special trains" that transported "about 3,000 prisoners collected from fifteen different police quarters" on "one-and-a-half hours" excruciating journey to Buchenwald. About "3–4 percent" of those transported to the camp with this prisoner were "Aryans" and "a few gypsies." The prisoners were met on arrival by "S.S. men" who heaped degrading insults and blows on the Jewish people among them. During his imprisonment at Buchenwald for 14 days, the camp, as he remembered it, held "about 10,000 men half of whom were Jews."[42] The prisoners lived under "awful conditions" with limited "straw sacks" to sleep on. Anyone who attempted to escape the camp's awful conditions or attack guards was stopped by the "1,000-volt charged wire" that surrounded the camp or was shot by any of the guards. Work at Buchenwald was relentless, and Jews were not expected to complain of illness or exhaustion; otherwise they could be classified as "work-shy" or feigning sickness to avoid work. Racial segregation was strictly enforced at the camp. "Non-Aryans" could not mingle with "Aryans." How the SS guards at Buchenwald distinguished Aryans from Jews was unclear to Herr Z. What was clear, however, was that Jews had to wear the "David Cross" with specific signs: red for "professional criminal," black for the "work shy," and lilac for the "Bible bug." At the camp, "one is compelled to sign oneself as a 'professional criminal' on one's index card." It was the back of the card that revealed one's "real profession." Refusal to follow this dictate could result in "heavy reprisals." Herr Z confirms that "twenty-five strokes" of lashes on the buttocks were the "normal punishment . . . carried out by two guards standing on each side with riding whips." If the victim cried out, the strokes could be "increased up to thirty-five."[43] There were other "punishments" beside this.

Another was "hanging up 3 meters from the ground by the arms which are violently bent back," done by "express orders from the commandant given through a microphone." A prisoner could hang in that position in public for "ten to twelve hours."[44] Herr Z describes the "S.S. men employed in the camp" as "mostly very young men of 17 to 20" years of age who had been specially "trained" to be brutal and sadistic. They "seemed to revel in inflicting torture." Herr Z wondered how this brutality and sadism of a younger generation of Germans could have been possible. While he survived his two-week experience of human despair at Buchenwald due, as he says, to "prayer," he thought it could have been "more merciful" if the SS guards had shot their victims "than to allow a life, which for all practical purposes had already been destroyed, to drag on to the prolonged infinite agony of the victim." Herr Z's survival of Buchenwald's hellish ordeal was more than the consequence of prayer. As his account reveals, he was "one of a small number" of Jews "who were released because all arrangements were ready for his emigration" from Germany to "South America" or bore no visible scars from the drudgery of work and daily flogging. Prisoners who had scars of their ordeal and who, after their release, could show them to the outside world were not allowed to leave the camp.[45] Those who were released were warned not to say a word about what they had gone through or witnessed at Buchenwald, or they would be rearrested and returned to the camp.

The anti-Jewish demonstrations in November 1938 forced many Jews to consider leaving Germany. Many encamped at various American consulates in Germany looking for exit visas. As Claire Gainer, the British Consul-General in Vienna, informed the British Embassy in Berlin, on 11 November 1938, the Jewish population of Vienna had been brutally abused on the streets "by crowds of hooligans."[46] It was not only Jews in Vienna who were assaulted but also Jews in Salzburg and Linz in Austria. Their shops were looted and synagogues burnt. In Cologne, Germany, similar anti-Jewish demonstrations erupted on 14 November. Intense and violent anti-Jewish acts drove some Jews to commit suicide. British Consul General in Cologne J.E. Bell noted in a dispatch to the British Embassy in Berlin that while angry mobs set the Jewish synagogue in Cologne ablaze, "the local fire brigade took no action."[47] Not all Germans, however, condoned the anti-Jewish atrocities seemingly endorsed by their government. But the majority of them did not voice their disapproval of what appeared to be the Fuehrer's orders. Some seemed to enjoy these acts against the Jews of Germany. Consul-General Bell's "German cook" reportedly admitted that it was "high time a certain neighboring Jew was 'washed up.'"[48] Attacks on "British subjects of Jewish race" appeared to have been minimal. That was because they had either left Cologne or kept off the streets completely. German Jews, however, continued to bear the brunt of the intensifying anti-Jewish persecutions in Cologne. Two translated "anonymous letters" the British Consul-General received "from a person who describe[d] himself as a "Beamter" and another who called himself judge" confirmed that fact and revealed new evidence.[49]

British diplomats in Germany had confidential corroborated information that *Kristallnacht* was not a spontaneous public reaction to the assassination of vom Rath in Paris. The reaction had been instigated by the Nazi regime, and the police had specific orders to remain aloof from or oblivious to the violent assault on Jews and Jewish-owned shops and synagogues. An anonymous informant had told the British Consul-General in Cologne that specific orders had been issued at dawn on the 10 November 1938 for Jewish synagogues and other places of worship to be set on fire beginning at 4:00 a.m. and "destruction and looting of shops and houses ... to begin in the city" at 6:00 a.m., and "[a]ll action ... to cease at 1 pm ... of the 10th November 1938." Informant Beamter also disclosed that "A list of names and addresses of all Jewish shops and flats was furnished, and the mob proceeded to do their work under the leadership of S.A. men." Seventeen shops belonging to Jews in Cologne were looted, and "a certain police commissioner" who dared to intervene "to save a shop" from being looted had reportedly been "placed on leave and relieved of his functions."[50] Ein Beamter's report was also corroborated by the second informant, who signed a name as Judex. He blamed the actions of 9 and 10 December on "Hitler, Hess, Goebbels, [and] Rosenberg" and "Reichsminister Dr. Gurtner."[51]

On 15 December 1938, the British Charge d'Affaires in Berlin Sir G. Ogilvie-Forbes also transmitted to British Secretary of State Viscount Halifax another detailed dispatch on "anti-Jewish persecution" from British Consul-General in Frankfurt-on-Main R.T. Smallbones.[52] Consul Smallbones had served in Germany for eight years and felt he "understood the German character." But, as he admitted, with a sense of pathos, "recent events have revealed to me a facet of the German character which I had not suspected."[53] Smallbones described his report as "a recital of what happened to a Jew, who was in the trenches during the war, who had a good business, and who is a well-educated man. His statements correspond in detail with what has been told to us by other persons who went through the same experience." The man, identified as Mr. Dowden, had been picked up by the German "secret police" at 3 p.m. on 11 of December 1938. He was sent to a nearby police station and kept there until enough other arrestees arrived to fill a lorry. From there, he and the other arrested people were driven to Exhibition Hall where at 5 p.m. on that day, "lorries manned by S.S. men" arrived, and the arrested people were loaded onto them "with blows and kicks." They "were taken across the town to a suburban railway station," and from there they were "entrained for Buchenwald near Weimar."[54] When they arrived, they were driven by SS guards with kicks and blows into a "wire enclosure" charged with electric current. Every prisoner had his hair shaved, and the guards "had great sport with the rabbis whose religious tenets do not allow them to have their beards touched with the scissors."[55] Dowden was among a group of 500 prisoners assigned to "shed No. 1." It was "about 200 feet by 80 and about 2,500 people were forced into it." At the time of Dowden's internment, the Buchenwald concentration camp was "under construction," compounding the discomfort of many prisoners sharing small sheds. According to Dowden, "there were no latrines," so those who wore hats and had the need to ease themselves "used their hats." Prisoners had "no water to drink the first day and never any water for washing." During the first night, guards came to the shed, picked up some prisoners at random and took them out for flogging. At Buchenwald, "flogging" could be up to 50 strokes for such "offences" as "not jumping to attention quickly or not obeying an order." Dowden tells the story of a rabbi who was "flogged because he refused to sign his name on the Sabbath." He yielded to threats of further flogging.[56] Some prisoners died after being flogged. The floggings took place in public "as a warning to others." Jews in the camp were especially singled out for this type of brutal and humiliating treatment. One case that Consul-General Smallbones felt had to be told was "a former Prussian officer" who was "ordered to kneel down and say: 'I am a dirty Jew and a traitor to my country.'"[57]

Amid the indignities meted out to Jews at Buchenwald, there were other extraordinary acts of courage. Among those who were interned at Buchenwald were "famous surgeons and doctors" who were often called upon, in the camp, to perform "operations in urgent cases." The rabbis who were subjected to vile treatment also "proved themselves worthy of their calling." Mr. Dowden recalled that "one rabbi when offered his release declined to leave the camp before the last of his flock." As was typical of Buchenwald's procedures of release, "when the prisoners were released they were first examined by the camp doctor and none with open wounds were allowed to depart." Those who were approved for release had their usual warning that "if they divulged anything they had seen in the camp, they would do so at their peril."

Consul-General Smallbones forewarned the Foreign Office, in his 14 December 1938 dispatch about an "imminent" new onslaught against Jews on 16 January 1939. The consul anticipated that on that day Jewish women will be placed in the concentration camps. According to the Consul, many Jews had been warned by their friends, who claim to have inside information, to get out of Germany before that date. He disclosed that he had heard that a new concentration camp was being built at "Obenrole, near Dieburg, in the Darnstadt district" to "house some of the victims of the contemplated drive."[58] The consul-general's warning to his superiors in Berlin and London was prescient about the genocide inherent in the mass arrests of "Jewish men" after the violent acts of 9 and 10 December. He wrote:

> As far as it is possible to mitigate the plight of the Jews in Germany, I venture to think that the policy indicated at present is not 'women and children first,' but men first: they are in the concentration camps and in imminent danger of death, and they are the potential bread-winners. If they die the problem of dealing with their families will be all the more formidable.

Smallbones wanted the information he had transmitted to be "treated as confidential" because it could "rouse world opinion to a higher pitch of indignation." His informants could be exposed and punished individually or with their families, and if his name were mentioned as the source of the dispatch, "it might lead to an incident." He advised that since "the rulers of Germany appear at present to be contemptuous of world opinion," a "useful" outcome of his dispatch "might . . . be to bring the facts reported to the confidential notice of those Governments which contemplate doing something towards the solution of this problem [the mitigation of the plight of German Jews]."[59]

Much of what was happening in Buchenwald was also taking place at the concentration camp in Dachau. British Consul-General at Munich J.E.M. Carvell's dispatch of 5 January 1939 reinforced many of the accounts his colleagues had gathered about Buchenwald and communicated to London. Consul Carvell reported that "the Dachau Camp appears to have been the place of concentration for all Jews arrested in South and West Germany as far as Neuss and in Austria." He estimated that "the maximum number of Jews in confinement [at Dachau before his dispatch] was 14,000."[60] However, about 200 or 300 Jews had been released daily in December 1938. Therefore, by the beginning of January 1939, about "5,000" Jews remained in custody there. Jews "over 65 years of age and all ex-service men who served at the front [possibly in World War I]" had been released. Only "[b]oys of 17 from the Jewish seminary at Wurzburg and professional men between the ages of 50 and 60" remained at the camp.[61] At Dachau, as in Buchenwald, "the first day of captivity was one of indescribable horror." Either because of the horrifying experience or the imposed gag order, the consul-general wrote that "no released prisoner has been able or willing to speak."[62] Those who were willing to share their experiences in confidence spoke about unimaginable horrors.

As at Buchenwald, every Jewish prisoner who entered Dachau had his hair shaved and was given "a coarse linen prison suit with a 'Star of David' stamped in yellow upon it." This is all the clothing Jewish prisoners at Dachau had even through "extreme winter weather." Prisoners had to buy their own underclothing "at the canteen." Residential conditions were no different from Buchenwald. At Dachau, "Two hundred to 300 persons were crowded together in huts originally built for sixty to eighty persons." Prisoners slept on straw or bare boards with one or two "thin blanket[s]." Food rations were similar to Buchenwald's, and "Jews receive[d] only half the quantities allowed to the Aryan prisoners." Family members of Dachau's prisoners were allowed to send them "15 marks a week," which the prisoners could use to buy "hot drinks, cheese, and also butter . . . at prohibitive prices at the canteen" to supplement their daily ration of food. The work routine was the same. Prisoners woke up as early as "5 a.m.," paraded at six, and "often kept on parade for five or six hours . . . without being allowed to leave . . . for any purpose." Prisoners could be "on their feet almost constantly from 5 a.m. until 7 p.m." The majority of those who were "unaccustomed to heavy military boots . . . suffer[ed] from sore and festering feet."[63]

Consul-General Carvell's dispatch contained consistent "[a]ccounts of brutal treatment at the hands of the [camp] guards." With only few exceptions in the testimonies of prisoners' encounters with guards who treated them well, the majority of prisoners were "buffeted, kicked, and even beaten . . . with steel birches." Some of Dachau's guards, like their counterparts at Buchenwald, "never speak to prisoners without hitting them across the mouth with the back of the hand." And "medical attendants are particularly callous in their disregard for prisoners requiring medical attention." Sixty prisoners who had suffered frostbite were released without treatment and "told that their affliction would eventually cure itself." Their "ordeal" on the day of release was deepened by an address from "the commandant who advise[d] them to leave Germany as soon as possible." Jewish prisoners were warned that spreading "atrocity stories" abroad would be detrimental to their "co-religionists remaining in Germany."[64] Released prisoners at Dachau followed the same release routine at Buchenwald. They were "required to sign a document stating that they have not been ill-treated, have acquired no infectious disease, and have received their personal effects intact."[65] Those who could walk to the lorry or train stations had to pay for their own transportation back to their homes. Those who were too weak to walk had to be carried "to the station unconscious." Since a list of those who died at the camp was not kept by the SS guards, an indication of their freedom to act, no one knew how many prisoners died at the camp "or shortly after reaching their homes." Consul-General Carvell could only confirm "the names of ten Munich Jews who died at Dachau between the 9 and the 25 of November." J.E.M. Carvell noted that while the accounts of his informants were consistent, they are "based on a series of isolated scraps of information" and that the Foreign Office should not take them "to mean that the treatment meted out was throughout so bad as it would appear." Some released prisoners had claimed that they were treated well, and the camp was "efficiently managed." However, Consul-General Carvell was quick to point out that "it is probable that the treatment of prisoners varied considerably with the character of individual guards."[66] Given the warning the guards issued as a prelude to the release of some prisoners, it is quite possible that those who claim to have been treated well said so under mental and memory duress realizing the consequences of admitting otherwise.

The longest and most detailed account of the wide-ranging atrocities against Jews in Germany and Austria following the consolidation of Nazi power was sent to the Foreign Office on 18 February 1939. It came from the British consul in Dresden, F.M. Shepherd, as a special memorandum on the experiences of another "former prisoner at the concentration camp at Buchenwald."[67] The prisoner was there for "six weeks."[68] His description of the location of Buchenwald, as "only a few miles from Goethe's Weimar," fenced with "barbed-wire," and "guarded by S.S. detachments and machine guns," is consistent with descriptions offered by other released prisoners such as Herr Z's. His testimony suggests that the arrests and detention in concentration camps of large numbers of Jewish men were not caused by the assassination of vom Rath. That merely accelerated a process of arrests of Jewish men that had begun earlier. This ex-prisoner was not part of the post-November arrestees. He had actually been arrested on 13 June 1938 in his home in Berlin at five o'clock in the morning and taken to the "police headquarters." There, he was informed that "as a Jew with a previous 'criminal record,'" he was "now under prevention detention" and would be sent to a concentration camp. At the police headquarters, he saw businessmen and university teachers whom he knew. The offense for which all of them, including him, had been arrested for "preventive detention" actually "dated back to a decade or more." Those offenses related to such crimes as "breaches of traffic regulations, or childishly unimportant escapades of one kind or another." In the course of the two days of 13 and 14 June 1938, "every male Jew with any sort of police record was arrested." Some of the arrested were over 70 years old. About 4,000 of them had been arrested in Berlin, and the number of the arrested for the entire country was "between 10,000 and 15,000."[69] All the arrested people were sent to the concentration camps at Dachau, Sachsenhausen, and Buchenwald. Before their imprisonment, they were told that they would be released only when they have procured documents that permitted them to leave Germany.

At the time of this former prisoner's confinement at Buchenwald in June 1938, there were 8,000 prisoners. Of that number, "2,000," according to him, were Jews and "6,000 non-Jews." The non-Jewish prisoners, as he describes them, consisted of five categories of people who were also visibly identified with degrading badges. Besides the Jews, there were, first, the political prisoners, mainly "Communist members of the Reichstag" and people "accused of having spoken abusively of the sacred person of the Fuhrer." Second, there were prisoners categorized as "work-shy." These were not "tramps" or "vagabonds" but businessmen, technicians, and other people who had left their low-paid jobs to seek new jobs and better-paid employment elsewhere and were arrested by the police and Gestapo on tip-offs from their previous employers. A third group of prisoners was the Bibelforscher, or Bible students. They are described as "a religious sect taking its doctrine from the Bible and having a considerable membership in every part of the country." Their religion had been banned by the Gestapo because "its members refuse military service." This group, the majority of whom were members of the Jehovah's Witnesses religion, were prominent in the camps with their lilac identification badges. They were reportedly treated "almost as badly . . . as the Jews." The fourth group of prisoners was "the homosexuals" or "those against whom the Gestapo thought fit to bring charges of homosexuality." As the former prisoner notes, charging people the Gestapo and secret police disliked "with this offense [of homosexuality] is a favourable tactic." The fifth group of non-Jewish prisoners was those regarded as "professional criminals."[70] And "the dress of every prisoner is marked with a special symbol." Those imprisoned for political reasons wore red stripe uniforms. Bible students [possibly Jehovah's Witnesses] donned a lilac stripe uniform, and the so-called "work dodgers" wore uniforms with black stripes.[71] The camp clothes that Jews wore in Buchenwald were "marked with the Star of David in black on a yellow patch." That was meant to mark one as a "work-shy Jew." This loose and degrading description of "independent businessmen," dentists, lawyers, doctors, professors, and other workers who had either been forced out of their jobs or who were not used to manual labor at Buchenwald was so inaccurate that it betrayed its own inherent purpose of demeaning the Jews of Germany. Moreover, at Buchenwald, one's prison number became a substitute for one's name.[72]

This informant believed, as did the British Consul who transmitted his testimony, that the arrests of Jewish men in June 1938 "were a purely political measure" designed by the Nazi regime to speed up "Jewish emigration, which in the Nazi view, was flowing too slowly."[73] That was the reason why the task of indiscriminately rounding up Jewish men, in particular, was given to the "ordinary criminal police ... and not ... to the Gestapo." In the view of Consul Shepherd, the explanation of these mass arrests by some German newspapers as the capture of "Jewish criminals" for "preventive custody" missed the actual intent of the Nazi regime.[74] Abusive treatments such as the "kicks and blows from fist and rifle butt" of SS guards run through the testimonies of released prisoners. Buchenwald was "guarded by machine gun posts," and over its gate was written the German equivalent of the English dictate, "My Country Right or Wrong!" Clearly, humane treatment was not a luxury afforded prisoners at the camp. Shaving the heads of prisoners and giving them "convict uniforms" were routine procedures. Periodic flogging for minor infractions such as drinking water during hours of work was part of the harrowing abuses at the camp. Work began very early in the morning and ended very late in the evening and included the breaking of stones in a quarry and carrying boulders over a mile to a new road under construction.[75] Very few sanitary places of convenience existed there. Prisoners, especially lawyers who refused to sign the usual forced declarations that Jews were "unwilling to work" were severely tortured into doing so.[76] These and other punishments such as strapping Jewish prisoners so tightly to a tree that in many cases, the blood of the victims could no longer circulate leading to collapse and death were a "daily occurrence" at Buchenwald.[77] This former prisoner observed that the death toll at Buchenwald, "both of Jews and of Aryans," was "far greater than in any of the other camps."[78] By 15 June 1938, there were about "2,000" Jewish prisoners. Eighty of them "died in the first four weeks" and "thirty more in the fifth week." Camp guards kept the mortality numbers low in their reports to the press and to the "Committee of the Berlin Jewish Community."[79] As this informant revealed, "most of the prisoners who die at Buchenwald die in the stone quarry." Prison guards who recorded these deaths claimed that the dead had been "shot while attempting to escape." In reality, genuine escapes from the camp hardly ever occurred.[80]

A harrowing story is told of the death of a young Jewish man of 22 years of age, Erich Lowenberg. He had been a cantor at a synagogue and had recently married. His wife was pregnant and expecting a child soon when he was arrested and sent to Buchenwald. On 15 July 1938, an SS guard drove Lowenberg "to the highway near the quarry and forced [him] in front of a heavy lorry driven by another S.S. man." The lorry crushed the young man.[81] Many prisoners also died because of lack of medical services in the camp. In the first weeks, camp doctors and ambulance drivers were forbidden to offer any medical help to Jews, an order that was also "responsible" for many of the deaths that occurred at the camp. SS guards claimed they could not alleviate the harsh conditions at Buchenwald because "they received their orders from 'higher up.'" That higher authority was "Herr Standartenfuhrer Kock, infamous as the perpetrator of nameless brutalities at the Kolumbiahaus in Berlin and at the camps of Esterwege and Sachsenhausen [and] now in charge of the Buchenwald camp." The few Samaritans at the camp, "some among the foremen," who dared to help Jewish prisoners were denounced as "Jew lovers" by other prisoners and publicly humiliated by flogging.[82]

The process of release from Buchenwald and Dachau bore close resemblance to each other, as prisoner accounts reveal. First, prisoners due to be released had to submit themselves to a rigorous medical examination. The purpose was to ensure that only those without any visible marks of abuse and torture could be discharged. Marks of such abuse could be the clearest evidence of the harrowing experiences they have endured, which could challenge official denials of bad treatment. Any prisoner "who still bore traces of his beatings was not allowed to leave until every mark was healed." That was meant to "prevent any knowledge of the physical maltreatment of prisoners reaching the outside world."[83] This former prisoner at Buchenwald, unlike Herr Z, was "one of the very few" Jewish prisoners released "without having obtained a visa" to leave Germany. He was warned against talking about his experiences when he was released and received a notice later "to quit the country within five weeks ... and not be allowed to re-enter it."[84]

The Holocaust and the African press

The *West African Pilot* shared aspects of these concentration camp testimonies from released prisoners with its readers on 2 November 1939.[85] The paper's front-page report of that day about the horrible treatment of Jews in a concentration camp was based on a British government "White Paper" and "evidence" given at tribunals the British government had established in Kent, to determine the cases of 3,600 Jews seeking refuge in Britain. Under the prevailing conditions of war against Germany, these persecuted German Jews who arrived in Britain faced initial suspicion and subsequent internment as enemy aliens. The testimonies of those who spoke in British courts confirmed the detailed accounts of the breakup of families and the harrowing "journeys by rail to prison or Concentration Camps" in the *Papers* that British diplomats in Germany had shared with the Foreign Office in March 1939.[86] These eyewitness accounts formed the core of the British government's White Paper of November 1939 on which the *West African Pilot* based its news report. The *Pilot* followed its 2 November 1939 report with another one on 8 November 1939, based on news sources in Budapest, about the "inhuman atrocities" against Jews "in Polish regions under German control."[87] As the 1930s drew to a close, it had become clear in West Africa that Nazi racism and brutality had destroyed the lives of many in Germany and German-occupied Europe and that the Jews in particular were "being persecuted with unqualified ruthlessness."[88]

More gruesome details of anti-Jewish persecutions appeared in African news outlets in the 1940s as Nazi persecution and legal restrictions on the lives of Jews moved into a new phase of actual physical annihilation in Germany, and countries in Europe now controlled by the Nazi regime. As usual, these reports in African newspapers were culled from a variety of European news sources. African editors and commentators analyzed them in the context of Nazi ideology, human decency, European claims to racial and cultural superiority, and the possible fate of Africans in a Nazi-controlled postwar world. The *East African Standard*, published in Nairobi by Indian immigrants, reported in October 1941, on its front-page, that "a Jewish purge" was underway in "a camp in Northern Poland."[89] This report about a "new [Nazi] order" of annihilation of Jews was derived from an unnamed "American journalist" in Berlin who reported on 30 October 1941 that "many hundreds of Jews" had been sent out of Berlin daily "over the last 10 days" to a destination "stated to be somewhere in Poland." The American correspondent reported that "the Jews are assembled in a goods yard in a Berlin suburb" and the German police try to make their departure by train "as inconspicuous as possible." The correspondent noted that "a certain fate awaits them in Poland" because Polish sources have confirmed that "recently several thousand Jews were sent to a camp in Northern Poland" where "many of them were forced to kneel in trenches and detachments of SS troops turned machine guns on them." Another massacre, reportedly, took place in Southern Poland where "several hundred more Jews" were "shot."[90] The *Tanganyika Herald* also reported on 20 June 1942, based on a "Stockholm dispatch to New York" dated 16 June 1942, that "60,000 Jews of Vilna," possibly Lithuanian Jews, had been "mowed down" by "German controlled Lithuanian Police" between 17 and 20 May 1942. According to the source, the "men, women and children" had been taken in the night "between sundown and dawn" in "trucks to a suburb of Ponary" and executed.[91] Two similar reports that appeared in the *Uganda Herald* and the *Gold Coast Independent* highlighted this critical transition from persecution and harassment to actual physical destruction of Jews in many parts of Europe. The *Herald*'s editorial page of 25 March 1942, based on Russian news sources, bemoaned the "horrible slaughter and pogroms" in German-occupied towns in Russia. Besides, "a large number of Jews, including women and children" had been "assembled in the Jewish cemetery" in Kiev, stripped naked, beaten up, and murdered later. The first and second batches of Jews executed had been made "to lie on the bottom of the ditch, face to the ground, and shot with automatic rifles."[92] The same report appeared in the *Gold Coast Independent* on 30 May 1942, indicating the extent to which colonial subjects in East and West Africa paid attention to the Holocaust. The minor difference in content was that the West African paper's report added "captured Russian soldiers" to the story about the murder of Russian Jews by Nazi soldiers.[93] These reports suggest that Africans were also reading Soviet news sources already translated into English.

Some of the press reports on different phases of the Holocaust came from official British sources. Such disclosures were certainly aimed at stimulating the interest of British subjects in Africa in the ongoing war by underscoring the implications of a German victory for them. In the Gold Coast, in particular, news bulletins and commentaries on the war, especially Nazi atrocities against innocent Jews and other groups of people, appeared in local languages, especially Twi, for the purpose of reaching a wider public beyond urban areas. The colony's influential educated people seized on the emotional effects of these atrocities to highlight the nature of the Nazi regime even if colonial authorities were not entirely forthcoming with every detail of Nazi atrocities. The infamous Nazi massacre of all men, women, and children in the Czechoslovak village of Lidice in June 1942 and the deportation of some to death camps to be gassed to death as revenge for the assassination of Gestapo chief Reinhard Heydrich attracted attention in the Gold Coast. The influential Gold Coast lawyer and member of the colony's Legislative Council, J.B. Danquah, had written to the acting colonial secretary on 29 June 1942 for "some accurate information or data on the war news item concerning what the Nazis have done to the village in Czechoslovakia where Heydrich, the Gestapo chief was shot." Danquah stated that "the destruction of all the men of that village, the evacuation of all its women, and the dispersion of all its children, seem to me to contain the kind of stuff to appeal to the emotions of the masses out here, and I have a mind to write an article on the subject if I could get hold of reliable information."[94] The response from the governor's office that the colonial administration did not have any "official" information on the massacre other than what the British Broadcasting Corporation had already broadcast in its news bulletins highlighted the tensions that often existed between colonial subjects and colonial administrators over the acquisition and management of war news that related to Nazi behavior or the Holocaust.[95]

Official weekly war pamphlets in English such as *Empire at War* and *Inside the News* kept the Gold Coast educated public informed about the war and the Nazi attack on European Jews. In a 9 July 1942 issue of *Inside the News*, colonial subjects read about the torture and murder of thousands of Jewish men and women in "prisons and concentration camps" in Poland. Of special emphasis in this issue was the reported "massacre of at least two hundred thousand Jews" through outright murder and "overcrowding and lack of food." The pamphlet also mentioned the murder and starvation of "approximately five hundred thousand more in Ghettoes" and "deportation of one and a half million people," whose identities were not given, to "slave labour in Germany."[96] For British officials in the colonies, unrestricted access of colonial subjects to information about the Holocaust was a double-edged sword. On one side, sharing information about Nazi atrocities against the Jews and other Europeans appealed to the emotions of influential colonial subjects in a manner that caused them to see their fate as tied to Great Britain's. That much can be established from the profuse pledges of loyalty to Great Britain in the course of the war by influential chiefs and leading African newspapers. On the other side, access to detailed information about Nazi behavior, such as J.B. Danquah requested, exposed the European claims about Western civilization, the teachings of Christian missionaries, and the pernicious structures of white supremacy in colonial society to renewed scrutiny.

What worried British colonial authorities was that colonial subjects in Africa associated the Holocaust and Nazi behavior with the entirety of European civilization and used the Holocaust as an analytical lens to expose its contradictions. Colonial Britain, however, wanted the crimes of the Nazi regime to be tied solely to Germany. A front-page news item in the *West African Pilot* of 17 December 1942 revealed the struggle between colonial subjects and colonial administrators over how to interpret the Holocaust.[97] The *Pilot* had reprinted a report from British Labor Party sources in London about "a statement" the Party had issued appealing to "the conscience of civilized mankind" to rise up in "passionate protest against the bloodiest crime in history" that was taking place in Europe "by and under the orders of the German Government with the complicity of their allies." According to the Party statement, "The homes of men and women of Jewish faith" have been "broken up," and Jewish families, in particular, have been "scattered, deported or ... driven to death by cold and hunger, [or] tortured and murdered with calculated scientific savagery." The Party was confident that "ample evidence" existed that "this crime has been methodically organized and is being carried out with such persistence and thoroughness that within a short time, the Jewish people within the frontiers of the new German order in Europe will have been exterminated." Party leaders wanted the world, including Britain's colonial subjects in Africa, to know that "[t]his unparalleled and stupendous act of barbarism will always be associated in history with the name of modern Germany."[98] People in Africa had a different view. Colonial subjects and even the sovereign peoples of Africa saw German anti-Semitism that led to the Holocaust in Europe and British racism that led to colonial exploitation in Africa as bedfellows on the same spectrum of prejudice and domination.

Arguably, African soldiers fighting in World War II may not have had the same information about the Holocaust that was available to their civilian counterparts at the home front. As already noted in Chapter Two, interviews conducted by the BBC, and the German radio network *Deutsche Welle*, with some African war veterans, in 2009 and 2015 respectively, (the latter to commemorate the 70th anniversary of World War II), have revealed specific and detailed knowledge that these respondents had about Hitler's dehumanization of Africans, in particular. The absence of the ex-servicemen's awareness of Hitler's comparable dehumanization of Jews, and their annihilation in the course of the war, suggests that British war bulletins intended for soldiers at the war front may have omitted references to the Nazi treatment of European Jews. Or African soldiers fighting in the war had limited access to war news or no access at all to information about the Holocaust compared to what Africa's educated elites and newspaper editors at the home front had, and the inferences newspaper editors made from the information they received.

The *Gold Coast Independent* published two detailed reports on the Holocaust in the last two years of the war. They were the accounts given by two people who had either escaped or survived the Nazi death camps at Treblinka and Oswecim (Auschwitz). Their testimonies confirmed some of the facts that had already become known to readers of newspapers in Africa and added some new information. In a long and detailed article written by one F.B. Ozarnomski and published as a feature article in the *Gold Coast Independent* on 6 November 1943, the author noted that "the extermination of Jews from Poland by methods of mass slaughter" continues "unabated."[99] It was not only Polish Jews who were being slaughtered in this new process of extermination but also Jews "from other occupied countries of Europe, including France, Belgium, Holland, Norway, [and] Czechoslovakia." Jews in these countries, according to the writer, were being "deported to special death camps and murdered by thousands without discrimination of age or sex."[100]

The author revealed the location of "the principal death camp" as "near the village of Treblink[a]" and close to "the main Bialystok-Warsaw railway line" in Poland. It was "situated in a wooded part of the country, completely isolated from the outside world." In area, it "cover[ed] about 10,000 acres and [was] entirely fenced in by two lines of barbed wire entanglements. A special railway siding ha[d] been constructed to connect the camp with the main railway carrying the trains of condemned Jews from Warsaw and other cities and towns."[101] According to Ozarnomski, the Germans had initially used Treblinka as a labor camp for Poles, and "thousands" of them had been killed there in March 1942. Later, the Nazi regime attached "a special death camp for the mass extermination of Jews" to this original "penal concentration camp" and began to exterminate Jews from Poland and other countries in Europe in this new death camp. The "execution chambers," Ozarnomski revealed, were "in a special building about 120 feet long and 45 feet wide." The building was "divided by an inner corridor about 9 feet wide into two rows of five chambers each." Each death chamber was "about 6 feet high and about 220 square feet." There were no windows in the room, only "hinged iron trap doors on the outside wall." The Treblinka camp, at the time Ozarnomski knew it, was guarded "by [a] small SS garrison under the command of Captain Sauer." A number of Jews called *kapos* were "forced to serve inside the camp." Their task included "burying the dead" and "disposing of the clothing and other belongings of murdered victims." They were "treated with utmost brutality," and those who were unable to discharge their forced tasks were "executed" immediately.[102] Ozarnomski's description of the architecture of Treblinka and of the treatment of Jews there is consistent with the standard portrait of the Treblinka and Auschwitz death camps in Holocaust historiography.[103]

Jan Wolny's account of his experience in a gas chamber at Oswiecim (Auschwitz), in southern Poland mirrored that of F.B. Ozarnomski's at Treblinka. Wolny had first published his ordeal in the *Sunday Express* newspaper in Britain. The *Gold Coast Independent* reprinted that account in its 16 September 1944 issue. Wolny confirmed what had become factual knowledge in the testimonies of people who had lived through the dehumanizing realities of life in Nazi concentration camps. As in Buchenwald and Dachau, "Prisoners at Oswiecim ha[d] no names, only numbers." Jan Wolny's "number was 1574," and he "left the camp after two and a half years."[104] By the time of his escape or release, the prisoners in this particular camp at Auschwitz where he was held "had reached 116,000." According to Wolny, "this figure did not include Jews or Russians."[105] He writes that all the prisoners at Oswiecim had been sent there "to die." However, "in the case of Jews and Russians death was intended to follow soon after the arrival that the Germans did not trouble [sic] to identify them." Newly arrived prisoners had to go through intense barefoot running drills and not even "the old and feeble" were spared this routine and the accompanying "blows from the guards' truncheons." As Jan Wolny noted, "Wounds never healed at Oswiecim." Guards killed prisoners who could not work. Wolny and most of the prisoners were assigned to "construction tasks" at the camp, which was "always being enlarged" as more huts were constructed each day. The prisoners "soon learned why Oswiecim was to become the slaughterhouse of Europe where mass executions could be scientifically carried out." Wolny recalled that he "once saw several hundred men all Jews captured in Russia" brought to the camp "in trucks." They were taken to the gas chambers, and when their bodies were brought out, they were "naked and they had the greenish colour of the soldiers who died of poison gas." After this ghastly deed, it was the task of the prisoners to load the corpses onto "farmcarts" and drag them to the "crematorium," a short distance away.

The crematorium at Oswiecim had "an immense red brick chimney." It was visible to every prisoner because "a thick black smoke rose from the chimney" every day. As Wolny noted, "There was not a prisoner at Oswiecim who was not at all times aware of the chimney and of its meaning." Wolny estimates that "the average number of corpses taken out of the gas chambers and burned was 50 a day." Whenever the "immense" crematorium "could not keep pace with the inflow of green-tinged corpses," the prisoners were ordered "to bury the unburned bodies." Oswiecim had "women prisoners" too. They included "several hundred French women wives and daughters of resistance fighters." The agony of life at this death camp was such that "[e]veryday, there were suicides in Oswiecim."[106] One can imagine what the subjects of the British colony of the Gold Coast, who read the galling details of Jan Wolny's account, must have thought. Their voices were channeled through the editorial columns of the newspapers they read.

While the editors of these newspapers paid particular attention to the treatment of Jews in Germany and countries occupied by Nazi troops, they also kept a close watch on Nazi treatment of Blacks in the same domains of Nazi control. From information that appeared in "A Stockholm Newspaper," the *West African Pilot* reported on 5 February 1943 that Heinrich Himmler, head of the German Gestapo, had issued an order to all "Negroes living in the Reich to register immediately with the Police."[107] This Swedish source also added the grim information that "the Negroes, now compelled to register, will no doubt receive the same treatment as the Jews." The consternation in the African press was immediate. In its editorial page of 6 February 1943, the *West African Pilot* asked the question that must have been on the minds of many in West Africa: Is it the Negro's turn now?[108] The paper reminded its readers of what it had published on the previous day about the Gestapo Chief Heinrich Himmler's order to all "Negroes living in Germany" to register with his organization. The *Pilot* wanted all its readers to remember that the German Gestapo "represents all the horror and wickedness of Nazism" and that in no other field of inhumanity had it made "a more calumnious name [for itself] than in the German persecution of the Jews." More frightening was the new fact that Gestapo notoriety for brutality and calumny had now extended "beyond the confines of the Third Reich" to "territories which the Hitlerites have temporarily overrun."[109]

Reports of arrests, deportations, and executions of Jews beyond Germany made an almost daily appearance in the *Pilot* after its pointed editorial. News of the treatment of European Jews acquired a more than ominous meaning especially when ten days after that editorial, the newspaper published, on its front page, another report, from "the British section of the World Jewish Congress" in London, that the "Nazis Will Destroy All Jews by March."[110] This particular news item, based on "direct reports" that the World Jewish Congress had received from several sources in "Central Europe," revealed that "German authorities have issued new orders to speed up and intensify the extermination, by mass massacre and starvation, of Jews remaining in occupied Europe." It also claimed that the Nazi regime has "ordered that by March 31 [1943], . . . the "Protectorate" of Bohemia and Moravia is to be cleared of Jews . . . and by that same date, no Jew is to be left in Berlin." Even more audacious was that this particular order or "decree" to exterminate the Jews of Bohemia and Moravia had been "published in an official gazette of the protectorate on December 1, 1942." The decree also required "local authorities" to "withdraw from the Jews cards for rationed foodstuffs." The *Pilot*'s front-page report also contained news that "Special Gestapo agents from Vienna" had already cleared that Austrian city of "almost" all of its Jewish population and "have been sent to Berlin and also to Holland to speed up expulsions." These Gestapo expulsions had not even spared "girls working in German war industries, whose parents have already been deported." The Nazi intent to wipe out every Jew from the face of Europe had also sparked "a new wave of suicide among Jews" as "mass execution of Jews in Poland . . . continued without respite." The source claimed, "Six thousand Jews are being killed daily in one area alone" in German-occupied Poland, and "130,000 Jews" had been deported from Romania, according to "special and well-authenticated report from Roumania." Regardless of its authenticity, this news report reinforced what had already become common knowledge in the African press that a different phase of Nazi policy of deportation of Jews for mass extermination had begun. That phase included the most humiliating fact that Jews due to be "massacred" were "ordered to take off their clothing."[111]

The accelerating pace of Nazi-ordered extermination of European Jews, as the year 1942 ended, revived conversation in Europe and in Africa about rescuing and resettling the remaining Jews who were still alive. A motion introduced in the British House of Lords on "Nazi pogroms" was the major front-page news item in the *West African Pilot* of 25 March 1943 based on a news report from London.[112] The report indicated that as a result of "the massacres and starvation of Jews and others in enemy-occupied countries," the Archbishop of Canterbury Dr. William Temple had addressed the British House of Lords and urged that eminent parliamentary body to support "immediate measures on the largest and most generous scale" by the British government to provide "help and temporary asylum to persons in danger of massacre who are able to leave enemy occupied countries." In the view of the archbishop, the world was "confronted with an evil of great magnitude the horror of which it is impossible to describe in words."[113] He did not consider "this sheer cruelty" as "vengeance" against any particular offense that the Jews of the world had committed, because he saw none beyond "a satisfaction of mere delight in power" by the Nazi regime and its collaborators. The archbishop's view was one, shared by colonial subjects and sovereign peoples in West and East Africa, that while human history is saturated with all kinds of "monstrous horror" and "even massacre," the type of monstrosity and destruction directed against the Jews was unparalleled.[114]

Interpreting the Holocaust

The persistent press accounts in East and West Africa on the Holocaust must put to rest the key question: Did Africans know about the Holocaust? But the now affirmative answer to that question raises another: If they knew, what did they say or think about the Nazi persecution and attempted destruction of Europe's Jews? Initial anticipation of a Nazi victory in the Second World War had triggered intense reflections, among educated segments of colonial African society, about the meaning and implications of the Nazi persecution of European Jews. For the colonized and sovereign peoples of Africa, caught in the same web as the Jews in Nazi racial obsessions, the Holocaust was as much a dire warning to peoples of African heritage as it was a threat to the physical existence of the Jewish people. As the *West African Pilot* noted, Black people in Africa had "borne the full brunt" of the type of racial mythologies and white supremacist ethos the Nazi regime espoused in their history of interactions with Europeans.[115] In the African mind, the calculus was very simple: the Jews today, Africans tomorrow, if Nazi Germany prevailed. This idea had been at the center of the thoughts of the managing director and chief editor of the *West African Pilot*, Nnamdi Azikiwe, when he wrote in his *Inside Stuff* column of 17 November 1938 on the subject of "Germanism." He argued that "the German Reich, under the influence of pseudo-scientific ideas of race is destined to exterminate people in Africa and Asia in order to make the world safer for the so-called Aryan races."[116] This thought, which large numbers of colonial subjects shared, had yielded two outcomes. First was a redoubled African commitment to the Allied war effort to defeat Nazi Germany and its allies. Second was a temporary pause in African anticolonial resistance. But while Azikiwe, for instance, repudiated Nazi racist beliefs and the fanaticism that gave it force and fire, he did not regard the use of murder as a legitimate response to them. It is therefore not surprising that the *West African Pilot* deplored Herschel Grynzpan's murder of Ernst vom Rath in November 1938. But the paper's publishers were in no doubt that the consequent attacks on Jews had been sanctioned by the top echelons of the Nazi regime.

Azikiwe wrote for many in Africa in his thoughts on *Kristallnacht* in his regular *Inside Stuff* column of 9 January 1939. He viewed the assassination of the German diplomat Ernst vom Rath as the "the act of a probably insane Polish Jew."[117] Yet the German reaction was equally perverse, in the view of Azikiwe and his colleagues. The paper's "own correspondent," possibly writing from London, had reported earlier, on 13 December 1938, that information available to British Prime Minister Neville Chamberlain's office "blame[d] Hitler himself for the anti-Jewish outrages in Germany" that followed the assassination of vom Rath. According to the correspondent, Hitler had reportedly "authorized the pogrom" under pressure from "extremists" within the Nazi party. Nazi officials such as "Propaganda Minister Goebbels, Deputy Fuehrer Rudolf Hess, and Heinrich Himmler, Chief of the Gestapo, organized the Police who carried out the persecution." Ordinary people eager to exploit the opportunity joined the looting.[118]

The events of *Kristallnacht* and reports of thousands of persecuted Jews fleeing Germany also made colonial subjects in Africa even more apprehensive about the Nazi regime and European appeasement diplomacy.[119] Exacerbating these fears were rumors about alleged Anglo-German negotiations to return former German colonies in Africa to Nazi Germany in addition to the transfer of portions of Nigeria to the Nazi regime. This allegation reinforced the view that was becoming axiomatic in West Africa that the "maltreatment of the Jews" was no longer "a Nazi domestic issue" but a matter that had significance for West Africa.[120] The *Pilot*'s editorial of 18 November 1938 on the issue of "Nazi Persecution" made this thought in Africa even more manifest. The editors made it clear that they took "great interest and concern" in Nazi reprisals against "innocent Jewish elements . . . in Germany and Austria" that had also caused some Jews living in these European countries to leave "for the Dominions" (Canada, Australia, and New Zealand).[121] The editors summed up the implications of these developments in Europe for colonial subjects in West Africa when they noted that "[i]t should be clear to any conscientious individual by now that if among white nations a line of demarcation could be drawn . . ., then there is hardly any prospect of any coloured nation coming under the Nazi regime to escape unwanton [sic] persecution or possible extermination like the Kulaks in Russia on grounds of blood inferiority."[122] A clear African perspective on the Holocaust is apparent in the *Pilot*'s editorial view. Colonial subjects in West Africa did not see European Jews, whether from Germany, Russia, or Austria, as different in their physical appearance or racial identity from the Germans who persecuted them. That made the Nazi treatment of White European Jews, and the inability of European nations to stop it, even more puzzling and particularly foreboding from the perspective of colonial subjects in West Africa. For the African who was conscious of Nazi ideology, the Holocaust was ominous for what the extermination of White European Jews meant for the fate of Black Africans in a Nazi-controlled world.

British colonial administrators in West Africa, who needed the loyalty of their subjects in the Allied fight against the Nazi regime, did not do much to assuage the palpable fears of those in Africa who saw the Holocaust and their own humanity as critically entwined. In fact, colonial authorities made sure that their subjects did not forget that correlation and its racial subtext and potential results. That was the objective when the colonial war pamphlet *Empire at War* reminded colonial subjects in Africa, in the aftermath of *Kristallnacht* and in the course of the Nazi anti-Jewish excesses in the 1940s, that "[s]uch is the German treatment of white people, some of them people of their own German race . . . Can Africans expect any better treatment from Germany than Europeans?"[123] The *Ashanti Pioneer* had already underscored that point in its editorial of 25 May 1940. Reminding its readers, possibly about *Kristallnacht*, the newspaper argued that "it is not long ago when Hitler and his gang of lunatics persecuted the Jews for the simple reason that these poor people had money which the Reichstag needed." Despite this rehashing of prevailing stereotypes of Jewish wealth, the paper's central point that the Nazi regime "pilfered" all the property of the Jews and "drove them from their soil" was consistent with the events of *Kristallnacht*. Like the colonial administration's racially coded message in *Empire at War*, the *Ashanti Pioneer*'s own racially tinged warning was that "if Hitler and his bloodthirsty hounds have been able to treat their old friends" who had fought and died for Germany in the "last Great War" in this "ungodly manner, it would be sheer madness for any Gold Coast African to expect something better from the Germans."[124] It was not only colonial subjects on the continent who viewed the rumors about the transfer of their territory to the Nazis through the prism of the Holocaust or saw the destruction of white European Jews by a white European nation as a fatal warning to Black Africans. Britain's African subjects who had left the continent to study abroad did too. Nigerian students in New York were reported to have concluded that "if Jews, who are members of the Caucasoid race as the Germans, are not good enough to be 'Aryans' and are expelled from Germany, then there is no telling to what extent the Nazis will go towards humiliating the Africans."[125]

The indiscriminate arrests and detention of large numbers of Jews in concentration camps across Germany and outside the country deepened comparisons between the plight of Jews under Nazi rule and what the Nazis could do to people in Africa. The specter of life in a Nazi-operated concentration camp on African soil was the imagery in the *West African Pilot*'s editorial of 2 November 1939 on the concept of a concentration camp.[126] It was an editorial response to a report the newspaper had carried, on the same day from European news sources, about the torture of Jews in concentration camps in German-occupied Poland according to the accounts of released prisoners seeking asylum in Britain. The *Pilot*'s editors waxed philosophical that "[t]he temper of any Government could be judged by its attitude towards those unfortunate persons who come into clash with its laws and dictates." While the editors of the *Pilot* were not ignorant of the long history of Britain's harsh treatment of its colonial subjects in Africa, they applauded the British parliament's discussion about what Britain could do to ease the lives of concentration camp prisoners as the temper of a government with "humanitarian inclinations" in contrast to those "states who arrange their affairs in such a manner that one who is against Government principles will not be alive to say so." For the editors, "the temper of the Nazi regime" was revealed through the concentration camps it built and operated, where "thousands of Jews" were destroyed for "no crimes [other than the fact] that they [were] German Jews and constitute[d] one of the things which the Nazi regime must stamp out." This African view of the Holocaust was consistent with the perspective that the Archbishop of Canterbury had expressed. Undoubtedly, the West African newspaper represented its own voice and those of its numerous readers when it concluded that the only good that could be done to deal with the "mental torture and physical excruciation [sic]" of life in the Nazi concentration camps is to fight "to stamp out Nazism."[127] That the *Pilot* spoke for many Africans is very clear here.

Responses to the Holocaust in West Africa were, in many ways, extensions of the views of colonized subjects on Nazism and racism as ideological travesties of human morality. The *West African Pilot*'s editorial page of 11 December 1941 summed up that perspective in the context of what Azikiwe and his editorial staff saw as the root cause of the world's problems: race discrimination. As they put it, "We believe that all the troubles in the world today could be traced to the question of one race, one group or class of people, claiming superiority over and trying to dominate or keep down others whom they consider inferior."[128] As an influential African newspaper, the position of the *Pilot* on racism as a root cause of the Holocaust could not have been clearer in the editors' opinion that "no race, class or group of people are [sic] superior to others, but that given equal opportunities, all races of mankind can rise to the highest pitch according to individual ability and energy."[129] That colonial subjects saw the Holocaust as the gruesome outcome of racism is undeniable. Given the fact that they lived under colonialism as another outcome of racism, it is reasonable to argue that colonial subjects in Africa saw the Holocaust and colonialism on the same spectrum, with the Holocaust as the extreme manifestation of colonialism.

From the accelerating Nazi persecution and extermination of Europe's Jewish population, Azikiwe and his newspaper saw a "lesson to all Africans." That was, indeed, the title of the *West African Pilot*'s editorial page of 15 June 1942 as the "Final Solution" gathered apace.[130] The three themes of that day's editorial are revealing. First, the editors reminded readers of the numerous reports the newspaper had published "from Allied and neutral sources" about alleged German atrocities "the like of which 'no eye hath seen, [and] no ears have heard' in the long history of mankind" that have taken place "both inside Germany itself and in the German-occupied countries." These atrocities included the German destruction of the "Bohemian town of Libce [sic]" and the killing of the men of the town and the transportation of its "women and children ... to concentration camps." This was the Nazi atrocity about which the Gold Coast barrister Joseph Boakye Danquah had inquired from the colony's administration. Second, the editors expressed their "deepest sympathy with the relatives" of those who have been killed by the Nazi regime. Third, the "lesson" the editors thought the British colony of Nigeria, in particular, could take from this Nazi atrocity and others beyond the Bohemian village was that "if the Germans could treat their own colour, as alleged [in this manner], how much more will they treat the African who, in Hitler's own words, is nothing but an ape."[131] This was the same question that colonial subjects in the neighboring British colony of the Gold Coast persistently asked about the Nazi treatment of European Jews and their own fate in a world controlled by Nazi Germany.

The day after the *West African Pilot* received news from Stockholm about a Gestapo order to "Negroes" in Germany to register with it, it responded with the standard editorial warning to Africans in Africa from the experiences of Jews in Europe.[132] That editorial put the fate of Africans under Nazi rule in the context of the ongoing extermination campaign against the Jews in Nazi Germany that had now become a well-known issue in the African press. The editors concluded that "[w]henever things have gone wrong with the Germans, they have always looked for a scapegoat." From this understanding of post–World War I German history, the publishers of the newspaper took the reported Gestapo order to "Negroes" to register with it as "an ominous sign" that the Nazi regime was about to pursue a "scientific persecution of Negroes" in Germany similar to the concentration camp annihilation of Jews for Germany's declining military fortunes in the ongoing war.[133]

While colonial subjects remained attuned to the accelerating pace of Nazi extermination of the Jews of Europe and what that meant for them, they shunned any theological and mystical interpretations of the Holocaust. The caveat of the editors of the *Uganda Herald* about a correspondent's view of the Nazi persecution of the Jews as an unfolding of a Divine plan has already been noted. Editors of newspapers in West Africa also recoiled from similar religious arguments. As much as they revered Mohandas Gandhi for his nonviolent anticolonial politics, Nnamdi Azikiwe and his colleagues who published the *West African Pilot* newspaper could not help but disagree with the view of the *Mahatma* (Saint) that the Jews should have submitted meekly to their persecution and death at the hands of the Nazi regime, as a sacred and dignified form of religious resistance.

The *Pilot* had published two letters from Gandhi in January 1939 on his views about "the Arab-Jews question in Palestine" and "the persecution of Jews in Germany."[134] In those letters, Gandhi had expressed opposition to the creation of a Jewish homeland outside of the European nations where the Jewish people lived, in response to the revival of discussions in the European press about the settlement of Jews on what Gandhi considered Arab lands in Palestine. Besides his position on the issue of a Jewish homeland outside of Europe, the Mahatma expressed his "sympathies" for the persecuted Jews of Europe. As a pacifist, the only war Gandhi supported and considered "justifiable" was "a war against Germany, to prevent the wanton persecution of a whole race." Like colonial subjects in East and West Africa, Gandhi believed that "the German persecution of the Jews" had "no parallel in history."[135] Yet, while Mahatma Gandhi saw the Holocaust as unparalleled, he found the best response to it in the history of Indian responses to state-organized persecution.[136] He argued that "if the Jewish mind could be prepared for voluntary suffering," the unparalleled massacre the Jews of Europe experienced under the Nazi regime "could be turned into . . . joy." As he observed, "For the God-fearing, death has no terror. It is a joyful sleep to be followed by a waking that would be all the more refreshing for the long sleep."[137] Gandhi's "prescription," as he called it, for a dignified Jewish response to a persecution he claimed had "no parallel in history" was the "parallel" situation he saw between the persecution of Jews in Nazi Germany and "the Indian satyagraha campaign in South Africa" in the 1920s. Gandhi argued that the Indian population in South Africa "occupied precisely the same place that the Jews occup[ied] in Nazi Germany" in the 1930s.[138]

The persecutions of Jews in Germany and Indians in South Africa, according to Gandhi, "had . . . a religious tinge." The racist government of South Africa had deemed Indians inferior to white Christians and consigned them to ghettos as the Nazi government had thought about Jews and done in Germany. But, as the Mahatma noted, the Indians in South Africa had "resorted to satyagraha [a form of passive, nonviolent resistance] without any backing from the outside world or the Indian government." Since the Jews of Germany were "a homogeneous community," "far more gifted than the Indians of South Africa," and have "organized world opinion behind them," they could "offer satyagraha under definitely better auspices than the Indians of South Africa" did. Gandhi concluded that "if someone with courage and vision can arise [sic] among them [the Jews] to lead them in non-violent action, the winter of their despair can, in the twinkling of an eye, be turned into the summer of hope."[139]

The *Pilot*'s editorial response on 18 January 1939 to Gandhi's first article took a different view. The editors praised the Mahatma for finding time to "put in a word or two regarding the Jewish problem, in our Newspaper." But they distanced their newspaper (and possibly its readers) from Gandhi's thoughts. Azikiwe and his editorial colleagues "endorse[d] all the Mahatma ha[d] said about the Jews and their right to live on any portion of God's earth which is theirs by reason of birth or domicile" and "support[ed] his condemnation of German atrocity" but not his "solution" to the condition of Jews in Nazi Germany. The *Pilot* found Gandhi's idea that "if a few thousands of Jews should sacrifice their lives" in civil disobedience as Indians in South Africa had done, it would somehow save "the lives of millions" to be a fantasy. As the editors put it rather controversially, that view "fails to appreciate that Jews, unlike Indians . . . have not cultivated that high spiritual sense so peculiar to the Orientals, who are born philosophers." In its editorial reaction to the "prescriptions" of Mahatma Gandhi, the *West African Pilot* associated itself rather with the thoughts of the

American Secretary of the Interior Harold Ickes that what the Nazi persecution and annihilation of the Jews of Europe actually signified was that "[t]he intelligence and culture of a humane people has [sic] been sunk traceless in the thick darkness of pre-primitive times."[140]

Even as Africa's colonial subjects and sovereign peoples acknowledged that the Nazi regime persecuted other groups of people in Germany and other parts of Europe, they found the Nazi treatment of Jews in particular to be singularly obtrusive and historically unparalleled. The *Ethiopian Herald*, a state-owned newspaper, summed up that African perspective on the Holocaust in its succinct editorial of May 1944 but not without its pathos and irony.[141] The paper observed that while "Jews are not the only people who are caught in the throes of unmitigated suffering; the scale of violence and torture against them and their agonies of frustration have never been so great as during the present generation." In the view of the *Herald*, the twentieth century had witnessed "man's inhumanity to man . . . expressed in brutal racial discrimination, in the agonies of concentration camps, in the torturings and killing of men, women and children." However, "the case of the Jew is a special one." The editors of the *Herald* acknowledged that the Jews have been "singled out, as no other group has, for special treatment by the political gangsters who delight in creating a shambles wherever they find cultural traditions of any kind different from the nihilism of their own barbaric creed."[142] In the view of this newspaper, "Nothing short of the complete extermination of Jews in Europe is what the Nazis are aiming at doing." The *Ethiopian Herald* echoed opinions that the *West African Pilot* also held that "[o]nly the final defeat of Hitler's regime can bring relief to the millions of sufferers in Europe today." As the editors of the *Herald* noted, "that victory may come too late to save those whose lives are hanging by a thread in the darkness and misery of Europe's ghettoes."[143]

The *Ethiopian Herald* saw any action that could be taken "to save the dwindling remnant of Jewish sufferers in Europe" as necessary and urgent. It is in that context that one should view the paper's endorsement of President Roosevelt's establishment of the "War Refugees Board" to "explore every possible means of saving Jews in Europe." Unlike the *West African Pilot*, the *Ethiopian Herald* saw the plight of Jews in Europe in the Nazi era as the "more compelling" reason for the revival of the idea mooted "after the last war of establishing a Jewish National Home in Palestine." For the editors of the *Herald*, "There is immense truth in saying that the present war did not begin in 1939, but [rather] the moment Hitler launched his campaign against the Jews some six years earlier." Even for the sovereign African nation that became one of the first victims of fascist aggression, the persecution and extermination of Europe's Jews, which followed in the wake of the rise of the Third Reich, represented the most significant development in the history of the Second World War. The editors of the *Ethiopian Herald* took the view that the "answer to present-day anti-semitism" as a precipitant of the Holocaust lay in making "the cause of the Jew" a universal "battle for social freedom."[144] Colonial subjects in Africa agreed with this tenor of the *Herald*'s editorial page.

That the *Ethiopian Herald* could be that forthright about the plight of European Jews in 1944 is very instructive. Haile Selassie's silence about Nazism and the Nazi persecution of European Jews in the 1930s had been noticeable and perplexing. However, by June 1941 the emperor had returned to his throne in Ethiopia, from his post–Italian invasion exile in Britain, with the help of the British government. While in London, top British officials had discussed the Nazi persecution of the Jews with the emperor and made a direct appeal to him to allow a number of Jewish refugees to resettle in Ethiopia.[145] The Emperor was noncommittal, as we will examine in the next chapter. The *Herald's* endorsement of a separate homeland outside of Europe (in Palestine, without mention of Ethiopia) for the persecuted Jews would appear to be an official Ethiopian view of how the emperor wanted the developing Jewish refugee and humanitarian crisis to be addressed. On the contrary, the *West African Pilot's* endorsement of Mahatma Gandhi's opposition to the idea of a Jewish homeland outside of Europe suggests that while colonial subjects and sovereign nations in Africa empathized with persecuted European Jews, their views on a homeland for the surviving Jews of the Holocaust as a place of refuge diverged.

Impact of the Holocaust on colonialism

The conduct of Nazi Germany in the course of the Second World War and the horrors of the Holocaust had stirred up intense conversation in colonial Africa about race and white supremacy. Thoughts about Nazism and the persecution of Jews in Germany also created room for other discussions about social justice. The Holocaust made educated Africans question the European claim to civilization. For educated Africans who scoffed at the European ascription of savagery and barbarism to Africans in the imperial discourse, the Holocaust provided evidence and arguments against European claims to civilization and moral superiority. Educated Africans saw the Holocaust in the heart of Europe as the extreme manifestation of colonialism and racism in the center of their lives in Africa. The European countries from which Hitler and Mussolini came, the Christian religious beliefs they claimed to represent, and the Christian nations and missionaries who could not restrain them were also not spared in the African indictment of the mindsets and circumstances that had produced the Holocaust. As a contributor of a feature article on "Christianity Today" to the *West African Pilot* noted, "[I]f Christianity means anything, let it now challenge the present-day imperialism—the exploitation of the weak by the strong." For "[a] nation … which does not allow equality of treatment of Jews and non-Aryans, is not one that is qualified to preach Christianity in Africa." To "Christian Missions," the author advised that they "humbly and wisely withdraw for a time from Africa and after 20 years to come back ready with something new." Or "start all over again by first retiring to Europe to teach their people the essentials of Christianity" and providing "a new spiritual basis for the rebuilding of European society which is in danger of decay." Only "when they have set their own house in order, … [and] removed the beams in their own and their brothers' eyes, to see clearly enough" could they "return to Africa the second time to preach anew."[146]

In that analytical atmosphere where colonial subjects associated the racist Nazi trope of *Aryan* with the racial adjective *European*, the maintenance of the latter in official colonial communication became a political burden. Britain could no longer ignore the tide that was clearly turning. That the tide towards the discontinuation of racial tropes in official colonial communications and the designations of public institutions in the Gold Coast turned after the governorship of Sir Arnold Weinholt Hodson (October 1934–October 1941) is particularly significant. Governor Hodson's conservative views on race and his convictions about "Europeans" as the architects of progress in colonial Africa had become outmoded and unsustainable by 1942 amid the Holocaust. The reform of racist designations was left to the colony's more progressive Governor Sir Alan Cuthbert Maxwell Burns (June 1942–August 1947).

The Holocaust had an early and significant effect on colonialism in the area of public health. The British had long pursued an especially racist public health policy in their colonies in West Africa. They divided public health spaces and services into two distinct categories: European and African. Hospitals for Europeans had better facilities and services. By contrast, those that catered to the African population had poor and substandard facilities. This health policy was based on the pernicious notion of white supremacy and the allocation of special privileges to White Europeans in the colonies. To discerning colonial subjects, these hospitals had become the visible embodiments of the type of Nazi racism that colonial subjects associated with the Holocaust. As the sordid details of the Nazi death camps became known in Africa and as talk about settling and employing certain categories of Jewish refugees in British colonies on the continent continued (as will be discussed in Chapter 5), especially the appointment of Jewish refugee doctors in the Gold Coast colony, the underlying rationale of the British race-based segregation and privileging of life-sustaining institutions in Africa came under assault from colonial subjects. In November 1942, the British government decided to change this policy and practice and replace it with a new policy. The carefully crafted official letters sent to colonial officials in the Gold Coast are worth quoting in full here. The initial letter dated 19 November 1942, signed by L.A. Northcroft for the colonial secretary, and filed as Circular No. 58/42 read as follows:

> I am directed by the Governor to inform you that His Excellency has ordered that the use of the word "African," in connection with appointments or posts, should be discontinued forthwith in all official communications and notifications. The racial adjective will not appear in future issues of the Colony Estimates; and it is desired that it be equally sedulously avoided elsewhere.[147]

If the initial discomfort with this particular "racial adjective" related to its use in "official communications and notifications" on appointments, it did not take long to affect the other racial adjective, *European*, in other colonial interactions. In the post-1942 phase of the war and the Holocaust, the juxtaposition of the two racial adjectives in references to "government buildings and institutions" became equally embarrassing. In 1947 and with particular reference to the 1942 decision, the British government authorized the removal of these racial descriptors from hospital buildings in the Gold Coast colony and the renaming of those hospitals after the towns and cities in which they were located. Again the directives on this policy are revealing in their actual content. On 14 July 1947, L.A. Northcroft signed Circular No. 58/47, on behalf of the colonial secretary, to "all Heads of Departments, Chief Commissioners and Provincial Commissioners" of the Gold Coast Colony. It read as follows:

> With reference to this office Circular No. 58/42 of the 19th of November 1942, regarding the use of the word "African" in connection with appointments and posts, I am directed by the Governor to inform you that His Excellency wishes the rule made therein to be extended as far as possible and in particular to titles of Government buildings and institutions. Thus hospitals should no longer be distinguished in their designations as "African" and "European." As in the case of the "Ridge" Hospital in Accra, formerly designated the "European" Hospital, appropriate names should be given to hospitals where more than one exists in a town. Where there is only one, it should be known by the name of the town.[148]

On 3 November 1947, Acting Colonial Secretary Kenneth Bradley sent Circular No. 87/47 to give concrete instructions on the implementation of the preceding decision. He wrote to the same recipients of the 14 July 1947 letter:

> With reference to this office Circular No. 58/47 of the 14th of July, 1947 regarding the application of the words "African" and "European" to Government buildings and institutions, I am directed by the Officer Administering the Government to inform you that His Excellency wishes the hospitals listed in the first column of the schedule hereunder to be given in future the titles shown in the second column.

Former Names	Approved Names
European Hospital, Accra	Ridge Hospital, Accra
European Hospital, Takoradi	Takoradi Hospital
European and African Hospitals, Kumasi	Kumasi General Hospital
African Hospital, Tamale	Central Tamale Hospital
European Hospital, Tamale	West Tamale Hospital.[149]

As symbolic an approach to rethinking race in colonial interactions as these may appear, they were revolutionary responses to the ongoing reports about the Holocaust. It is possible that anticipation of the appointment of a limited number of Jewish refugee doctors in the West African colony, as we will examine in Chapter 5, partly influenced this British decision. How could Jewish refugees who not long ago had been dehumanized and violently persecuted in Europe by the Nazi regime on the grounds of race be elevated to privileged status in Africa on the basis of their race as Europeans? The British colonial administration must have contemplated the irony of appointing Jewish doctors whose status as refugees had been created by Nazi racism and having them serve in hospitals in the Gold Coast colony demarcated by race and racial privilege. Therefore, contrary to the analyses Guilia Berrera has made about East Africa, drawing upon the work of Neil MacMaster, the British began to "reject the language of race" in their colonies in West Africa as early as 1942. That conceptual shift occurred in the course of the war and the Holocaust, not after "the disclosure of the horrors of the Shoah (Holocaust) at the end of the war," as Berrera argues.[150]

As the war and the Holocaust ended, colonial subjects could boldly proclaim the dawn of their own era of self-determination from European guardianship. The Holocaust had exposed the emptiness and contradictions of the promise of European tutelage. That egregious outcome of racial prejudice had undermined Christianity too as a reliable moral precept in colonial society. The conversation about racial equality and social justice that had been pushed under the commitment to fighting Hitler was resurrected. As the Gold Coast pan-Africanist and fervent anticolonialist Bankole Awoonor-Renner acknowledged in a speech to the West African Students Union of Great Britain and Ireland in London on 23 August 1943, people in West Africa could "no longer stand any form of exploitation, be it German, French, Italian, American or African.... The time has arrived when we Africans must take the responsibility of shaping the affairs of our own country [sic]."[151] That movement toward decolonization at the end of the Second World War was inspired partly by African perspectives on the Holocaust. The Holocaust gave the struggle against colonialism in Africa and the ideas and institutions that justified it the most potent and impenetrable moral argument.

Besides debating the place for the resettlement of the survivors of the Holocaust, colonial subjects also thought about where the champions of the philosophy that inspired the Holocaust ended up and about the lessons their "biographies" should teach humanity. In one of its most instructive editorials, toward the end of the war, the *West African Pilot* recalled on 2 May 1945 how Adolf Hitler had "basked in the sunshine of fame," how "by the majestic wave of his hand, the destiny of nations was sealed," and "by the stroke of a pen, life was given or life was taken ... from any person within the jurisdiction of the Third German Reich." But "today he is dead [having committed suicide in his bunker in Berlin on 30 April 1945] and his stinking carcass is food for the populations of the world of microbiology." Like Adolf Hitler, Benito Mussolini's "words, like lightning, destroyed those who dared to stand in his path.... Wherever he went, his pomposity and arrogance created terror in the minds of his people. They called him 'Duce.' Yet, like Hitler, "Mussolini is dead [captured and executed in Italy on 28 April 1945] and in spite of his callous invasion of Ethiopia, only six feet of earth await to swallow his bloated corpse."[152] The *Pilot* observed that "there must be a lesson for Africans from the biographies of Hitler and Mussolini." That lesson is that ambition and fame are noble, "but man must not allow his head to be swollen as to forget that life has a meaning—service to humanity."[153]

Conclusion

It is now possible to assert that news about the German treatment of Jews reached a wide public in East and West Africa. Colonial subjects and sovereign peoples in these regions learned about the Holocaust from the many reports that were reprinted in their local newspapers from various newspapers in Europe and from selected official colonial sources. Certainly, it is easier to conclude that the major newspapers in East and West Africa published numerous news reports and commentaries on the Holocaust than it is to know how many people in these regions of Africa actually read them. But the extent to which the editors of these papers continued to publish these reports on a daily and weekly basis and colonial authorities did not censor them suggests that a large number of readers showed interest in the Nazi treatment of European Jews and what that meant to Africans. Colonial authorities did not confirm or deny or even censor those news reports. When the colonial government directly shared information it had about the Holocaust, it did so selectively and through official war news bulletins and war propaganda newsletters. It is therefore accurate to conclude that Britain used information about the Holocaust as a political tool in its colonies in West and East Africa to whip up local support for the Allied war effort. It succeeded. The unintended outcome of that political act was that colonial subjects became aware of the unspeakable crimes of the Nazi regime against a group of people in Europe (Jews) whom many in East and West Africa saw as racially similar to all Europeans. That a white European government could target another group of white Europeans for annihilation, in the age of colonial-civilization rhetoric and Christian-missionary teaching, struck many colonial subjects as not only paradoxical but downright frightening. It was in the context of that interpretation of the Nazi harassment and physical destruction of European Jews that colonial subjects in particular saw their own dignity and fate as bound up with the total defeat of the Nazi state.

The African press did more than publicize the plight of European Jews to their readers. Colonial subjects and sovereign peoples in Africa who offered their thoughts on the Holocaust in newspapers or in public statements empathized with the Jewish victims of Nazi atrocities as if they shared a bond of historical and persecuted kinship. They also reflected on the cruelty of the perpetrators of the Holocaust. Colonized and sovereign peoples in Africa analyzed the ideologies that produced the perpetrators of the Holocaust, the societies that nurtured their worldviews, and the world that tolerated their indifference to basic human values. Above all, they reflected on what the Holocaust meant for their own struggle against racism and colonial subjugation. Their reactions to the Holocaust were therefore extensions of their views on Nazism. Because they had read Hitler's thoughts about "Jews" and "Negroes," colonized and sovereign peoples in Africa followed the Nazi persecution of Jews with great attention in the course of the Second World War. They did not learn about the Holocaust after the end of the war. They followed the Holocaust as it happened, throughout the 1930s and early 1940s, because they had access to the many and detailed reports in global news outlets, including Soviet reports in English, about the mass deportations and executions of Jews in ghettos and concentration camps, in Germany and in other parts of German-occupied Europe. Denunciations of the Holocaust in the African press were more than preemptive responses to what colonial subjects and sovereign peoples perceived could also happen to them. As victims of specious race theories and degrading colonial policies, Africans' empathy towards the Jews was borne out of a shared history of discrimination and persecution. But how far did that African empathy go in addressing the significant Jewish refugee crisis that the Holocaust created and that needed a humanitarian response in itself?

Notes

1 Eberhard Jackel, "The Holocaust: Where We Are, Where We Need to Go," in *The Holocaust and History*, 24.
2 Liebau et al., *The World in World Wars*, 8.
3 Jackel, "The Holocaust," 23. See also Wyman, *The World Reacts to the Holocaust*, xiii, xiv, xix.
4 Marrus, *The Holocaust in History*, 3. See also Sean Warsch, "A 'Holocaust' Becomes 'the Holocaust'," *Jewish Magazine*, October 2016, 5, www.jewishmag.com/107mag/holocaustword/holocaustword.htm.
5 Ibid., 3.
6 E.C.T. Herman, "Do We Want Fascism?" *The West African Pilot*, vol. II, no. 485, Tuesday June 20, 1939, 4. For more instances of the early use of the term *holocaust*, see Ben Kiernan, *Blood and Soil: A World History of Genocide and Extermination from Sparta to Darfur* (New Haven, CT: Yale University Press, 2007), 9–10.
7 Warsch, "A 'Holocaust' Becomes 'the Holocaust,'" 2, 4–5.
8 Saul Friedlander, *Nazi Germany and the Jews, 1939–1945: The Years of Extermination* (New York: Harper Perennial, 2008), xvi.
9 Donald Bloxham and Tony Kushner, *The Holocaust: Critical Historical Approaches* (Manchester: Manchester University Press, 2005), 3.
10 Steven T. Katz, *The Holocaust in Historical Context: The Holocaust and Mass Death Before the Modern Age*, vol. 1 (New York: Oxford University Press, 1994). For how Katz describes the Holocaust, see 3. For his conception of it as phenomenologically unique, see 28.
11 Ibid.
12 Ibid., 10.
13 Ina R. Friedman, "The Holocaust: The Other Victims of the Nazis," *Social Education* 59, no. 6 (October 1995): 339.
14 Ibid.
15 David E. Stannard, *American Holocaust: The Conquest of the New World* (New York: Oxford University Press, 1992), 151.
16 Ibid., 257.
17 Ibid., 150. See also 184.
18 Ibid., 256. See also xi, xii.

19 United States Holocaust Memorial Museum, "Introduction to the Holocaust," www.ushmm.org/wlc/en/article.php?Moduled=10005143.
20 Ibid.
21 United Nations Educational, Scientific and Cultural Organizations [UNESCO], *Education About the Holocaust and Preventing Genocide: A Policy Guide* (Paris: UNESCO, 2017), 22.
22 United Nations, *Resolution Adopted by the General Assembly on Holocaust Remembrance* (A/RES/60/7), November 1, 2005, www.un.org/en/holocaustremembrance/docs/res607.shtml.
23 The Holocaust Resource Center (Yad Vashem), "The Holocaust," 1, www.yadvashem.org/yv/en/holocaust/resource_center/the_holocaust.asp.
24 Ibid.
25 "Another Aspect of Germany and Her Jews," *The Uganda Herald*, Wednesday September 13, 1933, 9. Prior to the appearance of this news item in the *Herald*, the *Daily Guardian* newspaper in Freetown, Sierra Leone, in West Africa had also published, in April and May 1933, from official British wireless news sources, widespread persecution of Jewish professors and other professional men in German Upper Silesia. See "The Jews in Upper Silesia," *The Daily Guardian*, vol. 1, no. 85, Freetown, Sierra Leone, Wednesday April 12, 1933, 4; "Treatment of Jews in Germany," no. 119, May 24, 1933, 1.
26 "Another Aspect of Germany and Her Jews," 9.
27 Ibid.
28 *Daily Guardian*, vol. III, no. 629, Tuesday September 17, 1935.
29 *Liberian Crisis*, vol. 2, May 1934, 1.
30 Governor Mark Young, Tanganyika Territory, to Malcolm MacDonald, Secretary of State for the Colonies, March 29, 1939, FO 371/22954, *Political Central Germany*. Document No. 69–70; 71–72.
31 Ibid.
32 "Number of Germans Who Have Migrated into Kenya Since 1933," Parliamentary Question from Mr. Craven Ellis, Registry No. C5666/9/18, April 21, 1939, PRO. FO 371/22954. *Political Central Germany, 1939*. See also Registry No. C8822/9/18, June 21, 1939. FO 371–22/955, *Political Central Germany, 1939*.
33 *Papers Concerning the Treatment of German Nationals in Germany, 1938–1939*, Enclosure to Circular Note, November 3, 1939, *Documents Concerning German–Polish Relations and the Outbreak of Hostilities Between Great Britain and Germany*, PRAAD, GNA. File: CSO 26/2/31.
34 Ibid.
35 Ibid., 3–4.
36 Consul-General Claire Gainer, British Consulate in Vienna, Austria, to Sir G. Ogilvie-Forbes, Charge d'Affaires, British Embassy, Berlin, November 11, 1938, in *Papers*, 15.
37 Ibid.
38 "Statement by Jewish Ex-Prisoner: August 1938; No. 5, Statement Communicated to the Foreign Office on October 28, 1938, by a Charity Organization Working in Germany," in *Papers*, 9–10.
39 Herr X's Statement, no. 5, in *Papers*, 9.
40 Ibid., 10.
41 Translated "Statement by a Jewish-Christian Prisoner," in *Papers*, 10–11.
42 Ibid., 11–14.
43 Ibid., 23.
44 Ibid., 13.
45 Ibid., 14.
46 Ibid., 16.
47 Consul General J.E. Bell, British Consul-General in Cologne, to Sir G. Ogilvie-Forbes, British Charge d'Affaires, Berlin, November 14, 1938, in *Papers*, 17.
48 Ibid.
49 Enclosure 1 in Correspondence No. 7, Translated letter from Informant Ein Beamter to Consul-General J.E. Bell, British Consulate in Cologne, November 12, 1938, in *Papers*, 18.

50 Ibid.
51 Enclosure No. 2 in Correspondence No. 7, *Translation of a Copy of the Original Sent to the Reichsminister for Justice*, in *Papers*, 19.
52 Despatch No. 8, from Sir G. Ogilvie-Forbes, Berlin, to Viscount Halifax, London, December 15, 1938, containing report from Consul-General Smallbones, Frankfurt-on-Main, to Sir G. Ogilvie-Forbes, British Charge d'Affaires in Berlin, December 14, 1938, in *Papers*, 20.
53 Ibid.
54 Ibid., 21.
55 Ibid., 20.
56 Ibid., 22.
57 Ibid., 23.
58 Ibid.
59 Ibid., 23–24.
60 No. 9, Consul-General [J.E.M.] Carvell, British Consul-General, Munich, to Viscount Halifax, Secretary of State, London, January 5, 1939, in *Papers*, 24.
61 Ibid.
62 Ibid., 25.
63 Ibid.
64 Ibid.
65 Ibid., 26.
66 Ibid.
67 No. 11, Statement of a Former Prisoner at the Concentration Camp at Buchenwald–(Communicated to the Foreign Office on February 18, 1939), in *Papers*, 27.
68 Ibid., 36.
69 Ibid., 28.
70 Ibid., 35.
71 Ibid., 29.
72 Ibid., 29–30.
73 Ibid., 28.
74 Ibid.
75 Ibid., 31–32.
76 Ibid., 30.
77 Ibid.
78 Ibid., 33.
79 Ibid., 30.
80 Ibid., 33.
81 Ibid., 34.
82 Ibid.
83 Ibid., 36.
84 Ibid.
85 "Concentration Camp Is Horrible, Concentration Camp Exposed," *West African Pilot*, vol. II, no. 602, Lagos, Thursday November 2, 1939.
86 Ibid.
87 "Germans Persecute Polish Jews, Germans Torture Polish Jews," *West African Pilot*, vol. II, no. 607, Lagos, Wednesday November 8, 1939.
88 Ibid.
89 "How the Nazis' 'New Order' Is Being Applied," *East African Standard*, Nairobi, Friday October 31, 1941, 1. British Newspaper Library, Colindale.
90 Ibid.
91 *The Tanganyika Herald*, Dar es Salaam, vol. XIII, no. 41, Saturday June 20, 1942.
92 "Soviet Report on Nazi Atrocities in Russia—Massacre, Devastation and Outrage" [Editorial], *Uganda Herald*, Wednesday March 25, 1942, 13.

93 "Soviet Report on Nazi Atrocities in Russia," *Gold Coast Independent*, vol. XXV, no. 22, Accra, Saturday May 30, 1942, 162.
94 J.B. Danquah, Barrister at Law, Yiadom Chambers, to Acting Colonial Secretary, Accra, June 29, 1942, PRAAD, GNA. File: CSO 23/5/12. Subject: *War News from Foreign Countries.*
95 T.R.O. Mangin, Acting Secretary for Native Affairs, to J.B. Danquah, July 15, 1942. CSO 25/5/12.
96 "Poland," *Inside the News, Weekly War Commentary by "Veritas,"* vol. 2, no. 131, July 9, 1942, PRAAD, GNA. File: CSO 23/5/129.
97 "British Labour Party Appeals Against Nazi Pogrom of Jews," *West African Pilot*, vol. VI, no. 1554, Thursday December 17, 1942.
98 Ibid.
99 "Nazi 'Murder Camps': The Slaughter House of Treblinka," *Gold Coast Independent*, vol. XXVI, no. 45, Accra, Saturday November 6, 1943, 280. There is no indication that this article was reprinted from a European newspaper; neither is there any evidence of how the *Independent* got hold of this report.
100 Ibid.
101 Ibid.
102 Ibid.
103 Yisrael Gutman and Michael Berenbaum, *Anatomy of the Auschwitz Death Camp* (Bloomington, IN: Indiana University Press, 1994), 21.
104 Jan Wolny, "How the Germans Massacred 116,000 Jews, Truth About the German Gas Chambers," *The Gold Coast Independent*, September 16, 1944, 223. Reprinted from *Sunday Express*. British Newspaper Library.
105 Ibid.
106 Ibid.
107 "Gestapo Orders All Negroes in the Reich to Report," *West African Pilot*, vol. VI, no. 1599, Friday February 5, 1943, 4.
108 "Is It the Negro's Turn Now?" *West African Pilot*, vol. VI., no. 1595, Thursday February 6, 1943, 2.
109 Ibid.
110 "Nazis Will Destroy All Jews by March," *West African Pilot*, vol. VI, no. 1603, Tuesday February 16, 1943.
111 Ibid.
112 "Nazi Pogrom Is Subject of Motion in the House of Lords," *West African Pilot*, vol. VI, no. 1635, Thursday March 25, 1943.
113 Ibid.
114 Ibid.
115 "The 'Superior Race' Myth" [Editorial], *The West African Pilot*, vol. VI, no. 1604, Wednesday February 17, 1943, 2.
116 Zik, "Inside Stuff: Germanism," *The West African Pilot*, vol. 1, no. 310, Thursday November 17, 1938.
117 Zik, "Inside Stuff: That Volteface," *West African Pilot*, vol. II, no. 352, Monday January 9, 1939, 6.
118 Our Own Correspondent, "Foreign Affairs (3)," *West African Pilot*, vol. II, no. 334, December 16, 1938, 5.
119 "One Hundred Jews Emigrate to Dominions from Germany," *West African Pilot*, vol. I, no. 307, Monday November 14, 1938, 1.
120 Our Own Correspondent, "Foreign Affairs (3)," 5.
121 "Nazi Persecution" [Editorial], *West African Pilot*, vol. I, no. 311, Friday November 18, 1938.
122 Ibid.
123 Department of Information, Gold Coast Government, *Empire at War.*

124 "German Propaganda" [Editorial].
125 Special to the *West African Pilot*, "Nigeria's Alleged Transfer Causes Great Apprehension," *West African Pilot*, vol. I, no. 303, Wednesday November 9, 1938. This article was a front page news item in the day's paper.
126 "Concentration Camp," 4.
127 Ibid.
128 "No More Discrimination!" *West Africa Pilot*, vol. V, no. 1243, Thursday December 11, 1941.
129 Ibid.
130 "A Lesson to All Africans," *West African Pilot*, vol. V, no. 1395, Monday June 15, 1942, 2.
131 Ibid.
132 "Gestapo Orders All Negroes in the Reich to Report," 4; "Is It the Negro's Turn Now?" [Editorial], Saturday February 6, 1943, 2.
133 "Gestapo Orders All Negroes in the Reich to Report," 4.
134 Mahatma Ghandi, "The Jewish Problem (1)," *West African Pilot*, vol. II, no. 359, Wednesday January 18, 1939, 5, 7; "The Jewish Problem (2)," *West African Pilot*, vol. II, no. 360, Thursday January 19, 1939, 5.
135 Ibid.
136 Ghandi, "The Jewish Problem (1)," 5.
137 Ibid., 7.
138 Ghandi, "The Jewish Problem (2)," 5.
139 Ibid.
140 "The Mahatma Speaks" [Editorial], *West African Pilot*, vol. II, no. 359, Wednesday January 18, 1939, 4–5.
141 "The Jews' Plight," *The Ethiopian Herald*, vol. 1, no. 32, February 5, 1944, 2. Ethiopian National Library, Addis Ababa, Ethiopia.
142 Ibid.
143 Ibid.
144 Ibid.
145 Otto M. Schiff, Secretary, Jewish Refugees Committee, to unknown recipient, Bloomsbury House, London, September 1, 1942. FO 371/36628, Refugees File No. 25, *General, 1943*. See also Bob Howe, British Legation, Addis Ababa, Ethiopia, to Gilbert Mackereth, Foreign Office, London, May 29, 1943, PRO, File 371/36628, Refugees File No. 25, *General, 1943*.
146 J.O. Anyaduba, "Christianity Today (3)," *West African Pilot*, vol. II, no. 388, Wednesday February 22, 1939, 5.
147 Colonial Secretary's Office, Accra, November 19, 1942. Circular No. 58/42. File No. 1787/S.F.3, *Discontinuance of the Use of the Word "African" in Official Documents*, PRAAD, GNA, RG 3/5/523.
148 Ibid., July 14, 1947. Circular No. 87/47.
149 Ibid., November 3, 1947.
150 See Guilia Berrera, "Wrestling with Race on the Eve of Human Rights: The British Management of the Color Line in Post-Fascist Eritrea," in Judith Byfied et al., *Africa and World War II*, 261–262.
151 "Africans Should Now Control Their Own Destiny: Says Renner," *West African Pilot*, vol. VI, no. 1810, Thursday October 21, 1943.
152 "The Vanity of Human Wishes" [Editorial], *West African Pilot*, vol. VIII, no. 2273, Wednesday May 2, 1945, 2.
153 Ibid.

5 African and British proposals on Jewish refugees

> No full-length study yet exists which explores the overall record of the colonial Empire [about Jewish refugees during the Holocaust period]. When one appears, it will have to take into account a number of issues: what was meant, as well as what was said; the local autonomy of the colonies as distinct from the degree of control exercised from London; and the perceptions held by both the colonies and the metropolis about each other and the refugees. It will not be an easy task, but it must be attempted, as the response of the British Empire reveals a great deal about the moral, political, and humanitarian implications of being British at a time when the rest of the world looked to the United Kingdom as the standard-setter of international fair-play and honesty. This subject, one of the last to be addressed in analyses of the Free World's response to the Holocaust, awaits its historian.[1]

The preceding chapters have answered two of this book's principal questions: What did people in Africa know about the Holocaust? And what did they say or think about it? Now that we know some answers to both questions, the third question that requires an answer is: What did they do to help Europe's persecuted Jews who survived the Holocaust, and who arrived in their regions as refugees? The search for a homeland for the Jewish people, as an international aspiration, preceded the Holocaust. Underlying that aspiration was the blight on the conscience of European statesmen who had failed to tame anti-Semitism in Europe and who had to confront the embarrassing effects of that failure in the throes of the Second World War. Those effects included efforts to safeguard the security and dignity of Jews fleeing persecution and genocide in Nazi Germany. Some of the earliest proposals for a safer homeland for European Jews included a place of refuge on the African continent. This chapter examines some of these earlier proposals, especially the British interest in settling some categories of European Jews in East and West Africa before and after the outbreak of the Second World War. It pays particular attention to the politics and controversies that engulfed those proposals and to the responses their implementation provoked from colonial administrators, British settlers, colonial subjects, and sovereign nations in the two regions of Africa. The chapter argues that the idea of creating a homeland for some of Europe's persecuted Jews on African soil, through the settlement of Jewish refugees with agricultural and medical skills, received mixed reactions. Support and opposition came from people and governments that had initially been empathetic to the plight of Jews in Nazi Germany but later recoiled from receiving them as refugees. In the end, politics, policy, land, and climate ensnarled an aspiration that could only be partially pursued and eventually abandoned. It is also a study of the contradictions and brittleness of empathy.

Early ideas about a Zion in Kenya

As we have already noted in Chapter 1, the history of Jewish settlement in Africa is very well documented. It dates back to many years before the twentieth century. Historically, Northern Africa and South Africa had the largest number of Jews who lived on the African continent. It is only recently that Jewish diasporic communities in West Africa, in particular, and in East Africa, to a moderate extent, have been uncovered and seriously studied. In Kenya in particular, Naomi Musiker has shown in her work that the year 1903 marked the first time that Jews, mainly from East Europe and South Africa, began to settle in sparse numbers in that British East African colony. As Musiker and Peter Mwangi Kagwanjia have noted, in their respective research on this subject, the settlement of Jews in Kenya in the early twentieth century owed its origins to British policy. That policy had been prompted by a conscientious desire "to solve the problem of mounting persecution of Jews in Russia."[2] This early twentieth century effort at securing a safe haven for some of Europe's persecuted Jews had the support of Theodore Herzl, the influential leader of the Zionist Congress. The Zionist Congress expected this initial effort to be a temporary solution to the ultimate aspiration of creating a permanent homeland for Jews. In the end, differences of opinion over the location of that permanent national homeland for Jews within various Jewish organizations doomed this early pre–World War II British idea of a homeland for European Jews in East Africa. Jewish organizations such as the World Zionist Conference that advocated for a permanent Homeland for Jews saw the East Africa experiment as a diversionary ploy to stymie the Zionist commitment to a homeland in Palestine. Kenyan historians Peter Mwangi Kagwanjia and Mwangi wa-Githumo, who have studied the politics of this initial British project in East Africa, argue that the plan to settle thousands of East European Jews on a stretch of fertile land in the Kitale and Eldoret regions in Kenya (popularly known as the Uasin Gishu Plateau and that British settlers called the White Highlands) was bound to flounder long before the World Zionist Conference nipped it. British settlers in Kenya wanted to reserve the White Highlands for particular categories of European settlers. These British settlers, many of whom were retired officers of the British Army, did not think that the presence of Jews in that British colony enhanced the image of white supremacy that the aristocratic British settlers were eager to maintain in East Africa.[3] They opposed the settlement of "poor whites" or "lower class" Europeans in Kenya.

Reactions from British settlers

Studies of British settler reactions done by Mwangi wa-Githumo, Brett Shadle, and Adam Rovner have exposed the kinds of anti-Semitic attitudes and the ideologies behind them that British settlers brought to the East African colony or developed on the continent. As Githumo has argued, that British plan to settle persecuted Jews from Russia in the Uasin Gishu plateau in Kenya (a land area of about 5,000 square miles) "unleashed a wave of open anti-Semitism among White Anglo-Saxon Protestant settlers in Kenya" who wanted all rich cultivable land in the colony to be reserved for "settlers of the British race."[4] The "indignant" reaction of these European settlers and their protestant Christian counterparts was coordinated by Lord Delamere, a British settler who served as president of the Planters and Farmers Association and who also chaired a committee formed by the settlers to oppose Jewish settlement in Kenya. Delamere, in particular, dismissed the Russian Jews as "undesirable aliens" in his numerous written protests to the Foreign Office for daring to consider settling Jews "in the area originally reserved for the white race."[5]

Clearly, British settlers in Kenya distinguished between themselves and Jews from other parts of Europe, a distinction that must have seemed odd to indigenous Africans who saw all Europeans as racially white. But for Delamere and other British settlers such as W.H. Tiller, editor of the anti-Semitic and pro-Settler newspaper *African Standard*, and "Anglo-Saxon church leaders" such as W.G. Peel, the Bishop of Mombasa, and Reverend Bennett, Jews belonged to a different race of humanity. For these representatives of settler opinion in Kenya, Russian Jews lived in ghettoes, and "whatever their virtues, industry and misfortunes, were unlikely to command respect" among local Africans.[6] They also viewed Jews as unlikely to assimilate well into the colony given their "religion, customs and habits."[7] A.E. Atkinson, a British settler, for instance, claimed that if the British wanted to hurriedly populate Kenya with people, then the Foreign Office would do well to bring in "our own poor farm labourers from England." For Christian leaders in the British settler community, their hatred for Jews was based on religion. They claimed to fear the possible Jewish hindrance of the conversion of colonized Africans to Christianity. In one particular sermon that reflected this view, Bishop Peel claimed that he preferred "Christian settlers in Kenya to accursed Jews" for the sake of Christianity and "white civilization." As wa-Githumo has observed, these "deliberate anti-Semitic descriptions" by European settlers of British heritage were aimed at accomplishing "one goal, the monopoly and preservation of Kenya as a white Anglo-Saxon Protestants' country."[8]

British settler attitudes toward Jews transcended the goal of controlling land and saving souls in colonial Kenya. Their anti-Semitism also exposed the racial and colonial order that the British settlers wanted to enforce in Kenya and other British colonies in Africa. Brett L. Shadle has situated British settler views about Jews in the long and complicated history of British anti-Semitism and Anglo-Saxon imperial notions of race, civilization, and prestige. In his *The Souls of White Folk*, Shadle argues that while many Jews of British heritage had gained respect within official and aristocratic British circles and had even served as colonial officials in Britain's overseas Empire in the nineteenth and twentieth centuries, the same British aristocrats did not look so favorably upon non-British Jews.[9] For the settlers, European heritage did not necessarily confer the prestige of whiteness. British settlers in Kenya viewed Jews from East and Central Europe, the regions where the Jews intended for settlement in Kenya in the early years of the twentieth century were to come from, as not white.[10] Shadle locates the roots of British settler anti-Semitism in Anglo-Saxon ideological equation of "whiteness" with "civilization." In this ideology, only English-speaking European Jews qualified as truly "white" and "civilized." British settlers in Kenya regarded their conflation of whiteness and civilization as necessary to separate the large number of native Black Africans in the colony from the small number of White Europeans who exercised power over them and to ensure that native Africans did not deviate from the respect and deference for "whites" that the settlers required of them. The dominant settler view that "whites brought civilization to Africa" and therefore "Africans must defer to whites as higher beings" drove this racial narrative.[11] To maintain the prestige, honor, and safety that whiteness was supposed to confer on Anglo-Saxon Europeans in the colony, British settlers in Kenya opposed any form of sexual and physical intimacy between Europeans and native Africans that could suggest any type of racial and emotional equality.[12] From this premise, the settlers believed that every individual white person in Kenya will be safe "so long as the white race had prestige" in the eyes of the colonized people.[13] Whites who were "poor" or supposedly "backward" or who "liv[ed] like Africans" posed the greatest threat to white prestige. Such Europeans were presumed by the settlers to have "gone native" and therefore to have failed to maintain the posture and demeanor required to inspire prestige.[14]

From Shadle's analyses of British settler attitudes, one can discern that "the real complication" with the British proposal to settle Russian and Romanian Jews in the Uasin Gishu plateau was that the Jewish immigrants intended for that settlement were "poor" and many of them were "peasants or ghetto-dwellers." They were deemed by influential members of the English-speaking settler community to lack the financial resources, the social status, and "the bearing that whites in Kenya must have." As "impoverished, down-trodden victims of pogroms, the Jews would not appear civilized." For that reason, "Africans would not see them as superior, [and] would not respect them."[15] And if the dire economic and social circumstances of the Jewish settlers led them "to go native," with the unmarried having sexual interactions with Black Africans, the Jews could endanger the racial order in colonial Kenya. Therefore, for the sake of maintaining the prestige of whiteness, Russian and Romanian Jews, considered by the British settlers as "white vagrants" and therefore not purely white in nature and civilization, were unwelcome in Kenya.[16]

Opposition from the British settlers may have foreshadowed some of the challenges that awaited the British government's interest in establishing a homeland for persecuted Jews in East Africa. That, however, did not foreclose the official interest. As wa-Githumo and Adam Rovner have observed in separate research, the initial setback must have inspired the Balfour Declaration of 1917 which committed the British government to "the establishment in Palestine of a national home for the Jewish people" and the use of the "best endeavours" of the government "to facilitate the achievement of this object."[17] Continuation of the British commitment to creating a Zion in East Africa after 1917 seems to bolster Rovner's view that an East African stepping stone to a future Jewish homeland in Palestine was, for the Colonial Office, "a neat solution to several colonial dilemmas." One of them was that "a substantial colony of grateful Jews in East Africa would mean additional loyal subjects who would pose an obstacle to German expansionism" in that part of the British Empire.[18]

Prewar and wartime proposals on Jewish refugees

With the failure of the initial British effort in Kenya in the 1900s, British policymakers yielded subsequent initiatives to private individuals and Jewish organizations. One of the earliest private appeals to the British government for the rescue of Jews in Germany for safe settlement elsewhere arrived in the Dominions Office at Whitehall in July 1933. It was made by Simon Marks, owner of the British retail chain store Marks and Spencer, in a passionate letter to Secretary of State for the Dominions J.H. Thomas. The occasion for this communication seemed appropriate: a meeting, in London, at that time, of "the principal representatives of the Dominions." In his letter, Simon Marks sought the "advice and assistance" of J.H. Thomas on the "the magnitude of the catastrophe" facing German Jews in the wake of the Nazi ascent to power.[19] He pointed to the "resolute, deliberate and persistent effort" by the Nazi regime "to reduce to ruin and penury more than half a million people who have been settled for many centuries in Germany, and ... made most memorable contributions" to the development of the country. Marks disclosed that as a result of Nazi policy and practices about "twenty or thirty thousand Jews" have left Germany and now lived as "refugees" in neighboring countries. Simon Marks predicted that the number of Jews fleeing Germany would increase and that those who remained in the country would "face a miserable and hopeless prospect." He observed that while Jews all over the world grappled with "this terrible problem" of Jewish refugees, they could not, alone, resolve "the task imposed upon them" without the "collaboration" and "sympathy" of others. In view of that catastrophic reality, Simon Marks called upon the British government "to offer some assistance in finding homes" for the Jews who have fled Germany and those who remained there. He also underscored the fact that "[t]he Jews who have been driven out of Germany include very large numbers of men of exceptional scientific, technical, industrial, and commercial gifts and knowledge, and these gifts are certain to add strength to the reserves of any country" that offered them sanctuary and employment. But beyond their professional talent, "finding asylum for some of the persecuted Jews of Germany," would be a "greater ... act of humanity that could be performed in this hour."[20]

The secretary of state for the dominions shared Simon Marks's plea with representatives of these overseas outposts of the British Empire. As Louise London has demonstrated, despite the official request from the Dominions Office, the autonomous governments of Britain's Dominion countries (Canada, Australia, New Zealand, South Africa) were initially reluctant to accept Jewish refugees. Dominion governments that even cared to respond to the written request from Whitehall to take in a number of those refugees complained about Jews as "Communists" who could unsettle existing social structures with their revolutionary ideas or as the wrong type of immigrants who shun assimilation into the host country.[21]

Perhaps the most prominent of the pre–World War II intergovernmental conversations on the resettlement of "political refugees," many of whom were Jews fleeing Nazi persecution, were those undertaken at the Evian Conference. It was convened by President Roosevelt of the United States and held in the French city of Evian-les-Bains on 6 July 1938. Representatives from 32 countries, including Britain and France, attended. Evian aimed at considering the steps that could be taken to facilitate the settlement "in other countries" or overseas territories of people in Nazi Germany who wanted to leave the country because of persecution on grounds of religion, race, or politics, as well as those, like many Jews, who had already left for this specific reason. The conferees also intended to consider the steps that could be taken to encourage countries and territories willing to accept these "political refugees" to modify their existing immigration laws to make their entry and settlement possible. As far as Africa was concerned, the Evian conference was significant in one important respect. It was here that Britain formally disclosed its plan and interest in resettling a number of the Jewish political refugees in its colonies in East Africa, particularly Kenya, and its mandated territory of Tanganyika.[22] The temporary revival of British actions on the settlement of Jewish refugees in the Colonial Empire was partly a consequence of what had transpired at Evian and the continuing difficulty the British government had in eliciting positive responses from the governments of the Dominions for the acceptance of Jewish refugees.

Before and during the Second World War, discussions about the settlement of Jewish refugees in Africa took place, confidentially, among the Foreign Office, Home Office, and Colonial Office and certain Jewish organizations. Internal memoranda exchanged between various offices within the Colonial Office in London highlight some of the internal thoughts on what that settlement policy might mean for Britain's African colonies. Some bureaucrats saw the settlement of Jewish refugees in the Colonial Empire as a colonial development potential, but one that was certain to "generate strong opposition among settlers and colonial subjects.[23] Others concluded that it could reassure colonial subjects in Tanganyika, for instance, who were uncertain about British policy on the return of that former German colony to the Nazi regime. Settlement of Jewish refugees in that East African territory under British trusteeship could represent "an indirect but certain indication that His Majesty's Government did not intend to return Tanganyika to Germany." A few were "not sure" that it would be wise for Britain to convey that impression.[24]

Opinions varied in the three departments that decided British policy on the settlement of Jewish refugees in Britain's overseas Empire. Of special significance in this typical interdepartmental tussle over policy was the internal conflict over the scope and purpose of a Jewish refuge settlement in Tanganyika, in particular. A summary of the prevailing views in the Foreign Office on this subject from J.G. Hibbert to E.B. Boyd on 16 November 1938 is illuminating. According to Hibbert, initial letters that some Colonial Office staff had drafted to be sent as a telegram to Governor Mark Young of the Tanganyika Territory had "conveyed the impression that all we [at the Foreign Office] expected the Governor to do was to agree to an experimental scheme comprising the settlement of about 25 young Jewish trained agriculturists and their families." That was not the view of the secretary of state in the Foreign Office. His view, according to Hibbert, was a much larger project that would make "a large area of [the] country" available even "if not immediately suitable for settlement on a large scale could be rendered so if Jewish capital were available for the cost of clearance." Hibbert's summary of internal policy thoughts reveals that the Foreign Office wanted a clear statement in the British Parliament about "the possibilities of German refugee settlement in ... the Colonies." That statement, to be drafted by "representatives" of the Foreign Office, Home Office, and Colonial Office, was to "mention the extent of the areas that might be made available for the ultimate settlement of refugees on a fairly large scale in British Guiana and Tanganyika Territory."[25] Any definite official statement on the Tanganyika option was to await the advice of the British governor of the Tanganyika Territory bearing in mind the "safeguarding of native interests" in any refugee settlement policy.[26] The option for Kenya, however, was to be much smaller, perhaps because of strong opposition from British settlers in the colony.

The Colonial Office reaffirmed its position on what it called the Kenya project. It was meant to be "a small-scale settlement in the first instance of a small number of trained refugee agriculturists." These refugees could later be joined by their families. A total of "150 persons in all" was envisioned.[27] Even at this time, British officials in London understood that "the proposal to settle refugees" in some colonial territories "aroused great apprehension" within colonial administrations. In Kenya, in particular, the Foreign Office wanted to be very cautious about the refugee matter since "any impression among the settlers or the Indian population that a large influx of refugees was contemplated would render the prospect of settlement much more difficult." The British government was very clear that a Jewish refugee settlement in the colonies should be a self-financing or privately funded project since "Colonial Governments can make no financial contribution towards these projects."[28] Jewish refugees were to be settled "on farms purchased by Jewish organizations."[29] British policy took into account the importance of Jewish organizations sending their own representatives to the colonies to carry out their own studies of the feasibility of refugee settlement.

The Foreign Office and the Colonial Office remained sensitive to the idea of settling Jewish refugees in Kenya. That was in response to the determination of the colonial administration in Kenya to restrict and also control such emigration to exclude the admission of refugees who might later become a financial burden on the colonial government. The case of a "refugee named Liebenstein" was the subject of a confidential correspondence between the Colonial Office and the Foreign Office on 10 November 1938. A visa to Kenya had been granted to Liebenstein by the British consul in Basel, Switzerland, without regard to the instructions issued to British consular and passport control officers that "no visa for entry into Kenya should be granted, without prior reference to the Government of Kenya, in any case in which there is a doubt whether the applicant would be in possession of adequate means on his arrival in the colony, or as to his readmission to German territory." Liebenstein had arrived in Kenya, thanks to the help of a charitable organization. But his German passport was "due to expire in April, 1939" and "his resources over and above the immigration deposit of [£50] amounted to only [£9 pounds and 14 pence]." The immigration deposit of £50 was not intended to signify "the possession of "adequate means" for the purpose" of emigration but rather "to pay for repatriation if necessary." Since Liebenstein's German passport was soon to expire, it would be "difficult for him to be deported to Germany" as the only alternative to the refusal of admission into Kenya.[30] This particular condition of possible deportation back to Germany, in the event that a Jewish refugee was unable to support himself and his family, appears to have been a demand made by colonial administrators in Kenya. That point was underscored by both the Foreign Office and the Colonial Office.

The Foreign Office did not disguise its frustration over the stringent immigration conditions that "many of the British overseas governments" imposed to restrict their admission of Jewish refugees fleeing the Nazi state. One of them was that an entry visa would be granted only to Jewish refugees who had valid passports that also allowed them legal "readmission to Germany."[31] The Foreign Office found that regulation, along with the Colonial Office's deference to the sensitivities of colonial administrators, maddening. In the Foreign Office's response to the case of Liebenstein, Secretary of State for Foreign Affairs Viscount Halifax instructed Secretary of State for the Colonies Malcolm MacDonald to advise colonial administrators in Africa that insisting on returning Jewish refugees to Germany because they did not have valid passports or reasonable funds to live in a colony could result in their "lifelong imprisonment or incarceration." The Foreign Office was very clear in its view that on basic humanitarian grounds "the return to Germany of a person of the refugee class," especially Jewish, was intolerable and that the "insistence by colonial authorities" on any conditions beyond outright admission and settlement of such refugees violated their initial expressed interest to admit Jewish refugees into their territories.[32]

Frustration over the lack of cooperation from the African colonies on the issue of Jewish refugees and pressure from the Foreign Office prompted MacDonald to send a confidential circular to all governors of British colonies in Africa in December 1938. In that letter, the secretary highlighted the "desperate" situation that Jews in Germany faced and the "great concern" that Nazi persecution of German Jews was causing the British government and the governments of Germany's neighbors. Britain and Germany's neighbors had received "thousands of applications" from Jews in Germany who wanted to leave that country.[33] The secretary put British administrators in Africa in no doubt that he expected Britain's Colonial Empire to play a role in "the solution of this grave and most urgent problem."[34] That expectation was expressed against the backdrop of the Colonial Office's understanding of "the obvious difficulties" of any "large-scale settlement of refugees in the Colonial Empire." However, the Colonial Office seemed satisfied that "two territories [Kenya and Nyasaland]" could accommodate the settlement of Jewish refugees on some scale. Secretary MacDonald assured colonial administrators in Africa that the settlement of Jewish refugees in their jurisdictions, if it were to be backed by the British government, would not be funded from the public treasury. It would have to be planned and financed by "voluntary organizations concerned with the welfare of German refugees." That also meant bearing "the cost of transporting, training and settling" any number of Jewish immigrants in Africa.[35]

The Colonial Office saw the availability of Jewish refugees and the eagerness of Jewish organizations to fund their resettlement overseas, as an economic development opportunity for British colonies in Africa. What stood in the way of combining humanitarianism with self-interest in the admission of large numbers of Jewish refugees with particular professional skills into East Africa was the intransigence of some British officers administering the colonies. Officials in Whitehall thought that if these colonial administrators modified their immigration and employment regulations restricting the entry of Jewish refugees, they could receive "medical practitioners" and "dentists" who hold "qualifications registrable in the United Kingdom."[36] British settlers in Nyasaland (now Malawi) were in dire need of physicians who had expertise in tropical medicine and dentistry. Governor Harold Kittermaster of the Nyasaland Protectorate in southeastern Africa put this strategy of profiting from kindness best when he agreed with his counterparts in Whitehall that "providing employment in the Colonial Empire for Jewish doctors of Austrian and German origin" will "contribute not only to the cause of humanity, but also to the interests of the Protectorate."[37] It is fair to argue, however, that even in Nyasaland, much less in other parts of Africa, what the governor and his counterparts in Whitehall assumed was not what actually happened or was considered preferable.

In East Africa, the Colonial Office initially supported a selective and experimental refugee settlement program for Kenya in 1938. The Council for German Jewry (CGJ) in London devised the settlement program "in conjunction with certain Jews in Kenya."[38] Twenty-five "young German Jews, between the ages of 18 and 30" and half of whom "would be over the age of 25, and 5 of whom should be married" were to be selected "from Jews in Germany ... who had undergone a course of training at one of the agricultural training centres in that country ... established by Jewish organizations with the acquiescence of the German Government."[39] Upon selection, the men and their wives were to proceed to Kenya to be attached to suitable farmers in the colony for about six months or a year. Afterward, they would be settled "in groups on five or six farms" with "one married couple being included in each group." The cost of transporting the selected refugees to Kenya, and of training and maintaining them was to be borne by the CGJ. If this experimental project succeeded, then "the settlers [would] be joined by other members of their families up to a total number of about 150." The emphasis on married Jewish men for this refugee project was particularly instructive and was undoubtedly meant to assuage the sensibilities of the British settler aristocrats and their Christian missionary counterparts in Kenya who were afraid of possible sexual interactions between unmarried Jews of European heritage and local Africans. The Colonial Office had advised the representative of the Council for German Jewry and the Kenya representative of the East African Trade and Information Office in London, who were responsible for selecting the initial 25 men for the project, to pick Jews "of a good type" who were "likely to become speedily assimilated into the general social structure of the Colony." Moreover, it was important that the selected Jewish refugees obtained "the goodwill of the existing settler community for the success of any scheme of this kind."[40]

The emphasis that the Colonial Office put on the importance of assimilation of Jewish refugees into the social structure of colonial Kenya reflected prevailing British views and stereotypes of Jews as undesirable immigrants who are resistant to integration. That stereotype had been articulated by the governments of New Zealand, Australia, Canada, and South Africa as the basis for their opposition to Jewish emigrations into their dominions. Louise London has also noted that many officials in various departments and even embassies of the British government viewed the interest of Jews in preserving their identity as a group as one of the central causes of anti-Semitism in Europe.[41] Those British officials who took part in formulating Jewish refugee settlement policy for the colonial Empire or who endorsed policies already devised by private Jewish organizations sought to avoid a similar rise of anti-Semitism in the colonies. As far as Africa was concerned, British policymakers in the Colonial and Foreign offices did not need to worry about Jewish assimilation as a possible trigger of anti-Semitism in Kenya. After all, British settlers in the colony already harbored their own anti-Jewish prejudices and those feelings had nothing to do with Jewish assimilation. They were tied to competition for land and perceptions of how the lives of poor Jews in the colony could affect the preservation of white Anglo-Saxon identity in East Africa.

Before it began, the British-backed idea of settling Jewish refugees in Kenya was subordinated to the "goodwill" of British settlers there. The settlers hardly demonstrated that goodwill, and the project itself got off to a false start. A confidential Downing Street memorandum reveals that the "25 young Jewish trained agriculturists" intended for the experimental settlement project in Kenya were "selected in Germany by Mr. Stephany [possibly a member of the CGJ] and Colonel Knaggs [possibly the Kenya representative of the East African Trade and Information Office]."[42] No subsequent record is available to confirm the arrival of the 25 men in Kenya. What is available indicates that their arrival in East Africa was "delayed" because "a few days after" they were selected, possibly with the knowledge of the Nazi regime, the German authorities put them in a concentration camp.[43] The archival record is also silent over whether they were released at a later date and eventually made the journey to Kenya with the Jewish refugees who arrived there in the 1930s.

The other prewar British option for addressing the issue of Jewish refugees was the alternative plan to resettle them in Nyasaland. The Nyasaland model, also envisioned for British colonies in West Africa, was to follow what had become the standard metric for obtaining official British support for Jewish emigration to Britain's overseas Empire: a privately planned and funded resettlement project. Like the planned project in Kenya, the Nyasaland alternative was to be "confined to a limited number of selected young Jews trained in agriculture."[44] Jewish organizations were to bear the cost of transporting the refugees to Nyasaland, of training them for their agricultural occupation, of securing them land, and of repatriating them to another country if their resettlement failed after five years. Those in the Colonial Office who justified British refugee settlement proposals to the public and the colonies framed the Nyasaland option in the standard logic of the time as a humanitarian and economic endeavor aimed at settling "a limited number of German Jews of a type [who would] become useful citizens" and also "play their part in contributing to the development" of the Nyasaland territory. To safeguard the health and survival of the refugees, a small number of "Jewish refugee doctors," and "dentists" would be employed in the settlement camps, although these medical practitioners would hold foreign qualifications different from what the British colonies required for medical practice.[45] The Nyasaland project, however, met the same fate as the one formulated for the British colony of the Gold Coast. It hit a snag over the issue of land. The "unofficial members of the Legislative Council" of the Nyasaland protectorate expressed their concern that not enough land owned by the colonial administration existed to be set aside for the Jewish refugees.[46] In the face of the unenthusiastic support from the unofficial members of the Nyasaland legislative council, who were themselves British settlers, the Kenya experimental settlement project became the one the Colonial Office considered most seriously.[47]

Colonial Office support for the privately funded settlement of Jewish refugees in the colonies hobbled along until the outbreak of war with Germany put a temporary halt to all discussions about Jewish refugee settlement. A confidential circular of 23 October 1939 from Secretary of State for the Colonies Malcolm MacDonald to all colonial officials laid out the new "policy to be adopted" by the British government.[48] In the early years of the war, Britain suspended the grant of "permits" to Jewish refugees in Germany and those in German-occupied countries to enter Britain. The decision was strategic. Britain found it "impossible as a matter of principle ... to assist in any way the exodus of the nationals of a country with which [Britain was] at war." However, Britain was willing to work with private organizations "to find permanent asylum ... in overseas countries" for "refugees from Germany or countries occupied by Germany" who had already arrived in Britain, France, or any neutral country "at the time of the outbreak of the war." Those overseas countries included the sovereign nation of Ethiopia and the British colonies in East and West Africa. Relegation of the settlement of Jewish refugees outside of Europe to private organizations was intended to assist the new British policy of solving "the refugee problem" by concentrating the nation's and the Empire's attention and resources on "the eradication of the root cause of the problem, namely the existing regime in Germany."[49] By October 1939, the British government estimated that "roughly 50,000" German refugees, presumably Jews who had fled Nazi persecution, were in the United Kingdom. They had been "admitted on the assumption that they would eventually emigrate to other countries." To deal with the presence, in the United Kingdom, of such a large number of "alien enemies," described as "all Germans and Austrians," and also to "alleviate the position of friendly refugees," described as "citizens of the former republic of Czecho-Slovakia," the British Home Office set up special tribunals (about 100 of them) to determine which of these refugees "can properly be left at large" and which of them to subject to "other restrictions." Those in each category found to be friendly to British interests could be employed in domestic war-related services or enlisted for service in the British armed forces.

Britain's African colonies were especially encouraged under this new wartime policy to be sympathetic and helpful to Jews fleeing persecution in Nazi Germany. Viewing the offer of refuge to Jews from the perspective of economic self-interest more than a moral imperative became the familiar trope in public and private exhortations from the Colonial and Foreign offices in Whitehall. In an entreaty that echoed Simon Mark's appeal, in July 1933, to the Dominion Office to save Jews in serious danger in Germany and surrounding countries, the Colonial Office, in October 1939, asked "all Colonial Governments" to "bear in mind" that many of the Jews displaced by the war in Europe possessed "professional and technical qualifications of a high order" that "might well prove useful and valuable" to the colonial community.[50] It is in the context of this bewildering discourse about the economics of empathy that colonial administrators, sovereign nations in Africa, and some colonial subjects also placed their responses to the problem of Jewish refugees.

Changing circumstances of war, intensifying Nazi atrocities, and global public opinion forced British policy on Jewish refugees to take a new turn in the early 1940s. The plight of Jews in Germany and European countries under German occupation had become painfully desperate. Influential clergymen like the Archbishop of Canterbury had spoken out about the humanitarian need for Britain to seek places of refuge for the remaining Jews of Germany.

The *Ethiopian Herald* had editorialized on "the Jews' plight" in June 1943 and expressed support for a Jewish Homeland in Palestine. The paper's editorial view that victory over the Nazi regime might not come soon enough to save many of the imperiled Jews of Europe seemed a candid commentary on the wartime British policy of saving or rescuing the Jews of Germany primarily through the defeat of their government.

Proposed settlement of Jews in Ethiopia

Another of the many private efforts to win the support of the British government for a large-scale Jewish settlement plan was undertaken by a Jewish organization in New York. The plan of its leadership was to seek British support for the creation of a Jewish state in the Harar province of Ethiopia. In 1943, the British representative in Ethiopia R.G. Howe received such a proposal from a group in the United States that called itself the Council for an Autonomous Jewish Province in Harar. The objective of the Council was to "provide the necessary basis for and to carry through a large-scale settlement of European Jews in the Harar territory of Ethiopia and adjoining British Somaliland." This settlement project was to begin "at the earliest possible moment" after the end of the war and "under conditions of political autonomy."[51] Minister Howe did not respond to this communication, which sought his "approval in principle" for the envisioned settlement. He sent the letter to Gilbert Mackereth of the Foreign Office in London.[52] However, on the advice of a group called "The American Jewish Committee Research Institute of Peace and Post-War Problems," the Colonial Office and Foreign Office rejected the proposal made by the Council for an Autonomous Jewish Province in Harar and discontinued communication with it for what British officials viewed as the Council's colonization desires in Ethiopia.[53] Given its own experiences in colonial ventures, the British government appeared to have been sensitive to any Jewish refugee settlement proposal in Africa framed as a colonization project.

The economic rationale for the settlement of Jewish refugees overseas was also tested in the sovereign nation of Ethiopia. In that East African nation, the British government and the London-based Jewish Refugees Committee (JRC) envisioned the "employment" of certain German, Austrian, and Polish refugees, many of whom were Jewish and some "enemy aliens" in transit camps in Mauritius, India, and the Middle East, to fill strategic positions in the Ethiopian economy. As the JRC and the British government acknowledged, the arrival of these refugees and their employment depended on the issuance of entry permits to them by the Ethiopian government. If entry was permitted, the JRC and the British government hoped the refugees could meet Ethiopia's urgent need for "technicians and professional men" to repair and maintain roads, railways, and agricultural machinery that the Italian invasion had left in serious disrepair.[54] Doctors among the refugees could also offer essential medical and dental services, and the mechanical engineers and business administrators could replace Italian workers who occupied these important positions in the Ethiopian economy. Above all, the refugees could contribute to the Allied war effort by working in the factories the Italians had built in Ethiopia.[55]

The Ethiopian government, however, showed "little or no desire" to admit or employ the refugees. Not even the personal and direct appeals of R.G. Howe to Ethiopian officials to do so assuaged them. Ethiopia's hesitancy was partly due to the economic commitments it had made to retain the services of Italian technicians in the country's transportation industry. As Minister Howe admitted, "so long as Italians on the retention list" remained in Ethiopia, the government was "unlikely [to] make a serious effort to import other technicians."[56] Unlike the intense pressure British officials brought upon colonial administrators in East and West Africa to employ certain categories of Jewish refugees, these same officials were very cautious in their approach to this same issue in Ethiopia. Sensitivity to Ethiopia's sovereign status was a primary factor. But another was the fear of what could happen in Ethiopia after the war when German and Austrian Jews "recover[ed] their full rights of citizenship." The chief diplomat in the British Legation in Ethiopia warned the Foreign Office that German refugees in Ethiopia could become an influential German diasporic group and "form centres of German influence" in the East African nation. "For this reason," R.G. Howe argued, it was essential for the British and Ethiopian governments to "limit the numbers of [refugees] admitted."[57]

British hesitation to impose a Jewish emigration fiat on Ethiopia gave room for private individuals and groups to seek British support for the implementation of their own refugee settlement projects. Jacques Faitlovitch's proposal for the settlement of Jews with professional and technical expertise in Ethiopia was one of a few of such proposals. Jacques Faitlovitch was a Jewish philanthropist who had lived in Ethiopia for many years and knew the Ethiopian emperor personally. In April 1943, he sought British support for his interest in the settlement and among the Ethiopian Jewish population of the Gondar region of Jewish doctors, engineers, technicians and Jews "of other callings useful to the development of the country."[58] Jacques Faitlovitch was optimistic that information he had gathered from "many outstanding chieftains" in the interior of Ethiopia showed a favorable local interest in the settlement of "a considerable number" of Jewish immigrants in their regions. Those chiefs, according to Faitlovitch, preferred "people of liberal professions, physicians, [and] engineers," although they did not rule out "artisans" such as "carpenters, joiners, tailors and shoemakers."[59] Faitlovitch disclosed in his correspondence with the British Minister in Ethiopia that leaders of the Ethiopian Jewish community also favored the settlement of Jewish refugees in Gondar. Here, as in other parts of Ethiopia, where Faitlovitch had raised the issue of the settlement of Jewish refugees, the response had been positive with only one caveat: Local chiefs did not want a large number of Jewish refugees, and also "not . . . immigrants to be settled on land" that will be taken from local people to create a Jewish homeland within the Gondar province.[60]

Jacques Faitlovitch had a much broader and long-term view of Jewish settlement in Ethiopia than the British did. He saw European Jews as the means not only to "an intellectual regeneration of the Abyssinian Jewish population" but also to the improvement of "health conditions in Abyssinia in general."[61] Faitlovitch was confident that "the Emperor and the Ethiopian Government will naturally highly appreciate such an action from the part of Jewry" that would also bring "honorable credit to the Jewish name." Faitlovitch claimed that from his private discussions with the emperor and notable chieftains in the Ethiopian Jewish community, he had a good sense that "the settlement of European refugees in Abyssinia" is taken seriously and that "many outstanding personalities of the Ethiopian Government are anxiously looking forward to it."[62] Yet, he acknowledged that while the Emperor had "already consented to have about two thousand Greek refugees" settle in Ethiopia, the decision "concerning the Jewish refugees" was still "awaiting further discussion between the British Legation and the Ethiopian Government." Faitlovitch blamed the delayed action on the settlement of Jewish refugees in Ethiopia on stalled negotiations between the British Legation in Addis Ababa and the Foreign Office in London and between that office and private Jewish organizations that are also "interested in the matter."[63]

Eventually, the British Legation and the Foreign Office did not favor Jacques Faitlovitch's ideas. In the Legation's letter of 25 March 1943 to Foreign Secretary Anthony Eden, the British representative in Ethiopia R.G. Howe summed up what he had discerned from Faitlovitch's interactions with Ethiopian officials and influential people and what he thought.[64] First, in "conversations with the Emperor," Faitlovitch claimed to have "gained the impression that, as a temporary measure, the Ethiopian Government would agree to accommodate a limited number of Jewish refugees." Second, these refugees "would only be temporary visitors to Ethiopia, and would be expected to leave as soon as practicable after the end of the War." Third, "as a permanent measure, the Ethiopian Government would accept the immigration of a limited number of Jewish business men, technicians, and artisans, if they would be self-supporting." Fourth, according to Faitlovitch, "these were the views of His Imperial Majesty [Haile Selassie] only, and that educated and nationalist opinion would be opposed to such an incursion." The British representative disclosed that he had "mentioned" the issue of settling Jewish refugees in Ethiopia to the emperor. But although the emperor had "adopted a sympathetic attitude, and enquired how many persons it was [sic] proposed to send, . . . he ha[d] not, as yet, committed himself to a definite undertaking in principle to accept the entry of refugee Jews into Ethiopia as part of an organized scheme."[65]

R.G. Howe was also very skeptical of the feasibility of the Faitlovitch plan. He informed the Foreign Office that he "found it difficult to share th[e] view" offered by Faitlovitch that "it would be a relatively simple matter to settle Jewish artisans and traders among the Falashas in the Gondar region."[66] Besides the complicated negotiations for Ethiopia's approval that this would require, Minister Howe surmised that the Ethiopian Government would insist on the Jewish refugees adopting Ethiopian nationality. Moreover, "European Jews would find in Ethiopian villages, few, if any, of the amenities of civilization to which they are accustomed, and it is more than possible that many of them would not wish to remain, when they become acquainted with the conditions under which they would have to live and work." Against this background, the British Legation in Ethiopia did "not think that the expenditure of time and money necessary for the organization, transport[ation], and installation of any large body of Jews among the Falashas would be worthwhile."[67] Above all, "[t]he settlement of Jewish agriculturalists would meet with insuperable opposition from Ethiopians, if it involved the ownership of land." While the Legation saw vast possibilities for the employment of "Jewish artisans, technicians and professional men in the towns of Ethiopia," especially in the capital city of Addis Ababa, it concluded that such people had to be carefully selected and that any large-scale movement of them to Ethiopia "under present conditions" would not be feasible.[68]

Not everyone in the British Legation in Addis Ababa thought as the chief of mission did. Commercial Advisor to the Legation A.D. Bethell had an even bigger vision in mind that mirrored aspects of Faitlovitch's proposal. Bethell was blunt in his admission that the long-standing plan of the British to settle Jewish refugees or to create a permanent home for them in Palestine was "to all intents ... closed to Zionist aspirations." He argued, "Since the Balfour declaration, Palestine has received a few thousand [someone, possibly in the Foreign Office, appended 300,000 in ink to the side] Jewish immigrants and many millions of Jewish money, but it has proved disappointingly inadequate owing to the strong Arab opposition to Jewish agricultural competition in so small a country."[69] That hitherto unfulfilled aspiration in Palestine, Bethell argued, could actually be met through the creation of a homeland for European Jews in Ethiopia instead. For him, "Ethiopia has a still more ancient link to Israel and has for centuries provided a home for a tiny remnant of their scattered tribes." In view of the terrible treatment of Jews in Europe, "[t]he time has come when Ethiopia should once more open her gates and when the Lion of the Tribe of Juda should offer hospitality and security to his exiled kinsmen." Like Faitlovitch, Bethell wanted the plan to settle Jewish refugees in Ethiopia to be made on "financial and commercial grounds" as an endeavor to secure "the future of Ethiopia for all time." Bethell believed that the Palestine experiment had failed because the Jewish refugees who emigrated there were not carefully selected and "their land hunger, combined with their lack of suitable training," created "unnecessary and deepseated antagonisms." He was confident that Ethiopia could learn from "Palestine's mistakes" and since Ethiopia had much more land available, these antagonisms could be avoided. Bethell envisioned that in an African nation of "989,000 square kilometres," thinly populated, with large spaces of fertile land, and "a people enfeebled by war and disease and doomed to early decay unless reinforced by new blood," there was no blood "more suited to this transfusion than the vigorous streams of their legendary ancestors."[70]

A.D. Bethell anticipated that Ethiopia could sell some of its good agricultural land to Jewish settlers at an average price of £500 a *gasha* (acre). With Ethiopia's two and a half million *gashas* of land, a hundred thousand of that sold to Jewish settlers, which, Bethell estimated, is only "4% of the total land in the country" could yield "some fifty million sterling in hard cash."[71] After five years of residence in Ethiopia, Bethell expected the Jewish settlers to take Ethiopian nationality. That social and economic transaction could "provide the Imperial Government with all the occidental education and technical skill necessary to Ethiopia's survival as an independent and civilized state." With that, Ethiopia would bind itself even more closely to Great Britain and the United States "where Jewish wealth and influence is a power for good" and "permanent[ly] guarantee . . . her future place in the new world order." Anticipating that some in the Legation or the Foreign Office might "doubt that the Jews would come to Ethiopia," Bethell outlined five "advantages" that he thought Ethiopia possessed for the Jews of Europe which "no other country in the world" had. One was the mutual need that Ethiopia and the Jews of Europe had for one another, even more so for Ethiopia. Two was the availability in Ethiopia of vast unused land and a "healthy climate and magnificent scenery." Three was Ethiopia's proximity, by air travel, to Palestine, the "religious home" of the Jews. Four was Ethiopia's "untouched mineral resources," which Jewish settlers would help develop as citizens of their new nation. Five was the absence of an indigenous professional, technical, and commercial population in Ethiopia that would present any antagonistic competition to the Jews. Bethell saw his proposed "project" as one that is "both financially and economically sound." What he saw as "the only possible objections" to his proposals was "political" opposition. He viewed that as a "negligible" hazard compared to the "overwhelming advantages" for European Jews in Ethiopia and the "serious troubles which Great Britain has created for herself in Palestine" since the Balfour Declaration.[72]

On 29 May 1943, R.G. Howe gave the Foreign Office his confidential opinion on A.D. Bethell's plan for Jewish emigration to Ethiopia.[73] He advised that "any scheme which involved the alienation of appreciable areas of land to foreigners would be most unlikely to meet with the Emperor's approval." Also equally unlikely to excite the Ethiopian emperor was Bethell's idea that Jewish settlers could take Ethiopian nationality. Minister Howe saw that as an idea that would "in due course . . . probably produce friction." Although, as Howe noted, from his own "conversations with the Emperor," the Ethiopian monarch had appeared "quite willing to accept a small number of skilled or professional Jews," he was "definitely unwilling to sanction large-scale agricultural settlement by foreigners" in his kingdom. In the British representative's view, while Bethel's plan seemed attractive financially and could be appealing to the Emperor, it "definitely contain[ed] the seeds of foreign intervention in the internal affairs of his country, and this would probably weigh with him even more."[74] The Foreign Office agreed.

In its final response to the two plans (Faitlovitch's and Bethell's) for a large-scale emigration of European Jews to Ethiopia that the British Legation had shared with it, the Foreign Office concluded that "the case which [A.D. Bethell] attempts to make out in favor of Jewish colonization of Ethiopia is not altogether convincing."⁷⁵ The Foreign Office appeared to have learned something from British colonial experiences in East and West Africa. It was especially critical of Bethell's suggestion "that Jewish immigrants should settle agricultural land amounting to 4% of the total area" of Ethiopia on the payment of £50 million. The Foreign Office viewed that amount of money as financially helpful to Ethiopia but at the cost of losing "a larger percentage of cultivable area" of the country. As the response letter made clear, "for foreign immigrants to occupy so much" cultivable land in a sovereign nation "would surely . . . cause dissatisfaction and anti-Jewish feeling." Certainly, the Foreign Office appears to have been mindful of the anti-Jewish feelings in Germany that had produced the Holocaust in Europe. The Foreign Office also found no convincing evidence to support the underlying premise of Bethell's plan that Jewish immigrants were willing to settle in Ethiopia, and the Ethiopian government was equally willing to accept them. The Foreign Office agreed with Minister Howe that the British government had received only the emperor's "consent in principle" to the settlement of "a small number of skilled or professional Jews" in Ethiopia, not his firm and definite commitment to any large-scale emigration of Jews to Ethiopia. Regarding Faitlovitch's plan of settling a large number of professional Jews among the Ethiopian Jewish community, the Foreign Office dismissed that as "Dr. Faitlovitch's pet uplift scheme."⁷⁶ This conclusion from the Foreign Office is particularly revealing. It is clear that following the Nazi persecution and destruction of European Jews and Britain's mobilization of its national resources and those of the colonial Empire to defeat the Nazi regime, the British became sensitive to arguments that harkened back to the civilizing mission discourses of the nineteenth century that British imperialists had used for their colonization of much of Africa.

The Foreign Office conceded, however, that the Bethell plan seemed "less far-reaching" than others it had received, including the proposal from a Jewish organization in New York "advocating the creation of a Jewish state in the Harar region [of Ethiopia] and part of British Somaliland." To the Foreign Office, these proposals were "too wide in their scope for the Emperor" and fraught with future problems. Officials in the Office found it "highly improbable that any responsible Jewish body would accept this or any other such far-reaching scheme except under guarantees which would involve the possibility of foreign intervention in Ethiopian affairs." The Italian occupation of Ethiopia, the Nazi occupation of much of Europe, and the comparisons that colonial subjects in Africa had begun to make between Nazi ideologies and British colonialism at this time must have played key roles in the conclusions the Foreign Office drew. Equally pressing on the minds of officials in the Foreign Office about the settlement of Jewish refugees in Ethiopia was the nascent experiment in Palestine. A.W.G. Randall of the Foreign Office admitted in his letter to the British Minister in Ethiopia that "the Palestine experiment, whatever its future may be, has made similar enterprises . . . more difficult than before since prospective settlers, hosts and, . . . guarantors will all, from their various points of view, regard Palestine and its concomitant difficulties as arguments against starting something similar elsewhere." What the Foreign Office found practicable and sustainable in Africa, beyond the Palestine experiment, was the settlement of "small numbers of Jewish professional men and technicians . . . if their employment could be arranged without upsetting local susceptibilities." Even here, British officials feared that the presence of German and Austrian Jews as refugees in Ethiopia might create "centres of German influence" that could be counterproductive.[77] With these thoughts, the Foreign Office proceeded cautiously in its support of the Colonial Office's proposals of settling Jewish refugees in parts of Africa under British colonial rule.

Jewish refugees in Tanganyika and Uganda

Information on the precise numbers of Jewish refugees who arrived in East Africa and West Africa in the course of the Holocaust is spotty. That may be due to the secrecy, anxiety, and ambiguity that surrounded the refugee settlement experiment and the nature of communication and transmission of information at this period. Colonial Office records indicate that "176 Jewish Cypriots" arrived in Tanganyika in December 1941.[78] They were initially accommodated in "hotels and houses" in the "moderately malarious" towns of "Mwanza, Bukoba, [and] Shinyanga in the Lake Province and Tabora in the Western Province." A large number of them, reportedly, secured employment immediately "in various parts of Tanganyika," but "reacted to the climate" and the trauma of their experiences. According to the director of medical services of the Tanganyika territory, this group of Cypriot Jews who came to Tanganyika "suffered periodically from malaria." They were also prone to "nervous irritability" because of their "previous hardships."[79] However, they lived "in a manner very similar to free European business people" in the territory. Only 40 percent of the Polish refugees who were "deported from Eastern Poland to Russia" in the course of the war and later mobilized specifically for sanctuary in Tanganyika eventually made it to this former German colony under British trusteeship. The rest reportedly "died of hardship and disease before reaching" this part of Africa or "disappeared in Russia."[80] The majority of the Polish refugees who arrived in Tanganyika were Jewish. They lived in four settlement camps at Tengeru, close to the towns of Arusha, Kondoa, Kidugalla, and Ifunda. The Tengeru settlement camp was located in a "malarious, agricultural, [but] well-watered" area close to the "moderately cool climate" of Arusha. Between 1943 and 1944, the Tengeru settlement had about "3000 persons, mostly women and children." The Kondoa settlement, located in the Central Province and "moderately malarious in the wet season," had "about 400 refugees, mostly women and children." The Kidugalla and Ifunda camps were located in "cool, almost non-malarial" regions of Tanganyika. Unlike the Greek and Cypriot Jews, a "large proportion of the Polish refugees arrived in Tanganyika with malaria parasites in their blood," and the young adults and children among them had severe dental problems. Polish doctors and nurses lived in the camps with the refugees and attended to their health needs.[81]

Polish refugees in Tanganyika had to contend with malaria and other tropical diseases, but none on any calamitous scale. What was bothersome was their "contempt of the sun." While the director of medical services found that new experience of the African climate "worthy of notice for future experiment and guidance," he also noted that the complaints of the refugees about the African sun "should not be taken too seriously because the length of time spent in bright sunlight in a residential camp will not be comparable to the exposure incurred by ... others working through the heat of the day continuously out of doors."[82]

Climate was less of a problem in the refugee camps than the outbreaks of conflicts among the refugees themselves. As the director of refugees noted in a confidential letter to the Commissioner of the East African Refugee Administration, "a good deal of quarrelling" took place "among the Jewish refugees themselves." The director attributed that to the "nervous irritability" that the director of medical services had claimed Jewish refugees experienced as a result of their persecution and circuitous travel from Europe, through Asia to their settlement camps in East Africa.[83] The requests of some refugees, especially from Greece, "for permission to employ African personal servants" to do camp work such as bread baking for them did not endear them to the East African Refugee Administration. The women refugees from Poland, who formed the majority of settlers in the Kondoa camp, earned high praise for their hard work in contrast to the men. Polish male refugees who were used to hard manual work in Poland showed little eagerness to do the same in their settlements in Tanganyika.[84]

The lives and experiences of Polish Jewish refugees who arrived in Uganda were no different from those who settled in Tanganyika. About "5,800" Polish Jews, comprising 10.5 percent adult males, 43.7 percent adult females, and 45.9 percent "children under 16 years of age," arrived in Uganda between 1942 and 1943.[85] Since the war disrupted their lives, these refugees had moved from the "mild continental climate of Poland to the sharp continental climate of Siberia." For about a year, many of them lived in subarctic climates. From there, they were "transferred to the hot continental climate of Middle Asia, the steppes of Kazakhstan," and sent to Persia, then to India, before their final destination in tropical East Africa.[86] Their exhausting exodus exposed them to "physical and mental strain." The majority of them suffered from anemia, tuberculosis, heart and gastric conditions, trachoma, eye diseases, insomnia, malnutrition, and other health problems. The refugees were encamped at Koja "on the shores of Lake Victoria" and at Nyabeya in Uganda's Western Province. Koja had an annual rainfall of about 46.12 inches with a mean maximum temperature of 81.9 degrees Fahrenheit and a mean minimum of 61.8 degrees. Nyabeya camp was close "to large expanses of water," and the location had variable winter and summer climatic conditions ranging from a maximum temperature of 86.7 degrees Fahrenheit in January to a minimum of 73.8 in August. As a result of the Nyabeya camp's proximity to water and the location's frequent rainfall patterns, it was vulnerable to mosquitoes and malaria. However, the East African Refugee Administration considered it "suitable for European habitation under reasonable conditions." Compared with Nyabeya, Koja was an extensive breeding ground for malaria-carrying mosquitoes. However, the East African Refugee Administration took "constant" steps to "detect and deal with natural and artificially created breeding places" in both camps.[87]

Refugees in Nyabeya and Koja lived in "brick or mud and wattle cottages with thatched roofs and unglazed windows."[88] Since it was impossible to give every refugee family a separate house, lack of privacy was one of the major discomforts of refugee life in Uganda. The overall health condition of Polish refugees in Uganda improved after their arrival. According to the Refugee Administration's reports, "among the 3,450 inhabitants of the Nyabeya settlement 308 had suffered from malaria before reaching Africa." About 1,112 developed malaria for the first time. By contrast, in Koja, where 2,338 refugees lived, 1,647 were reported to have contracted malaria between their arrival in the camp in September 1942 and the end of December 1943. Polish and British medical officials who monitored the health conditions of the refugees attributed some of these malaria infections to relapses of the disease. The Refugee Administration noted, however, that "deaths" in the Koja and Nyabeya settlements that were definitely caused by malaria were "approximately 12, which is a case mortality of 0.27% and a death rate of 0.21%."[89]

The *Uganda Herald* reported on the arrival of Jewish refugees in Uganda and the help they received from colonial subjects. On the front pages of its issues of 23 and 30 September 1942, the paper announced the arrival of "about one thousand Polish refugees" by train from Kenya.[90] The editors of the paper took special interest in reminding readers about the Nazi invasion of Poland in September 1939 as the principal reason for the departure of the refugees from their country to Uganda. Added to that notification was the exhausting journey the refugees had made from Poland through Russia, Iran, Iraq, and India before arriving in Uganda through Kenya. By underscoring these facts, the editors of the paper wanted readers to take notice of the "harrowing experiences" of the refugees "during their long trek in search of safety." The paper noted that "now they have come to us for help in Uganda, where they hope to find peace and rest until such time as they can return to their native land."[91] The emphasis on the temporary nature of the presence of the refugees in Uganda was especially noteworthy. In East and West Africa, empathy for Jewish refugees who fled the Holocaust came also with anxiety over their length of residence and ownership of land in African societies with complicated family and communal land tenure systems. The *Herald* newspaper emphasized that, unlike the refugees, the people of Uganda have been spared the ravages of the war, and "now is the time to pass a little of that good fortune on to people who . . . have suffered to the full the horrors of modern war." Items of greatest need which the paper requested its readers to send to the majority of the refugees, who were "women and children," included clothing, toys, magazines, books, and toilet articles. Readers who were willing to help were asked to send "articles of clothing, or anything else likely to prove useful" to "Mrs. Lukya Williams, c/o 2 Allidina Visram Street, Kampala."[92]

The paper's major report in its issue of 30 September 1942 was a call for help. It underscored the joy that some of the refugees felt on seeing the "little homes prepared for them" and the "little plots of gardens" attached to them.[93] A letter in that day's paper from one Mrs. D.G. Gorton applauded the free gifts of "clothes, hats, shoes, etc" that "the people of Uganda" have given to the Polish refugees who have arrived. However, in view of the fact that "more Poles are coming here," Mrs. Gorton suggested the opening of a "Polish Relief Fund" to have "money in hand to buy needles, sewing cotton, toys, comb" and other needs when the next batch of refugees arrive.[94] By 2 December 1942, about 2,500 Polish refugees, the majority of whom were Jews, had arrived in Uganda. On that day, the *Uganda Herald* tied the needs of the refugees to the humanity of the people of Uganda and called on all Ugandans to open their hearts and pockets in the most humane demonstration of compassion for "some of Hitler's victims of aggression."[95] While colonized subjects in Uganda welcomed Hitler's victims of aggression to their homeland, albeit temporarily, British settlers in Kenya did not want Jewish refugees at all in the fertile lands of the settlers' so-called White Highlands. For its part, the *Ethiopian Herald* offered its empathy for Hitler's victims of aggression in the most solemn of words but wished that a permanent homeland would be found for them instead in Palestine.

West Africa

Compared to East Africa, Britain's colonies in West Africa were not expected to receive a large number of Jewish refugees. As a result, the active West African press did not write as much about Jewish refugees arriving in the region and what that meant for colonial subjects, as it did about the Holocaust in Europe. Because the British envisioned only a limited settlement of Jewish doctors in a West African region notorious for its endemic tropical diseases and their deadly impact on Europeans, the reaction to the arrival of Jewish refugees in West Africa was limited to the views of colonial administrators in the region and a few African members of the colonial legislative councils who knew about this very confidential British proposal. Like the Nyasaland project, the proposal for West Africa encountered opposition on similar grounds of land availability to the refugees and the effects of climate on them. For the Gold Coast in particular, an additional reason for opposition surfaced: the impact of the arrival of Jewish doctors on the training of colonial subjects for the colonial medical service.

As a general policy directive, the Colonial Office in London had asked the colonial authorities in the Gold Coast in December 1938 to take in Jewish refugees. In response to that request, the Gold Coast government agreed "to offer appointments to two Jewish male clerks."[96] Beyond that, the government could assure the Colonial Office only that it would investigate the "possibility of finding employment for other refugees in the Medical and Public Works Department." That investigation was left to Director of Medical Services of the Gold Coast Colony J.W.P. Harkness. In his edited book *False Havens: The British*

Empire and the Holocaust, Paul Bartrop argues that "[n]o Jews were recorded [by the Colonial Office] as having entered Gambia, Gold Coast, Nigeria [in West Africa] ... as of 31 March 1939."[97] However, records of the Gold Coast colony mention that a limited number of Jewish refugees entered in 1938 and 1939, although no figures are given. The colony's Executive and Legislative councils also discussed "actions to be taken" to employ Jewish refugees as doctors or as laboratory technicians in the colonial medical service or as foremen in the Public Works Department to supervise work on the construction of roads and buildings. The difficulty of finding, in the colony's archival records, the actual numbers of Jewish refugees who emigrated to the Gold Coast and who lived there between 1933 and 1945 suggests that the colonial authorities may have actually admitted none or a very negligible number over that period of the Holocaust. These are some of the silences and exclusions in official archives that Ann Laura Stoler and Kirsten Weld have written about. While records of the actual number of Jews who arrived and lived in the Gold Coast are difficult to find in the colony's archives, the same archives contain some figures of Jewish refugees who arrived in East Africa before and during the Holocaust.[98] Those figures are corroborated by other records of the Colonial Office.

The numbers may be hard to locate, but not the responses. Some of the earliest attitudes of the Gold Coast colonial administration to the proposed employment of a few Jewish refugees in the colony appear in colonial correspondence in 1938 and 1939. The director of medical services (DMS) of the Gold Coast colony J.W.P. Harkness had already informed the colonial administration, as early as August 1938, about the limited prospects for Jewish refugees in West Africa. The DMS wrote that "prospects of a Jewish doctor of German or Austrian origin making a living as a private practitioner in this Colony are not very bright."[99] He conceded, however, that as a temporary measure, the arrival of Jewish doctors could be "an excellent opportunity to obtain some very good doctors ... to relieve colonial governments of the difficulty of obtaining candidates for the Colonial Medical Service."[100] Nevertheless, one of his major concerns was that "it would not be politic to encourage them to set up as private practitioners if this is likely to interfere with legitimate practice by African doctors, a class which is likely to increase in numbers as the years go on." As a general principle, the Gold Coast Executive Council agreed that "the Gold Coast should do what it could" to assist Britain's efforts "to relieve the suffering of Jews of German and Austrian origin" who have become "refugees."[101]

In July 1939, the Gold Coast government received a letter from one Mr. W. Gips, of Luanshya, Northern Rhodesia, asking for information "about the possibility for Jewish refugees from Germany to enter your [Gold Coast] colony." The request was for the entry into the Gold Coast of three Jewish refugees—an electrical engineer, a doctor, and a lady trained in "medical laboratory work." Mr. Gips asked for "clearance for at least one of them."[102] In a draft response letter prepared for the approval of the Gold Coast governor, a clear indication appears that the colonial administration did not favor the arrival of such refugees. The draft letter stated that "few opportunities for private practice exist, and the difficulties of securing professional and living accommodation are great" in the Gold Coast. Moreover, the colonial authorities wanted Mr. Gips to know that "the Gold Coast is not suitable for the permanent residence of Europeans who normally have to take health leave in a temperate climate after about 18 months in West Africa."[103] This prewar request for the employment of Jewish refugee doctors in the Gold Coast, similar to another made by the Colonial Office to Governor Harold Kittermaster of the Nyasaland Protectorate, had been backed by Secretary of State for the Colonies Malcolm MacDonald in a letter to Governor Arnold Hodson of the Gold Coast.[104] In the secretary's letter, he reminded the governor of his request to the colonial administration in Nyasaland to amend the existing Medical Practitioners and Dentists Ordinance to permit the administration there to "recognize, for registration purposes, foreign medical and dental degrees which are excluded by the operation of the Ordinance in its present form." This Colonial Office request came one year after the Evian Conference where this particular immigration regulation issue was discussed. Secretary MacDonald wanted Governor Arnold Hodson to "introduce similar amending legislation" in the Gold Coast to make it possible for Jewish doctors to emigrate there.[105]

The secretary's letter conveyed the broader British policy of settling Jewish refugees in Britain's Colonial Empire. The Gold Coast colonial administration was not convinced. That was a clear indication of the autonomy the colonies sought to maintain over Jewish refugee policy from the control London tried to exercise. The DMS of the Gold Coast colony communicated his impressions about the interest of the Colonial Office to implement the Nyasaland model of settling a limited number of Jewish doctors in the Gold Coast to the governor's office ahead of an upcoming Executive Council meeting in February 1940. In that memorandum, the DMS was adamant in his view that he did "not consider . . . the Nyasaland proposals . . . suitable for adoption or necessary in this colony where the circumstances appear . . . to be entirely different." In his view, "four government scholars studying medicine in England" and three more students "due to go to the United Kingdom this year" meant that "the employment of Jewish refugee doctors by Government except on a very temporary basis would be likely to arouse criticism." The DMS's larger concern appeared to have been the possible impact of the arrival of Jewish refugee doctors in the Colonial Empire on other policies endorsed by the Colonial Office in London. The DMS echoed the policy that "if a foreign university degree was recognized by this country refugee doctors possessing a state qualification which Government might not feel justified in recognizing could as a rule obtain the recognized degree or diploma under easier conditions than they can at present obtain a British registrable qualification." That, the DMS argued, "would inevitably lead to a lowering of the standard in this country."[106]

The DMS was also worried about two other possible effects of the admission of Jewish doctors with foreign degrees on some colonial policies, including the colonial idea that Britain sought to foster. J.W.P. Harkness saw the opening of the Gold Coast colony to Jewish medical practitioners as "detrimental to the policy of encouraging Africans to take up the study of Medicine, and to the plan for the ultimate establishment of a West African Medical School." That was his charitable objection. The more insidious objection was that education controlled by colonial governments had the object of producing "obedient servants" of the Empire and an educated African elite beholden to British values. Therefore, recognition of foreign degrees from foreign universities, such as those that professional Jewish refugees possessed, for the colonial civil service, other than degrees acquired in Great Britain, would "open these [foreign] universities to African students where apart from obtaining a . . . qualification on a lower standard . . ., they might pursue their studies in an atmosphere critical if not actually hostile to British imperial policy."[107] Harkness was silent on the possible implications of the arrival of Jewish doctors in the Gold Coast for the prevailing British policy of racializing medical services in the colony or how Jewish doctors, aware of Nazi racial science, might react to practicing medicine in an African colony where hospitals were segregated and designated as African and European.

The Gold Coast Executive Council, a small body of European officials who advised the governor on policy matters, took up the subject of the settlement of Jewish refugees at its meeting on 2 February 1940.[108] The topic was actions to be taken in regard to the acceptance of Jewish medical doctors in the Gold Coast. The Executive Council concluded that the Colonial Office should be sent a copy of the report on this subject prepared by the director of medical services, with an accompanying letter addressed to the secretary of state for the colonies. The Executive Council recommended a strong emphasis in that letter that "conditions in the Gold Coast were not similar to those in Nyasaland" and that, contrary to the request made by the secretary for the modification of colonial laws to allow Jewish doctors to practice in the colonies, the existing laws could not be altered for Jewish refugee doctors. The Executive Council was to make it clear also that it found it "undesirable to recognize foreign degrees" because "the possession of such a degree in itself was no guarantee that the holder thereof was up to the required standard" and because "African students might seek the opportunity of evading the labour entailed in gaining British degrees by obtaining foreign degrees of less value."[109]

Following this Executive Council meeting, Governor Hodson sent a confidential letter to the secretary of state for the colonies. It echoed the DMS's memorandum, with the additional statement that the DMS, the Executive Council, and the governor himself had agreed on the following four principles regarding the issue of Jewish refugees in the Gold Coast. One, conditions in the Gold Coast differed widely from those in Nyasaland, and the Gold Coast could not accept the employment of Jewish refugee doctors. Two, existing laws in the colony already permitted British missionaries to practice medicine, under certain conditions, and foreign (non-British) degrees are not recognized in the Gold Coast. Three, recognition of foreign degrees is no guarantee that the holders of such degrees can competently operate in the colony. Moreover, African students might also seek the opportunity to obtain foreign degrees of inferior value and avoid "the study necessary to obtain British qualifications." Four, an influx of foreign doctors "at a time when the establishment of a West African Medical School is contemplated" would have an "unfavourable effect on African students" and "undoubtedly lead to considerable political repercussions."[110] Like the British settlers in Kenya who opposed the settlement of Jews in the British East African colony out of a perception that their presence might lead to a lowering of white European social standards, British colonial administrators in the Gold Coast opposed the admission of Jewish refugee doctors to the British West African colony based on a similar perspective of maintaining British standards of education and medical practice.

For the African members of the Legislative Council, the concern was not the maintenance of abstract British standards of education. Theirs related to the tangible matter of land. The most candid native Gold Coast opinion on Jewish refugees that appears in the Gold Coast colonial records is the one expressed in the Legislative Council, in the aftermath of the war, by notable chief Nana Amanfi III, *Omanhene* of Asebu. In his address to the presiding new Governor Alan C. Burns at the legislative council meeting in March 1946, Nana Amanfi described "the immigration of aliens" into the Gold Coast as a "vital matter which [gave] the people of this country a real cause for alarm as to the future of our lands."[111] He singled out the presence of "Syrians and Lebanese" in the colony as creating the possibility that the Gold Coast "would be faced with a crisis similar to those which took place in . . . Lebanon, Syria and Palestine." The chief referred particularly to the emigration of "Jews" into Palestine and the social and economic conflicts that have arisen there in the wake of that immigration. He was blunt in his appeal to the governor that "we do not want to see . . . Zionism, National Home, Diaspora or a place of refuge for those escaping from political and economic troubles to be established in this country."[112] To the extent that none of the other African members of the Legislative Council, who also spoke on that day, differed in their views from the paramount chief's, this suggests that he must have articulated their concerns as well. That perspective in the Gold Coast colony belies the deeply rooted philo-semitic attitudes in West Africa and the empathetic native African response in the Gold Coast colony to the plight of Jews in the course of the war. While the chief's view may not be representative of a regional sentiment, it nevertheless exposed a lingering grievance.

By opposing the settlement of Jewish refugees with reference to Syrian and Lebanese migrants in the Gold Coast, Nana Amanfi echoed an existing antipathy towards Syrians and Lebanese as a diasporic community in the British colony. As Emmanuel Akyeampong and Toyin Falola have documented in their respective research on this subject in the Gold Coast and Nigeria, that antipathy followed the emigration of Syrian and Lebanese refugees to West Africa in the late nineteenth century through to the twentieth. They arrived in the Gold Coast after 1914 as poor migrants fleeing war and displacement in south Lebanon and "in search of a home and nationality."[113] By the time World War II broke out, their numbers had increased to several thousand as new migrants joined them. With time, the Syrian and Lebanese migrants became too closely tied to the colonial state as recipients of colonial patronage.

In the 1940s, the Syrian and Lebanese community in the Gold Coast filled the critical intermediary position between the large European import and export companies and the majority local African consumers and peasants. As "beneficiaries of British imperialism and colonial capitalism," the Syrians and Lebanese inevitably became the "targets of indigenous west African hostility" in the 1930s' economic depression and the 1940s' nationalist fervor.[114] Anti-Syrian and Lebanese feelings in the Gold Coast and Nigeria also stemmed from prevailing local beliefs that the Syrians and Lebanese had become detached from the larger colonial society in which they lived and had engaged in questionable business practices.[115] Negative perceptions of Lebanese trading practices and land uses provoked anti-Lebanese petitions and riots in southwestern Nigeria.[116] It is therefore possible that hostility towards Syrian and Lebanese emigres in the Gold Coast shaped local opposition to any talk about the possible settlement of Jewish refugees in the colony. More comparative studies may be necessary to document perspectives on the Jewish refugee resettlement issue in Nigeria or in Senegal, in particular, where Jewish settlement had a long and well documented history. Meanwhile, one can argue that the feelings expressed about the settlement of Jews in the Gold Coast resembled those expressed against Jewish emigration into Kenya by British settlers and into Ethiopia by the emperor and notable Ethiopian chieftains. These responses related to the anticipated alienation of land to Jewish refugees. The African perspective on this central moral issue highlights the contradictions and brittleness of human empathy.

Conclusion

British thinking about settling certain categories of European Jews in British colonies in Africa began before the outbreak of the Second World War, and it was not only in Kenya and Ethiopia that the settlement of Jewish refugees was envisioned. Plans to settle Jews from Germany in Tanganyika, Northern Rhodesia, and Nyasaland formed part of such discussions in 1938, before the Second World War severely disrupted the lives of European Jews. Britain's interest in resettling some Jewish refugees in its colonial Empire in Africa was more than a selfless humanitarian act. Two political motives were apparent. The first was harnessing Jewish capital and professional expertise to develop the colonies for British benefit. In this calculation, only Jews considered useful for particular colonies, economically and technically, were considered for resettlement. That meant Jews with expertise in tropical agriculture and tropical medicine. The second was envisioning a large-scale settlement of Jews, regardless of economic and technical background, in a British-mandated territory in Africa and a former German colony the Nazi regime wished to repossess. Given the well-known Nazi anti-Jewish proclivity, this British intention is open to a variety of interpretations, one of which may have been to discourage Nazi interest in reclaiming Tanganyika. It was on the issue of resettling Jewish doctors in the colonies that the policy of the Colonial Office and the Foreign Office, as well as the politics of colonial administrators and other officials, clashed.

Reactions in Africa can be seen in two broad spheres: the feelings of British settlers and administrators and the responses of colonized and sovereign peoples. British settlers in Kenya saw the arrival of Jews as potentially the beginning of the end of the British aristocratic and patrician vision of the supremacy of White Europeans that British settlers had fostered in Africa. The obvious impact of Jewish settlement on land acquisition and retention lurked in the background of that British settler reaction. Ethiopia had its own policy on Jewish refugees motivated by possible land alienation. That was a principal source of Ethiopia's discomfort about the establishment of an autonomous Jewish territory within the sovereign Ethiopian nation. Land tenure issues generated a similar discomfort among colonized subjects in the Gold Coast about the arrival of Jewish refugees in that British colony.

What the secret conversations in London, Addis Ababa, and the African colonies on Jewish refugee settlement issues revealed was that the Holocaust exposed more than the anti-Jewish proclivities of the Nazi regime. It also revealed the limits and paradoxes of human empathy. The hesitation bordering on reluctance of those in Africa who bewailed the destruction of Jewish life from a distance, to accommodate, in their homes, those whom the Holocaust rendered homeless is a bewildering fact of African and Holocaust history that often lies frozen in the archives. This book has revived this cold case and has examined its complexities and contradictions from the African perspective.

Notes

1 Paul R. Bartrop, "The British Colonial Empire and Jewish Refugees During the Holocaust Period: An Overview," in Paul R. Bartrop, ed., *False Havens: The British Empire and the Holocaust* [Studies in the Shoah, vol. X] (Lanham, MD: University Press of America, 1995), 14–15.
2 Musiker, "The Jews of Kenya," 21; Kagwanjia, "Unwanted in the 'White Highlands,'" 63, 74.
3 Ibid., 63–65.
4 Mwangi wa-Githumo, "Controversy over Jewish Ante-Chamber in Kenya: British Settlers' Reaction to the Proposed Jewish Settlement Project in Kenya, 1902–1905," *Transafrican Journal of History* 22 (1993): 88, 91.
5 Ibid., 91.
6 Ibid.
7 Ibid.
8 Ibid., 92–93.
9 Brett L. Shadle, *The Souls of White Folk: White Settlers in Kenya, 1900s–1920s* (Manchester: Manchester University Press, 2015), 72–73.
10 Ibid., 72.
11 Ibid., 26.
12 Ibid., 7–8.
13 Ibid., 5.
14 Ibid. See also 61.
15 Ibid., 72–73.
16 Ibid., 78.

17 Quoted in wa-Githumo, "Controversy over Jewish Ante-Chamber in Kenya," 97. See also Adam Rovner, *In the Shadow of Zion: Promised Lands Before Israel* (New York: New York University Press, 2014), 78.
18 Ibid., 53.
19 Simon Marks, Michael House, London, to The Rt. Hon. J.H. Thomas, M.P., Dominions Office, Whitehall, July 14, 1933, PRO, LAB 2/1189/ETAR 5513. 1933, File: *Mr. Dennis Cohen, Letter from Mr. Cohen on "Settlement of German Jews in the Dominions and Colonies."*
20 Ibid.
21 London, *Whitehall and the Jews*, 9, 43–45. See also Bartrop, *False Havens*, 66–67, 81, 101, 127.
22 For more information on the Evian Conference and its significance for British colonies in Africa, see Eric Estorick, "The Evian Conference and the Intergovernmental Committee," *The Annals of the American Academy of Political and Social Science* 203 (May 1939): 136–137; Chatham House, The Royal Institute of International Affairs, "The Evian Conference on Refugees," *Bulletin of International News* 15, no. 14 (1938): 16; Bartrop, *False Havens*, 54, 59.
23 J.G. Hibbert to E.B. Boyd, November 3, 1938, PRO. CO 525/176/19, Nyasaland Protectorate: *Settlement of Refugees from Central Europe.*
24 Ibid.
25 Ibid.
26 Ibid.
27 Memorandum on meeting between J.E. Shuckburgh, Downing Street, and Mr. Anthony de Rothschild, December 23, 1938, PRO, CO 525/176/19.
28 Ibid.
29 From the Secretary of State for the Colonies to the Governor of Nyasaland, November 18, 1938, PRO, CO 525/176/19. The Secretary's telegram to the governor contains references to the envisioned settlement project in Kenya as the context for a similar project in Nyasaland.
30 J.J. Paskin, Colonial Office, to the Under Secretary of State, Foreign Office, November 10, 1938, PRO, CO 525/176/19.
31 R. Dunbar, Foreign Office, to the Under Secretary of State, Colonial Office, December 1, 1938, PRO, CO 525/176/19.
32 Ibid.
33 Malcolm MacDonald, Secretary of State for the Colonies, Downing Street, CIRCULAR, December 1, 1938, PRO, CO 525/182/21, 1939. File No. 44227, *Settlement of Refugees from Central Europe*, Subject W. 1805.
34 Ibid.
35 Ibid.
36 Ibid.
37 Governor of Nyasaland to Malcolm MacDonald, Secretary of State for the Colonies, January 3, 1939, PRO, CO 525/182/22, Nyasaland Protectorate, 1939. File No. 44227/1: *Settlement of Refugees from Central Europe/Jewish Doctors of German and Austrian Origin.*
38 Colonial Office, *Note on Experimental Scheme for the Settlement of a Small Number of Young German Jewish Refugee Trained Agriculturalists in Kenya*, Enclosure in circular dispatch dated December 1, 1938, PRO, CO 525/182/21, 1939. File No. 44227.
39 Ibid.
40 Ibid.
41 London, *Whitehall and the Jews*, 32–33, 44.
42 Memorandum of meeting between Shuckburgh, and de Rothschild, December 23, 1938. This information is also contained in an internal communication between J.E. Shuckburgh and Mr. Hibbert regarding the former's conversation, over lunch, in London, with Mr. Anthony de Rothschild, Mr. Lionel Rothschild, Major Stern and "another guest," December 30, 1938, PRO, CO 525/176/19.
43 Shuckburgh and de Rothschild, December 23, 1938.

44 Telegram from Secretary of State for the Colonies to the Governor of Nyasaland, November 16, 1938, PRO, CO 525/176/19.
45 K.L. Hall, Acting Governor, Nyasaland Protectorate, to Malcolm MacDonald, Secretary of State for the Colonies, September 30, 1939, PRO, CO 525/182/22, Nyasaland Protectorate, 1939. File No. 44227.
46 Governor Harold Kittermaster, Nyasaland Protectorate, to Malcolm MacDonald, Secretary of State for the Colonies, December 22, 1938, PRO, CO 525/182/21, 1939. File No. 44227.
47 From Harold Kittermaster, Governor, Nyasaland, to Malcolm MacDonald, Secretary of State for the Colonies, December 22, 1938, and enclosure from Mr. W. Tait-Bowie, dated December 12, 1938, outlining the views of the three unofficial members of the territory's Legislative Council on the settlement idea, PRO, CO 525/182/21. 1939. File No. 44227.
48 Malcolm MacDonald, Downing Street, October 23, 1939, Confidential Circular, PRO, CO 525/182/22, Nyasaland Protectorate, 1939. File No. 44227/1. *Settlement of Refugees from Central Europe, Jewish Doctors of German and Austrian Origin.*
49 Ibid.
50 Ibid.
51 From Otto Norden, on behalf of Hermann Fuernberg, Council for an Autonomous Jewish Province in Harar, June 1943, to Mr. R.G. Howe, Minister of the United Kingdom, Addis Ababa, Ethiopia, PRO, FO 371/4014, *Zionist Activities of the African Continent*, 1944. File #405.
52 R.G. Howe, British Legation, Addis Ababa, to G. Mackereth, Foreign Office, London, January 5, 1944, PRO, FO 371/4014.
53 From Max Gottschalk, Director, The American Jewish Committee Research Institute of Peace and Post-War Problems, 386 Fourth Avenue, New York, to Sir Herbert Emerson, High Commissioner for Refugees, London, February 12, 1944, PRO, FO 371/4014.
54 Secretary of Jewish Refugees Committee Otto M. Schiff, to Bloomsbury House, London, September 1, 1942, PRO, FO 371/36628, Refugees File No. 25, *General, 1943*. See also R.G. Howe, British Legation, Addis Ababa, to the Right Honorable Anthony Eden, M.P., March 20, 1943, PRO, FO 371/36628, Refugees File No. 25, *General, 1943*.
55 R.G. Howe, British Legation, Addis Ababa, to the Right Honorable Anthony Eden, M.P., March 20, 1943, PRO, FO 371/36628.
56 Ibid.
57 Ibid.
58 Dr. Jacques Faitlovitch, Asmara, Erythrea, to R.G. Howe, His British Majesty's Minister, Addis Ababa, Ethiopia, April 12, 1943, PRO, FO 371/36628.
59 Ibid.
60 Ibid.
61 From Dr. Jacques Faitlovitch, Dr. Faitlovitch's School, Addis Ababa, to Mr. Goodman, Director, Jewish Section, Religious Division, His Majesty's Ministry of Information, London, April 23, 1943, PRO, FO 371/36628.
62 Ibid.
63 Ibid.
64 Howe to Anthony Eden, Secretary of State, March 25, 1943, PRO, FO 371/33628.
65 Ibid.
66 Ibid.
67 Ibid.
68 Ibid.
69 "*Fifty Millions Sterling for Ethiopia.* A Suggestion Which Could Work," Memoranda written by A.D. Bethell, Commercial Adviser, British Legation, Addis Ababa, March 24, 1943. Submitted to the Foreign Office by the British Minister R.G. Howe as Enclosure to dispatch No. 156/21/43 of May 29, 1943, PRO, FO 371/36628.
70 Ibid.

71 Ibid.
72 Ibid.
73 Bob Howe, British Legation, Addis Ababa, to G. [Gilbert] Mackereth, Foreign Office, London, May 29, 1943, PRO, FO 371/36628. Refugees File No. 25, *General, 1943*.
74 Ibid.
75 A.W.G. Randall, Foreign Office, London, to R.G. Howe, British Legation, Addis Ababa, July 27, 1943, PRO, FO 371/36628.
76 Ibid.
77 Ibid.
78 Director of Medical Services, Tanganyika Territory, to A.J. Pennington, Director of Refugees, Dar es Salaam, *Preliminary Memorandum on the Reactions of European Refugees to Tanganyika Climates*, PRO, CO 822/117/2, *Accommodation for Refugees in East Africa, 1943–45*.
79 Ibid.
80 Ibid.
81 Ibid.
82 Ibid.
83 Director of Refugees, A.L. Pennington, Dar-es-Salaam, Tanganyika, to The Commissioner, East African Refugees Administration, Nairobi, Kenya, September 29, 1944, PRO, CO 822/117/2.
84 Ibid.
85 "Review of Health Conditions of Polish Refugees in Uganda," PRO, CO 822/117/2.
86 Ibid.
87 Ibid.
88 Ibid.
89 Ibid.
90 "The Polish Refugees—First Batch Now in Uganda," *The Uganda Herald*, Wednesday September 23, 1942, 6. British Newspaper Library.
91 Ibid.
92 Ibid.
93 "Help," *The Uganda Herald*, Wednesday September 30, 1942. British Newspaper Library.
94 Ibid.
95 "Polish Refugees—This Concerns You," *The Uganda Herald*, Wednesday December 2, 1942, British Newspaper Library.
96 *Minutes of the Meeting of the Executive Council held at Government House, Christiansborg, Accra, at 10:00 am, on Friday November 25, 1938*. PRAAD, GNA. File: ADM 13/1/14. This meeting was attended by the Governor, Arnold Hodson. See also Minutes of the Executive Council Meeting of January 27, 1939, PRAAD, GNA. File: CSO 11/1/436.
97 Bartrop, *False Havens*, 6.
98 In the closing years of the war, Sir John Shuckburgh, retired deputy under-secretary of state in the Colonial Office, drafted a general history of the Second World War with details of various parts of Africa that received European war refugees including Jews. A copy of this draft history was sent to the governor of the Gold Coast for comments. See "History of the War, 1939–45," no. 5867, PRAAD, GNA. File: CSO 22/4/284.
99 Director of Medical Services to Colonial Secretary, 8/1/38. *Jewish Doctors of German and Austrian Origin—Possibility of Employment in the Colonial Empire, 1938–1939*. PRAAD, GNA. File: CSO 11/1/436.
100 Ibid.
101 *Minutes of the Meeting of the Executive Council, Friday November 25, 1938*, PRAAD, GNA. File: ADM 13/1/14.
102 Undated handwritten draft letter in response to Mr. Gips's letter to the Colonial Secretary, Gold Coast Colony, Accra, July 13, 1939. PRAAD, GNA. File: CSO 11/1/444. *Jewish Refugees—Applications for Information Regarding Settlement in the Gold Coast*.
103 Ibid.

104 Malcolm MacDonald, Secretary of State for the Colonies, London, to the Officer Administering the Government of the Gold Coast [Arnold Hodson], July 27, 1939, PRAAD, GNA. File: CSO 11/1/436.
105 Ibid.
106 Director of Medical Services, Gold Coast Colony, to Colonial Secretary, January 16, 1940, PRAAD, GNA. File: CSO 11/1/436.
107 Ibid.
108 *Minutes of the Meeting of the Executive Council Held at Government House, Christiansborg, Accra, at 10:00 am, on Friday February 2, 1940*. PRAAD, GNA. File: ADM 13/1/15.
109 Ibid.
110 Governor Arnold Hodson, Accra, to Malcolm MacDonald, Secretary of State for the Colonies, February 29, 1940, PRAAD, GNA. File: CSO 11/1/436. The governor's letter to the Colonial Office was based on DMS J.W.P. Harkness's memorandum on the subject of Jewish refugee doctors in the Gold Coast sent to the colonial secretary of the Gold Coast colony dated January 16, 1940.
111 Nana Amanfi III's address to Governor Alan Burns, *Legislative Council Debates*. Session 1946, Issue 1 of the *Proceedings of the Meeting of the Legislative Council Held in the Supreme Court (Court C), Accra, at 9:30 am, on Thursday March 21, 1946*. PRAAD, GNA, 126.
112 Ibid.
113 Emmanuel K. Akyeampong, "Race, Identity and Citizenship in Black Africa: The Case of the Lebanese in Ghana," *Africa* 76, no. 3 (2006): 303.
114 Ibid., 307–308, 311.
115 Ibid., 300, 311.
116 Toyin Falola, "Lebanese Traders in Southwestern Nigeria, 1900–1960," *African Affairs* 89, no. 357 (October 1990): 532–534, 539, 541, 544–548.

Conclusion

This book has answered three important questions and offered the historical, diplomatic, and intellectual contexts for those answers. One, what did people in Africa know about the Holocaust? Two, what did they think or say about it? Three, what did they do to help the Jews, as the primary victims of the Holocaust? The answers to these questions provide some insights into how oppressed people who had borne the brunt of racism in their history reacted to oppression and racial prejudice beyond their borders, and what they did beyond the expression of empathy from a distance when they had to confront the reality or prospect of accommodating the subjects of their empathy on their own land. In that regard, the preceding chapters have been a critical study of colonized and sovereign people's thoughts on genocide and of the contradictions of human empathy in two regions of Africa. They have also been a study of how the Holocaust rendered the theory and practice of British colonialism flimsy in Africa and empowered colonial subjects in their quest for self-determination.

As a study of ideas and social bonds forged in the common history of persecution, the book has demonstrated that Jews and Africans lived together in Africa for many centuries. Amid their different historical experiences in different regions, Jews and Africans shared a common historical misfortune. In the prewar period they were the victims of dehumanizing racism and discrimination. The exception was West Africa where the philosemitic attitudes of native populations among whom migrant Jews lived protected them from the types of anti-Semitic persecution and occupational discrimination their coreligionists endured at certain moments of their lives in parts of North, East, and South Africa. Nonetheless, it was in Nazi racism that Africans and Jews faced a common existential threat. That made Africans who lived under colonial rule in Africa, even those who lived in their sovereign domains, pay keen attention to the experiences of Jews in Europe.

Whether colonized or sovereign, Africans on the continent became even more attentive to Nazism's particular disdain for Jews and Africans. Notwithstanding Ethiopia's silence on Nazi anti-Semitic and anti-African racism, colonial subjects in East and West Africa and the free people of Liberia vigorously discussed Nazism as an ideological affront to Jewish and African humanity. News and rumors of the possible transfer of former German colonies in Africa to Nazi Germany, the cession of other colonized territories to the Nazi state, and the addition of Liberia to this Faustian diplomacy intensified anxiety in Africa. It is not solely the inherent perfidy of this reported appeasement bargain in Europe over African lives that aggravated Africans but also what Nazi ideology revealed to them about European civilization and its intellectual foundations. Henceforth, events in Europe and Nazi Germany's actions became, for people in East and West Africa, the most important barometer for measuring colonial rule, European Christianity, and the potential fate of Africans under Nazi rule. African anxieties about Nazism became more palpable from the Nazi response to the assassination of the German diplomat Ernst vom Rath by the Polish-Jewish student Herschel Grynszpan on 7 November 1938. For many in Africa, that marked a significant stage in the history of the Holocaust.

The organized destruction of Jewish synagogues and shops by mobs and hooligans in many parts of Germany and Austria, from the 9 to 10 November 1938, bore the horrifying marks of Nazi brutality and retribution. The events of *Kristallnacht* provided the Nazi regime the opportunity it sought to accelerate the process of deporting Jews from Germany. British diplomats in Germany and Austria documented this state-authorized vandalism, along with the government-ordered arrests, detention, and torture of a large number of Jewish men between the ages of 17 and 60, and shared aspects of that dossier with colonial administrators in Africa. Colonized people in West Africa whose social institutions upheld the sanctity of family and children and respect for the elderly read the details of these anti-Jewish deportations and persecutions with understandable dismay. In this context, the African participation in World War II was more than an expression of loyalty to Great Britain and its allies in their fight against Nazi Germany. It was, in part, a self-preservationist response to all that Adolf Hitler and his Nazi regime had come to represent in the minds of the educated African who had read Hitler's *Mein Kampf* and of the ordinary colonial subject who contemplated the implications of living under Nazi rule. The use of Hitler's disdainful views of Africans and Nazi Germany's genocide against European Jews as military recruitment tools by Great Britain in Africa deepened awareness of the Holocaust and its meaning for colonial subjects and sovereign peoples on the continent.

It is now possible to state that Africans knew about the Holocaust in all its transitions and thought about it in profound ways. The African perspective on the Holocaust can therefore be summarized in five interrelated ways. First, for Africans the Holocaust was an incremental process of the state-authorized and society-condoned persecution and physical destruction of Jews, not only in Europe but also in Africa, soon after the National Socialists came to power in Germany. Since the main targets of the Holocaust were Jews, it was their experiences under the Nazi regime that preoccupied the African observers. And because the principal perpetrators of the Holocaust were not different in their physical appearance from the main victims of that crime, people in Africa saw the Holocaust as an ominous signal of what potentially awaited them under Nazi rule. Second, colonial subjects saw the Holocaust as the gruesome outcome of the twin forces of racism and colonialism, both of which had defined their lives and relations with their colonial states and interactions with Europeans. Third, they surmised that the Holocaust could happen in Europe at the time it did because the majority of Europeans harbored racial prejudices and colonial sentiments against Jews and other groups. Fourth, colonized subjects in Africa saw the Holocaust as a human-created catastrophe and refrained from interpreting it in religious and mystical terms. Fifth, in the eyes of colonial subjects, the Holocaust shattered the European claim to legitimate tutelage over Africans and gave the anticolonial struggle in Africa new and moral impetus.

The earliest effect of the Holocaust on British colonial policy and racial thought in Africa was the revision of how appointments to the colonial service would henceforth be communicated. That decision in 1943 was probably the result of the anticipation of the appointment of a limited number of Jewish refugees into the colonial civil service. In colonial Kenya, where a small number of Jews lived in the course of World War II, the native African view of Jews as no different from other Europeans had been confirmed by the colonial administration's classification of Jews in East Africa as "Europeans," although British settlers in Kenya maintained their own views of Jews as a different category of Europeans. Unlike Kenya, the Gold Coast did not have any recognizable number of Jewish immigrants. Thus, colonial authorities did not have to make any racial classifications of colonial society that assigned "European" status to Jews, although in the minds of colonial subjects in the region, Jews were no different from Europeans in their racial identity. What actually existed in colonial relations on the Gold Coast was the strict dichotomy British administrators had maintained since the late nineteenth century between themselves as "Europeans" and their colonial subjects as "Africans" and the social privileges the colonial state accorded or denied each of these racial categories in the twentieth century. In the course of World War II, Nazism's privileging of Europeanness and white supremacy and Nazi Germany's destruction of European Jews made racism and race-based privileges embarrassing social and intellectual anomalies. Therefore, scrapping the use of racial adjectives in official appointment letters in the Gold Coast colony after 1943, because of their connotations of racial superiority (European) and racial inferiority (African), removed what had already become incongruous racial constructs in the course of the Holocaust. After all, how would the Jewish victims of the Holocaust and of Nazi racism be addressed in their appointment letters in the Gold Coast when they were employed in the colonial civil service, and how would Jewish refugee doctors as victims of Nazi racial and segregation laws feel if they had to serve in hospitals segregated into "European" and "African"? This thought, undoubtedly a consequence of the Holocaust, must have influenced the British official abolition of the racial adjectives *European* and *African* in colonial appointment letters in the Gold Coast colony and the complementary decision to also remove such references from the names of medical facilities and substitute them with the names of the towns or cities in which these facilities were located.

While colonized and sovereign peoples in Africa did not take part in the direct rescue of Jews from the inferno of persecution in Europe, they participated in giving refuge to some of the rescued and other Jews who survived the Holocaust. Africa became one of the places the British considered resettling some of the Jewish refugees. But the reluctance of those who bewailed the destruction of Jewish life from a distance to accommodate those whom the Holocaust rendered homeless, on their land, is one of the known facts of Holocaust history but not a well-known reaction in African history. Some colonized and sovereign people in Africa who spoke loudly and humanely against the persecution of European Jews by the Nazi regime, in the course of the Holocaust, recoiled at the prospect of welcoming the persecuted Jews onto their lands. Yet, as in all human circumstances and contradictions, there are conscientious exceptions to even the most mundane. Colonial subjects in Tanganyika and Uganda showed the side of human empathy that was rare in some of the African responses to the survivors of the Holocaust.

Bibliography

Primary sources

British National Archives [Public Record Office], London

Foreign Office [FO] 660/167. *Jews in North Africa.*
FO 371/22954; FO 371–22/955. *Political Central Germany.*
FO 371/36628. *General File, 1943.* [Refugees File].
FO 371/4014. *Zionist Activities of the African Continent, 1944.* [File #405].
Colonial Office [CO] 691/160/13/1938. *Confidential dispatch from Governor Mark Young, Tanganyika Territory, Dar es Salaam, to Malcolm MacDonald, Secretary of State for the Colonies.*
CO 525/176/19. *Nyasaland Protectorate: Settlement of Refugees from Central Europe.*
CO 525/182/21. 1939. File No. 44227: *Settlement of Refugees from Central Europe.* Subject W. 1805.
CO 525/182/22. Nyasaland Protectorate, 1939. File No. 44227/1: *Settlement of Refugees from Central Europe/Jewish Doctors of German and Austrian Origin.*
CO 691/160. File: *Tanganyika 1938. Permanency of Mandate. German Aspirations: Nazi Activities.*
CO 822/117/2. *Accommodation for Refugees in East Africa, 1943–45.*
CO 875/13/5. *Press Censorship, Nigeria.*
CSO 875/6/9. Ministry of Information, Colonial Section. Public Relations File: *Propaganda, Gold Coast.*
LAB 2/1189/ETAR 5513. 1933. File: *Mr. Dennis Cohen, Letter from Mr. Cohen on "Settlement of German Jews in the Dominions and Colonies."*

Ghana National Archives [Public Records and Archives Administration Department], Accra

ADM 1/1/523. *Despatches of Secretary of State to Governor* [1940].
ADM 13/1/14. *Minutes of the Meeting of the Executive Council Held at Government House, Christiansborg, Accra, on Friday, 25 November 1938.*
ADM 14/2/36. Gold Coast Government. *Proceedings of the Meetings of the Legislative Council, 1939–1946.*
ADM 14/2/35. *Legislative Council Debates.* Session 1940, Issue 2.
ADM 14/2/38. *Legislative Council Debates.* Session 1942, Issue 1.
ADM 14/2/44. *Legislative Council Debates.* Session 1945, Issue 1.
Legislative Council Debates. Session 1946, Issue No. 1: *Proceedings of the Meeting of the Legislative Council Held in the Supreme Court (Court C), Accra, at 9:30 am, on Thursday, 21 March 1946.*
Colonial Secretary's Office [CSO]
CSO 11/1/436. *Jewish Doctors of German and Austrian Origin—Possibility of Employment in the Colonial Empire, 1938–1939.*

CSO 11/1/444. *Jewish Refugees—Applications for Information Regarding Settlement in the Gold Coast.*
CSO 22/4/284. No. 5867: "History of the War, 1939–45." [Draft].
CSO/23/1/75; CSO 11/1/436. *Minutes of the Executive Council, 1939–41* [German Propaganda Archive].
CSO 23/5/12. Subject: *War News from Foreign Countries.*
CSO 23/5/32. *Correspondence Between Gold Coast Information Officer, John Wilson, and Colonial Office, 1940:* "Public Opinion in the Gold Coast Towards the War"; "Further Report on Public Opinion in the Gold Coast"; "Empire at War: Britain's Might Forbids the Slavery of Africa."
CSO. Vol. 1, No. 2420: *Confidential Report on Conference of Information Officers, Accra, February 1942.*
CSO 23/5/168. *West Africa and the War,* Robert Gardiner.
CSO 26/2/31. *Papers Concerning the Treatment of German Nationals, 1938–1939.*
CSO. Circular Nos. 58/42; 87/47. File No. 1786/S.F.3.
CSO. RG 4/5/523.

Africana Library, University of Liberia, Monrovia

"American Liberian Relations During World War II." Unpublished Paper.
Collections of the Honorable Louis Arthur Grimes, 1883–1948. Uncatalogued Papers.

Newspapers and pamphlets

University of South Florida Library, Tampa, Florida, United States

East Africa and Rhodesia.
East African Standard.
New Times and Ethiopian News.
West African Pilot.

British Library Newspapers, Colindale

Daily Guardian.
Gold Coast Independent.
Gold Coast Spectator.
Tanganyika Herald.
Uganda Herald.

Ghana National Archives, Accra

The Ashanti Pioneer. File CSO 23/1/75.
Empire at War; Inside the News. Department of Information, Gold Coast Government.

University of Liberia Library, Monrovia

African Morning Post.
African Nationalist.
Daily Observer.
Liberian Crisis.

Ethiopia National Library, Addis Ababa

The Ethiopian Herald.

Secondary sources: journal, book chapters, and online articles

Acheampong, Emmanuel K. "Race, Identity and Citizenship in Black Africa: The Case of the Lebanese in Ghana." *Africa* 76, no. 3 (2006): 297–323.

Akingbade, Harrison. "U.S. Liberian Relations During World War II." *Phylon* 46, no. 1 (1985): 25–36.

Amenumey, D.E.K. "German Administration in Southern Togo." *Journal of African History* 10, no. 4 (1969): 623–639.

BBC News. "The Africans Who Fought in World War II." http://news.bbc.co.uk/2/hi/africa/8344170.stm.

Bernhard, Patrick. "Behind the Battle Lines: Italian Atrocities and the Persecution of Arabs, Berbers, and Jews in North Africa During World War II." *Holocaust and Genocide Studies* 26, no. 3 (Winter 2012): 425–446.

Berrera, Guilia, "Wrestling with Race on the Eve of Human Rights: The British Management of the Color Line in Post-Fascist Eritrea." In *Africa and World War II*, ed. Judith A. Byfield and Carolyn A. Brown. New York: Cambridge University Press, 2015.

Boum, Aomar. "Saharan Jewry: History, Memory and Imagined Identity." *The Journal of North African Studies* 16, no. 3 (September 2011): 325–341.

Dickson, Kwesi A. "'Hebrewisms of West Africa'—The Old Testament and African Life and Thought." *Legon Journal of the Humanities* 1 (1974): 23–34.

Estorick, Eric. "The Evian Conference and the Intergovernmental Committee." *The Annals of the American Academy of Political and Social Science* 203 (May 1939): 136–141.

Falola, Toyin. "Lebanese Traders in Southwestern Nigeria, 1900–1960." *African Affairs* 89, no. 357 (October 1990): 523–553.

Friedman, Ina R. "The Holocaust: The Other Victims of the Nazis." *Social Education* 59, no. 6 (October 1995): 339–341.

Gilbert, Shirli. "Jews and the Racial State: Legacies of the Holocaust in Apartheid South Africa, 1945–60." *Jewish Social Studies: History, Culture, Society* 16, no. 3 (Spring/Summer 2010): 32–64.

Green, Tobias. "Further Considerations of the Sephardim of the Petit Cote." *History in Africa* 32 (2005): 165–183.

Hirschberg, H.Z. (J.W.). "The Problem of the Judaized Berbers." *Journal of African History* 4, no. 3 (1963): 313–339.

Kaplan, Steven. "Did Jewish Influence Reach Ethiopia via the Nile?" In *The Nile Histories, Cultures, Myths*, ed. Erlich Haggai and Israel Gershoni. London: Lynne Rienner Publishers, 2000.

Kesting, Robert W. "Blacks Under the Swastika: A Research Note." *Journal of Negro History* 83, no. 1 (Winter 1998): 84–99.

———. "Forgotten Victims: Blacks in the Holocaust." *Journal of Negro History* 77, no. 1 (Winter 1992): 30–36.

Laumann, Dennis. "A Historiography of German Togoland, or the Rise and Fall of a 'Model Colony.'" *History in Africa* 30 (2003): 195–211.

Massin, Benoit. "The Science of Race." In *Deadly Medicine: Creating the Master Race*, ed. United States Holocaust Memorial Museum. Washington, DC: United States Holocaust Memorial Museum, 2004.

Musiker, Naomi. "The Jews of Kenya." *Jewish Affairs* 59 (Winter 2004): 21–23.
Owino, Meshack. "Africa and the Second World War." In *The Palgrave Handbook of African Colonial and Postcolonial History*, ed. Martin S. Shanguhyia and Toyin Falola. Vol. 1. New York: Palgrave Macmillan, 2018.
Prussin, Labelle. "Judaic Threads in the West African Tapestry: No More Forever?" *Art Bulletin* 88, no. 2 (2006): 328–353.
Royal Institute of International Affairs, and Chatham House. "The Evian Conference on Refugees." *Bulletin of International News* 15, no. 14 (1938, 16 July): 16–18.
Shain, Milton. "South Africa." In *The World Reacts to the Holocaust*, ed. David S. Wymann. Baltimore, MD: Johns Hopkins University Press, 1996.
Smidt, Wolbert. "Germany, Relations with [Ethiopia]." In *Encyclopaedia Aethiopica*, ed. Siegbert Uhlig. Vol. 2 (D-Ha). Wiesbaden: Harrassowitz Verlag, 2005.
Stoler, Ann Laura. "Colonial Archives and the Arts of Government." *Archival Science* 2 (2002): 87–109.
United Nations. *Resolution Adopted by the General Assembly on Holocaust Remembrance* (A/RES/60/7), 1 November 2005. www.un.org/en/holocaustremembrance/docs/res607.shtml.
United States Holocaust Memorial Museum. "Introduction to the Holocaust." www.ushmm.org.
wa-Githumo, Mwangi. "Controversy over Jewish Ante-Chamber in Kenya: British Settlers' Reaction to the Proposed Jewish Settlement Project in Kenya, 1902–1905." *Transafrican Journal of History* 22 (1993): 87–99.
Warsch, Sean. "A 'Holocaust' Becomes 'the Holocaust.'" *Jewish Magazine*, 26 October, 1–13. http://www.jewishmag.com/107mag/holocaustword/holocaustword.htm.
Yad Vashem. "The Holocaust." www.yadvashem.org.

Books and unpublished sources

Abebe Zegeye. *The Impossible Return: Struggles of Ethiopian Jews, the Beta Israel*. Trenton, NJ: Red Sea Press, 2018.
Achebe, Chinua. *No Longer at Ease*. London: Heinemann Educational Books, 1960.
Adibe, Jideofor. *Who Is an African?: Identity, Citizenship and the Making of the Africa-Nation*. London: Adonis and Abbey Publishers, 2009.
Bairu, Tafla. *Ethiopia and Germany: Cultural, Political and Economic Relations, 1871–1936*. Wiesbaden: Franz Steiner Verlag, 1981.
Baranowski, Shelley. *Nazi Empire: German Colonialism and Imperialism from Bismarck to Hitler*. Cambridge: Cambridge University Press, 2011.
Bartrop, Paul R., ed. *False Havens: The British Empire and the Holocaust. Studies in the Shoah*. Vol. X. Lanham, MD: University Press of America, 1995.
Berenbaum, Michael, and Abraham J. Peck. *The Holocaust and History: The Known, the Unknown, the Disputed and the Reexamined*. Bloomington, IN: Indiana University Press, 1998.
Bloxham, David, and Tony Kushner. *The Holocaust: Critical Historical Approaches*. Manchester: Manchester University Press, 2005.
Boahen, Albert Adu. *African Perspectives on Colonialism*. Baltimore, MD: Johns Hopkins University Press, 1987.
Bodian, Miriam. *Hebrews of the Portuguese Nation: Conversos and Community in Early Modern Amsterdam*. Bloomington: Indiana University Press, 1997.
Byfield, Judith A., and Carolyn A. Brown, eds. *Africa and World War II*. New York: Cambridge University Press, 2015.
Calvert, Albert F. *German East Africa*. New York: Negro Universities Press, 1970.
Carlebach, Julius. *The Jews of Nairobi, 1903–1962*. Nairobi: Nairobi Hebrew Congregation, 1962.

Dawit, Wolde Giorgis. *Red Tears: War, Famine and Revolution in Ethiopia*. Trenton, NJ: Red Sea Press, 1989.

Dunn, Elwood D. *The Foreign Policy of Liberia During the Tubman Era, 1944–1971*. London: Hutchinson Benham, 1979.

Echenberg, Myron. *Colonial Conscripts: The Tirailleurs Senegalais in French West Africa, 1875–1960*. Portsmouth, NH: Heinemann, 1991.

Erhlich, Avram M., ed. *Encyclopedia of the Jewish Diaspora: Origins, Experiences and Culture*. Vol. 2. Santa Barbara, CA: ABC-CLIO, 2009.

Freeman, Dena, and Alula Pankhurst, eds. *Peripheral People: The Excluded Minorities of Ethiopia*. Lawrenceville, NJ: Red Sea Press, 2003.

Friedlander, Saul. *Nazi Germany and the Jews, 1939–1945: The Years of Extermination*. New York: Harper Perennial, 2008.

Gellately, Robert. *Backing Hitler: Consent and Coercion in Nazi Germany*. Oxford: Oxford University Press, 2001.

Gutman, Yisrael, and Michael Berenbaum. *Anatomy of the Auschwitz Death Camp*. Bloomington: Indiana University Press, 1994.

Hirchberg, H.Z. (J.W.). *A History of the Jews in North Africa: From Antiquity to the Sixteenth Century*. Vol. 1., 2nd Rev. ed. London: E.J. Brill, 1974. [Translated from the Hebrew].

Hitler, Adolf. *Mein Kampf*. Unexpurgated ed. Delhi: Jaico Publishing House, 2010.

Hull, Richard. *Jews and Judaism in African History*. Princeton, NJ: Markus Wiener Publishers, 2009.

Kagan, Richard L., and Philip D. Morgan, eds. *Atlantic Diasporas: Jews, Conversos and Crypto-Jews in the Age of Mercantilism, 1500–1800*. Baltimore, MD: Johns Hopkins University Press, 2009.

Kagwanjia, Peter Mwangi. "Unwanted in the 'White Highlands': The Politics of Civil Society and the Making of a Refugee in Kenya, 1902–2002." Unpublished PhD dissertation, Department of History, University of Illinois, Urbana Champaign, 2003.

Katz, Steven T. *The Holocaust in Historical Context: The Holocaust and Mass Death Before the Modern Age*. Vol. 1. New York: Oxford University Press, 1994.

Kiernan, Ben. *Blood and Soil: A World History of Genocide and Extermination from Sparta to Darfur*. New Haven, CT: Yale University Press, 2007.

Killingray, David (with Martin Plaut). *Fighting for Britain: African Soldiers in the Second World War*. Woodbridge, Suffolk: James Currey, 2010.

Killingray, David, and Richard Rathbone, eds. *Africa and the Second World War*. New York: St. Martin's Press, 1986.

Kolapo, Femi J., and Kwabena O. Akurang-Parry, eds. *African Agency and European Colonialism: Latitudes of Negotiation and Containment*. Essays in Honor of A.S. Kanya Forstner. Lanham, MD: University Press of America, 2007.

Lawler, Nancy Ellen. *Soldiers, Airmen, Spies and Whisperers: The Gold Coast in World War II*. Athens: Ohio University Press, 2002.

Lenhoff, Howard M. *Black Jews, Jews and Other Heroes: How Grassroots Activism Led to the Rescue of the Ethiopian Jews*. Jerusalem: Gefen Publishing House, 2007.

Liebau, Heike, et al., eds. *The World in World Wars: Experiences, Perceptions and Perspectives from Africa and Asia*. Leiden and Boston: Brill, 2010.

London, Louise. *Whitehall and the Jews, 1933–1948: British Immigration Policy, Jewish Refugees and the Holocaust*. Cambridge: Cambridge University Press, 2000.

Lusane, Clarence. *Hitler's Black Victims: The Historical Experiences of Afro-Germans, European Blacks, Africans and African Americans in the Nazi Era*. New York: Routledge, 2002.

Lydon, Ghislaine. *On Trans-Saharan Trails: Islamic Law, Trade Networks and Cross-Cultural Exchange in Nineteenth-Century Western Africa*. Cambridge: Cambridge University Press, 2009.

Mann, Gregory. *Native Sons: West African Veterans and France in the Twentieth Century*. Durham, NC: Duke University Press, 2006.
Mark, Peter, and Jose da Silva Horta. *The Forgotten Diaspora: Jewish Communities in West Africa and the Making of the Atlantic World*. Cambridge: Cambridge University Press, 2011.
Marrus, Michael. *The Holocaust in History*. New York: Meridian Books, 1987.
Massaquoi, Hans J. *Destined to Witness: Growing Up Black in Nazi Germany*. New York: Perennial, 2001.
Miles, William F.S. *Jews of Nigeria: An Afro-Judaic Odyssey*. Princeton, NJ: Markus Wiener Publishers, 2013.
Moore, Bob, and Kent Fedorowich, eds. *Prisoners of War and Their Captors in World War II*. Oxford: Berg, 1996.
Nunneley, John. *Tales from the King's African Rifles: A Last Flourish of Empire*. London: Cassell, 2000.
Ochonu, Moses. *Colonialism by Proxy: Hausa Imperial Agents and Middle Belt Consciousness in Nigeria*. Bloomington: Indiana University Press, 2014.
Osbourne, Richard. *World War II in Colonial Africa: The Death Knell of Colonialism*. Indianapolis, IN: Riebel-Roque, 2001.
Pankhurst, Richard. *Sylvia Pankhurst, Counsel for Ethiopia: A Biographical Essay on Ethiopian, Anti-Fascist and Anti-Colonialist History, 1934–1960*. Hollywood, CA: Tsehai Publishers and Distributors, 2003.
Parfitt, Tudor. *Black Jews in Africa and the Americas*. Cambridge, MA: Harvard University Press, 2013.
Parsons, Timothy H. *The African Rank and File: Social Implications of Colonial Military Service in the King's African Rifles, 1902–1964*. Portsmouth, NH: Heinemann, 1999.
Primack, Karen. *Jews in Places You Never Thought Of*. Hoboken, NJ: KTAV Publishing House, 1998.
Reed-Anderson, Paulette. *Rewriting the Footnotes: Berlin and the African Diaspora*. Berlin: Die Ausanderbeauftragte des Senats, 2000.
Richardson, Nathaniel R. *Liberia's Past and Present*. London: Diplomatic Press and Publishing Company, 1959.
Rovner, Adam L. *In the Shadow of Zion: Promised Lands Before Israel*. New York: New York University Press, 2014.
Satloff, Robert. *Among the Righteous: Lost Stories from the Holocaust's Long Reach into Arab Lands*. New York: Public Affairs, 2006.
Scheck, Rafael. *Hitler's African Victims: The German Army Massacres of Black French Soldiers in 1941*. Cambridge: Cambridge University Press, 2006.
Shadle, Brett L. *The Souls of White Folk: White Settlers in Kenya, 1900s–1920s*. Manchester: Manchester University Press, 2015.
Smidt, Wolbert G.C. *Ethiopia and Germany: 100 Years of Diplomatic Relations*. Addis Ababa: Goethe-Institut, 2005.
Stannard, David E. *American Holocaust: The Conquest of the New World*. New York: Oxford University Press, 1992.
Stewart, Andrew. *The First Victory: The Second World War and the East Africa Campaign*. New Haven, CT: Yale University Press, 2016.
Stoecker, Helmut, ed. *German Imperialism in Africa: From the Beginnings Until the Second World War*. London: C. Hurst & Co, 1986.
Teshale, Tibebu. *The Making of Modern Ethiopia, 1896–1974*. Lawrenceville, NJ: Red Sea Press, 1995.
Townsend, Reginald E. *President William V.S. Tubman of Liberia Speaks: Major Addresses, Messages, Speeches and Statements, 1944–1959*. Monrovia: Department of Information and Cultural Affairs, 1959.

United Nations Educational, Scientific and Cultural Organization (UNESCO). *Education About the Holocaust and Preventing Genocide: A Policy Guide.* Paris: UNESCO, 2017.

United States Holocaust Memorial Museum. *Nazi Ideology and the Holocaust.* Washington, DC: United States Holocaust Memorial Museum, 2007.

Weld, Kirsten. *Paper Cadavers: The Archives of Dictatorship in Guatemala.* Durham, NC: Duke University Press, 2014.

Wexler, Paul. *The Non-Jewish Origins of the Sephardic Jews.* Albany: State University of New York Press, 1996.

Wyman, David S., ed. *The World Reacts to the Holocaust.* Baltimore, MD: Johns Hopkins University Press, 1996.

Zucker, George K., ed. *Sephardic Identity: Essays on a Vanishing Jewish Culture.* Jefferson, NC: McFarland & Co, 2005.

Index

Note: *Italic* page references indicate figures.

Abraham 30
Abyssinia, Italy's invasion of 77–78
Abyssinian Jewish population 157
acculturation 22
Achebe, Chinua 44
Africa/Africans: archival materials in researching Holocaust perspective of 13; British settlers in 107–108, 145–147, 151, 168; Christianity in 19, 27, 133–134; criteria in researching Holocaust perspective of 12–13; defining *African* and 11–12; education and attitude about World War II 80–81, 83–84; education in German schools 53; education and reaction to colonialism 87, 91, 95; education and view of Nazism 62–63, 121, 176; fascism in 77–79, 91; German war propaganda portraying 8–9; Germany's relationship with 6; Germany's treatment of 3–4; Germany and, visions before era of Nazism and 45, 51–53; gold mines 35; Hitler's view/policy of 44, 49, 51, 67, 79; Holocaust knowledge during World War II 2–3, 105, 175–177; Holocaust and, voices/perspectives on 11, 13–15, 127–129; Islam in 29; Jewish refugees and 3–4, 9–10, 178; Judaism in 19; in *Mein Kampf* 45–51; Nazism and, reactions to 11, 44–45, 70–71, 175–176; newspapers in researching Holocaust perspective of 13; paradox in 27; in prisoner of war camps during World War II 4, 7–9; soldiers fighting in World War II 1, 71, 90–91, 122; sources/scope of knowledge of Holocaust 105–108; World War II, attitudes about 81, 83–88, 96–97, 176;
World War II literature relating to 1–2; World War II, promoting healthy interest in 88–93; *see also* historical perspective of Jews in Africa before Holocaust; *specific country*
African, defining 11–12
African Morning Post (newspaper) 64
African Nationalist (newspaper) 66–67
African press and reports on Holocaust 105–106, 119–126; *see also specific newspaper*
African Standard (newspaper) 145
Africanus, Leo 21, 32
Afrikaners 26–27, 108
Afro-Germans 3–7, 66, 103, 124–125, 130; *see also* Africa/Africans
Afro-Judaic Odyssey, An (Miles) 19
Agau people 28
Akan people 29, 81, 88–89
Akyeampong, Emmanuel 168
Akyem Abuakwa 80
Alexander the Great 19
Aliens Act (1937) 27
Allied Powers 1, 85
Almada (Portuguese trader) 33
Amanfi, Nana III 86–87, 90–91, 168
Amhara emperors 28
Among the Righteous (Satloff) 9
anti-Semitism: in Egypt 25; against Ethiopian Jews 28–29, 37; in Europe, causes of 152; in Germany 26, 176; Hitler's 45–46, 69; in Holland 31; Nazism and 3, 26, 56, 93–94; in North Africa 20–23; in Portugal 31; in South Africa 27; *see also* Holocaust
Anyaduba, J.O. 60
appeasement diplomacy 62, 76, 83, 127, 176

Index

Arab collaborators with Nazi Germany 9–10
Arab conquest of North Africa 20–21
archival thinking 14
Ark of the Covenant 18, 28–29
Armistice of 1918 45
Aryan races 1, 4, 46–49, 71n12, 126, 128
Ashanti Pioneer (Gold Coast newspaper) 13, 54, 81, 83, 128
Ashkenazi Jews 21, 25–26, 30
Askia Mohammed 29
assimilation 37, 50, 148, 152; *see also* integration, social
Atandaso, Assin 80
Atkinson, A.E. 145
Auschwitz (Oswiecim) concentration camp 123–124
Auschwitz-Birkenau concentration camp 1
Austria 62, 76, 78, 98n18, 110, 112, 176
Awooner-Renner, Bankole 136
Azikiwe, Nnamdi 56, 58–61, 63–66, 76, 88, 96–97, 126–127, 129–130; *see also West African Pilot*

Baby Sy 55, 93
Ballhaus, Jolanda 64
Barclay, Edwin J. 85
Bartrop, Paul 165
Beevers, John 59
Bell, J.E. 112
Bennett, Reverend 145
Berber traders 20, 34–35, 42n89
Berlin Conference (1885) 52
Berrera, Guilia 136
Beta Israel 28
Bethell, A.D. 158–159
Bismarck, Otto von 6
"Black No More" editorial 67
Blacks 1, 9, 103, 124, 130; *see also* Africa/Africans
Block, Sarah 30
Blomberg, Werner von 64
Bloxham, Donald 102
Boer War 108
Bohemian Jews 125
Boum, Aomar 29, 31
Boyd, E.B. 149
Bradle, Kenneth 135
British Broadcasting Corporation (BBC) 121
British Labor Party report 122
British Legation 157–158
British National Archives 13
British Newspaper Library 13
British news sources 120–122; *see also specific name*
British settlers in Africa 107–108, 145–147, 151, 168
Buchenwald concentration camp 110–111, 114–115, 117, 119
Burns, Sir Alan 84, 95

Caine, Mr. 92
Cameron, Sir Donald 91–93
Cameroon 62, 64, 76–77
Cape Verde 32–33
Carlebach, Julius 37–38
Carstairs, Mr. 92–93
Carvell, J.E.M. 115–116
Chamberlain, Neville 127
Christianity 19, 27, 35, 50–51, 133–134
"Christianity Today" serial 60
Cold War period 14
colonialism: Africa's reactions to Nazism during era of 53–56, 57, 58–61, 58, 61; British 23–25, 30, 54–55, 80–81; education of Africans and reaction to 87, 91, 95; education under 167–168; ethnic group identification and 38; French 23–24, 55; German 6, 49, 52, 61–69, 79, 101–102; Hitler's view of 49, 61–62; Holocaust's impact on 133–137, 177; in Liberia 65–67; Nazism and 59–65; in North Africa 23–24; in West Africa 62, 64; World War II and, explaining 80–81
Colonial Medical Service 165
Colonial Office 96, 149–155, 164, 166
concentration camps 102, 115–119, 122–126, 134; *see also specific name*
conversion of Jews 20, 28–29, 32, 145
Cooper, Harold 54–55
Council for an Autonomous Jewish Province in Harar 155
Council for German Jewry (CGJ) 151–152
crematorium 124
C. Woermann and Jantzen and Thomaehlem (German trading company) 52
Czechoslovakia 62, 76, 121

Dachau concentration camp 115–116, 119
Daily Guardian (Freetown newspaper) 106–107
Danquah, J.B. 89–90, 121–122, 130
Darre, Richard-Walther 5
Darwinist evolutionary theory 48–49
death camps 102, 115–119, 122–126, 134; *see also specific name*

Decker, Thomas 106
Delamere, Lord 145
Der Deutsch Togo Bund 53
Destined to Witness (Massaquoi) 4–5, 69
Deutsche Welle (German broadcasting network) 55
dhimmis 22, 33–34
Dickson, K.A. 29
disabilities, persecution of people with 1, 103
"documents of exclusion" 14
Dolobran, Lord Lloyd of 90
Dowden, Mr. 113–114
Dutch East Indian Company 26

East Africa: German colonialism in 52; historical perspective of Jews in Africa before Holocaust 29–30; Holocaust knowledge and 106–108; Jewish refugees and 151–152; Nazism and, reactions to 53; *see also* Africa/Africans; *specific country*
East African Refugee Administration 162–163
East African Standard (Nairobi newspaper) 12, 120
East Africa and Rhodesia (newspaper) 62
Eden, Anthony 157
education: of Africans in German schools 53; Azikiwe's view of 59; under colonialism 167–168; colonialism and, Africans' reaction to 87, 91, 95; Hitler's view of race and 50–51, 55; impact of Holocaust on colonialism and 133; interpreting Holocaust and 126; Jews and 24, 27; in Nazi propaganda 53–54; Nazism and, Africans' view of 62–64, 121, 176; racism and, countering 59; UN's agency for and Holocaust 104; World War II and, Africans' attitude about 80–81, 83–84
Education About the Holocaust and Preventing Genocide (UNESCO policy guide) 104
Egypt 19–20, 23–25
Einstein, Albert 59
emigration of Jews: to Ethiopia 27–29, 159–160; to Israel 29; to Kenya 30, 150, 156, 169; Nazism and 110, 118; to North Africa 20–21; Nyasaland settlement camp and 153; opposition to, by other countries 152; to Palestine 168; to South Africa 25–27; to South America 112; to United States 29; *see also* Jewish refugees; *specific country*

emigration of Syrian and Lebanese refugees 168–169
Empire at War (weekly publication) 80, 89, 121, 128
Epp, Frantz Ritter von 64
Ethiopia: emigration of Jews to 27–29, 159–160; Great Britain and 159; historical perspective of Jews in Africa before Holocaust 27–29; Italian invasion of 77–78; Jewish refugees in 155–161; Nazism and, reaction to 67–69; United States and 159; *see also* Ethiopian Jews
Ethiopia News (newspaper) 63
Ethiopian Herald (newspaper) 132–133, 155
Ethiopian Jews: anti-Semitism against 28–29, 37; Ark of the Covenant and, stealing of 18, 28–29; migration story and 27–28; Solomon legend and 18, 27; status of 36; terms for 28
Europe 78, 80, 152; *see also specific country*
Evian Conference 166
Executive Council (Gold Coast) 83, 167
extermination of European Jews *see* Holocaust

Faitlovitch, Jacques 156–157, 160
falasha 28
Falola, Toyin 168–169
False Havens (Harkness) 164–165
fascism 51, 77–79, 91
Ferreira, Joo 33
Fighting for Britain (Killingray and Plaut) 1
"final solution" 102; *see also* Holocaust
First World War *see* World War I
Foreign Office 108, 150, 155, 157, 159–160
France: assimilation policy of 50; colonialism 23–24, 55; declaration of war against Germany 8; fascism and, attitude about 78; Germany's invasion of Europe and 80; Hitler's view of 49–50; Vichy 9–10, 24
Freeman, Dena 28
Freire, Jeronimo Rodrigues 34
Freud, Sigmund 59
Friedlander, Saul 102
Friedman, Ina R. 103
Funck, Casmir 59

Gainer, Claire 112
Gandhi, Mohandas 130–133
Gardiner, Robert 84–85, 96–97
Germany: Africans' visions of before Nazi era 45, 51–53; Africa's relationship

with 6; annexation of Austria and Czechoslovakia by 76, 98n18; anti-Semitism in 26, 176; Blacks in 3–7, 66, 103, 124–125, 130; citizenship of Jews in, Hitler's questioning of 48; colonialism 6, 49, 52, 61–69, 79, 101–102; Ethiopia and 67–69; Europe invasion by 78, 80; France's declaration of war against 8; Gestapo and 117–118, 121, 124–125, 127, 130; Liberia and 65–67; Poland occupation by 77; Third Reich 60, 63, 67, 105, 132, 136; treatment of Africans and 3–4; war propaganda 8–9

Gestapo 117–118, 121, 124–125, 127, 130

Ghana 13, 29

Ghana National Archives 13

ghettoes 22, 121, 131–132, 138, 145–146

Gilbert, Shirli 27

Gips, Mr. W. 165–166

Goebbels, Josef 55, 127

Gold Coast: Akan people and 29, 81, 88–89; Executive Council 83, 167; German colonial claims and 62; grievances against colonial government and 81, 83; Holocaust's impact on colonialism in 134–136; Jewish refugees in 134, 164–169; Legislative Council 80, 86–88, 91, 93–94, 168; Nazism and, reaction to 54–55, 81; promoting interest in World War II and, healthy 88–90; World War II and, attitudes about 81, *82*, 83–84, 86–88; World War II and, support for 80–81; *see also* West Africa

Gold Coast Independent (newspaper) 119, 122–123

Gold Coast Spectator (newspaper) 13, 55–56, 57, 61, 78

gold mines in West Africa 35

Goring, Hermann 64

Gorton, Mrs. D.G. 164

grand boubou (great robe) 35

Great Britain: African interest in World War II, promoting healthy 88–93; archival material from 13; colonialism 23–25, 30, 54–55, 80–81; Ethiopia and 159; fascism and, attitude about 78; Germany's invasion of Europe and 80; Holocaust knowledge 108, *109*, 110, 122–126; Jewish refugees in 3; Jewish refugees policy of 149–150, 153–154; news sources 120–121; *Papers* and 108, *109*, 110, 119; persecution of Jews and 108; World War II in West Africa, attitude about 83–84; *see also* British settlers in Africa

Grynzpan, Herschel 127, 176

Guatemalan National Police archives 14

Gutmann, Franz 107

Gypsies, persecution of 1, 102–104

Habe, Hand 66–67

Halifax, Viscount 150

Hall, David 68, 79

Harkness, J.W.P. 164–167

"Hebrewisms of West Africa" (Dickson) 29

Herman, E.C.T. 101–102

Herr X story 110–111

Herr Z story 111–112

Herschel, Sir William 59

Hert, Heinrich 59

Hess, Rudolf 127

Heydrich, Reinhard 121

Hibbert, J.G. 149

Himmler, Heinrich 124–125, 127

Hirschberg, H.Z. 20

historical perspective of Jews in Africa before Holocaust: activities 32–36; attitudes 36–38; background information 18–19; Cape Verde 32–33; cultural influences 30–33, 37–38; documentation 144; East Africa 29–30; economic influences 32, 34–35; Egypt 19–20; Ethiopia 27–29; Ghana 29; gold mines 35; interactions 36–38; Kenya 30, 36–38; Mauritania 37; Morocco 21, 31; Nigeria 29; North Africa 19–25; overview 38–39, 175; Senegal 31–32, 37; Sierra Leone 32; social science studies 18; Songhai 29; South Africa 25–27; status 32–36; trans-Saharan trade period 31; weaving industry 35; West Africa 29–31

Hitler, Adolf: Africans and, view/policy of 44, 49, 51, 67, 79; anti-Semitism of 45–46, 69; Aryans as superior people and 46–49; Christianity and 50–51; citizenship of Jews, questioning 48; colonialism and, view of 49, 61–62; Darwinist evolutionary theory and 48–49; education and race, view of 50–51, 55; fascism and 51; France and, view of 49–50; goal of 51; interracial sexual contact and 47; Jewish intellectual power in Germany and 48; Jews and, view/policy of 45–51, 67, 70, 79, 102; *Mein Kampf* and 45–51, *61*, 76; military alliances and 69, 79; Mussolini and 78,

98n18, 98n23; Nazism and 51; political career of 46, 52–53; procreation and, control of 47; racial theories/policies of 9, 46–47; Selassie and 44–45, 78–79; South Tyrol and 79; sports and race, view of 55–56; white supremacy and 46–49, 55–56; World War I and, view of 45–46
Hitler's African Victims (Scheck) 5, 7
Hitler's Black Victims (Lusane) 5
"Hitler's New Order" (Cameron's letter) 91–93
Hodson, Sir Arnold Weinholt 80–81, 94–95, 134, 167
Holland, anti-Semitism in 31
Holocaust: African press reports on 105–106, 119–126; Africans' knowledge of during World War II 2–3, 105, 175–177; African sources/scope of knowledge of 105–108; African voices/perspectives 11, 13–15, 127–129; archival materials in researching Africans' perspective on 13; Black Germans' persecution 1, 103; British diplomats in Germany and 113–115; British news sources about 120–122; British settlers in Africa and 107–108; circumstances leading to 108, *109*, 110–119; colonial authorities' revelation of African perspectives of 14; colonialism and, impact on 133–137, 177; concentration camps and 102, 115–119, 122–126, 134; criteria in researching Africans' perspective of 12–13; defining 101–105; disabilities and, persecution of people with 1, 103; East Africa's knowledge of 106–108; European tutelage and 136; Gandhi and 131; Great Britain's knowledge of 108, *109*, 110, 122–126; Gypsy people's persecution 1, 103; Herr X story 110–111; Herr Z story 111–112; historical reality of 101; homosexuals' persecution 1, 103; imprisonment and 113–115; interpreting 126–133; Jehovah Witnesses' persecution 103; *Kristallnacht* and 108, 110, 176; Mr. Dowden's story 113–114; Nazism and 1, 101–102, 125–126; newspapers in researching Africans' perspective on 13; overview 105, 137–138; *Papers* and 108, *109*, 110, 119; persecution of Jews and 102–105, 108, 110–113; racial constructs of 177; racism as cause of 129; Roma people's persecution 1, 102–103; Russian news sources about 120; scholars' views of 102–104; significance of 101; Sinti people's persecution 1, 102–103; Smallbones and 113–115; terms applying to 102; UNESCO and 104; United States Holocaust Memorial Museum and 13, 104; West Africa and 106–107, 129; *West African Pilot's* information about 12, 119, 122, 124–133, 136–137; Yad Vashem Holocaust Resource Center and 104–105

holocaust, defining 101–102
Holocaust Remembrance Day 1, 104
"Holocaust, The" (Friedman) 103
homeland for Jews143 *see* Palestine
homosexuals, persecution of 1, 103
Horta, Jose da Silva 31–33, 37
Howe, R.G. 155–157, 159
Hull, Richard 18–19, 22, 24, 28, 31
human decency, World War II and conversations about 93–96
humanity, issue of 13–14, 56, 59, 62, 66, 76, 94, 137, 148, 164

Ickes, Harold 132
Ifunda settlement camp 161
Igbo people 29
Indians in South Africa, persecution of 130–131
inhumanity 125, 132; *see also* Holocaust
Inquisition 31–32
Inside News (Gold Coast newspaper) 121
"Inside Stuff" column (Azikiwe) 56, 58, 65, 76, 126–127
integration, social 22, 33, 37, 152; *see also* assimilation
intermarriages 34, 47, 67, 106–107
International Holocaust Remembrance Day 1, 104
interracial sexual contact 47
Islam 29, 35
Israel, ancient 12, 18, 28, 158
Israel, Jonathan 22
Israel, state of 29–30
Italy 77–78

Jackel, Eberhard 101
Jehovah Witnesses, persecution of 103
Jesus 59
Jew, defining 107
Jewish refugees: African land for, request for 3; Africans and 3–4, 9–10, 178; assimilation and 152; background

information 143; British policy and 149–150, 153–154; British settlers' reactions to 145–147; conflicts among 162; in East Africa 151–152; in Ethiopia 155–161; in Gold Coast 134, 164–169; in Great Britain 3; homeland for, searching for 143–144; in Kenya 30, 144–146, 149, 151–153; Liebenstein case 150; in Nyasaland 151, 153; overview 143–144, 169–170; in Palestine 158–161, 168; prewar proposals on 147–155; from Russia 30; in South Africa 25; in Tanganyiak 161–162; in Uganda 162–164; wartime proposals on 147–155; in West Africa 164–169
Jewish Refugees Committee (JRC) 155
Jews: acculturation and 22; Ashkenazi 21, 25–26, 30; assimilation of 148, 152; Bohemian 125; conversion of 20, 28–29, 32, 145; defining 18–19; education and 24, 27; German citizenship of, Hitler's questioning of 48; Hitler's view/policy of 45–51, 67, 70, 79, 102; Holocaust and persecution of 103; integration of, social 22, 33, 37, 152; intermarriage of 34; Jesus as 59; *Kristallnacht* and 5, 108, 110, 113, 127–128, 176; in *Mein Kampf* 45–51, 70; Moravian 125; Nairobi 30; Nazism's stereotype of 3; persecution of 26, 103, 108, 112, 176; pogroms against 20, 93–94, 126; Polish 102, 108, 123, 125, 162, 176; reconversion of 23; Russian 30, 120, 144–145; Sephardi 21–22, 25, 33–34, 36; Star of David patch and 10, 111, 115, 117; *see also* emigration of Jews; historical perspective of Jews in Africa before Holocaust; Jewish refugees
Jews and Judaism in African History (Hull) 18, 31
Johnson, Cornelius 72n57
Judaism 18–19

Kaplan, Steven 28
Karlow, Rudolf 63–64
Katz, Steven 102
Kenya: emigration of Jews to 30, 150, 156, 169; German colonial claims on 62; historical perspective of Jews in Africa before Holocaust 30, 36–38; Jewish refugees in 30, 144–146, 149, 151–153
Kesting, Robert W. 4–5, 9
Kidugalla settlement camp 161
Killingray, David 1–2, 77

Kittermaster, Harold 166
Knaggs, Colonel 153
Kock, Herr Standartenfuhrher 119
Koja settlement camp 162–163
Kondoa settlement camp 161–162
Kristallnacht (Night of Broken Glass) 5, 108, 110, 113, 127–128, 176
Kushner, Tony 102

Laumann, Dennis 52
Lebanese refugees 168–169
Left Book Club, Sierra Leone Branch 63
Legislative Council (Gold Coast) 80, 86–88, 91, 93–94, 168
Le Jour (French newspaper) 62
Lemba people 25
Liberia: Allied Powers and, support of 85; archival materials from 13; colonialism in 65–67; Germany and 65–67; interracial marriages and 107; Nazism and, reaction to 65–67; Poland and 61; United States and 65, 67, 85; World War II and, attitude about 85–86
Liberian Crisis, The (monthly newspaper) 67, 107
Lidice massacre (Czechoslovakia) 121
Liebau, Heike 101
Liebenstein (Jewish refugee) 150
London, Louise 3, 152
Lorimer, E.O. 60
Louis, Joe 7, 56, 57
Lowenberg, Erich 118
Lusane, Clarence 4–7, 9

MacDonald, Malcolm 62, 107–108, 150–151, 153, 166
Mackereth, Gilbert 155
Mark, Peter 31–33, 37
Marks, Simon 147–148
Marrus, Michael 2
Marx, Karl 59
Massaquoi, Hans J. 4–5, 55, 66, 69
Mauritania 37
Maxwell, Sir Alan Cuthbert 134
Medical Practitioners and Dentists Ordinance 166
Mein Kampf (My Struggle) (Hitler) 45–51, 61, 70, 76
mellahs 24
Menelik (Solomon's son) 18
Menelik, Emperor 68
Miles, William F.S. 19
Minkowsky, Oskar 59

Monrovia 85, 107
Moore, G.E. 87, 96–97
Moravian Jews 125
Morocco 21, 23–25, 31
Musiker, Naomi 30, 144
Muslims 24
Mussolini, Benito 68, 78–79, 98n18, 98n23, 136–137
Mwangi Kagwanjia, Peter 144
Mwangi wa-Githumo 144–145

Nairobi Jews 30
National Party (South Africa) 27
National Socialism 61
National Socialist Democratic Labor Party (NSDAP) 45, 51, 53
Nazi Germany and the Jews (Friedlander) 102
"Nazi Plan for Negroes, The" (Habe) 66–67
Nazism: Achebe's novel and 44; Africans/Africa's reactions to 11, 44–45, 70–71, 175–176; Africans' opinion of, before World War II 44–45; Africans' visions of Germany before era of 45, 51–53; anti-Semitism and 3, 26, 56, 93–94; Arab collaborators with 9–10; *Ashanti Pioneer* articles on 54; Azikiwe's view of 60–61, 64–65; Blacks and 124; colonial Africa's reactions to 53–56, 57, 58–61, 58, 61; colonialism and 59–65; as cornerstone of Hitler's anti-Semitism 69; East Africa's reactions to 53; education of Africans and view of 62–63, 62–64, 121, 176; education in propaganda of 53–54; emigration of Jews and 110, 118; Ethiopia's reaction to 67–69; Gold Coast's reaction to 54–55, 81; Hitler and 51; Holocaust and 1, 101–102, 125–126; Jewish policy/persecution 102; Jews' stereotypes and 3; Liberia's reaction to 65–67; massacre of Lidice (Czechoslovakia) residents and 121; *Mein Kampf* and 45–51, 76; in 1930s 3; overview 69–71; propaganda 53–55; racism and 61–65, 93–94, 175; Selassie and 44–45; sports and race, view of 55–56; tenets of, central 56; in Togoland 53; Vichy collaborators with 9–10; in West Africa 53, 76–77; *West African Pilot* and information about 66, 127; white supremacy and 56, 59; *see also* Holocaust
Neurath, Konstantin von 64

newspapers, African 13; *see also specific name*
News Review (London newspaper) 62
New Times (newspaper) 63
Nigeria 29, 62, 77, 87–88, 102, 130
No Longer at Ease (Achebe) 44
North Africa: anti-Semitism in 20–23; Arab conquest of 20–21; Ashkenazi Jews in 21; colonialism in 23–24; Egypt 19–20, 23–25; emigration of Jews to 20–21; historical perspective of Jews in Africa before Holocaust 19–25; Morocco 21, 23–24; Ottoman Turkish rule 21–23; pogroms 20; poll tax on Jews 22; Roman rule in 20; Sephardi Jews in 21–22; *see also specific country*
Northcroft, L.A. 134–135
Nuremberg Laws (1935) 67, 106–108
Nyabeya settlement camp 162–164
Nyasaland (present-day Malawi) 151, 153, 166–167

Ofori Atta, Nana 80, 86, 90, 93–94
Ogilie-Forbes, Sir G. 113
Olympic Games (1936) 7, 56, 72n57
Oswald Pirow plan 62
Ottoman Turkish rule of North Africa 19, 21–23
Owens, Jesse 56, 72n57
Ozarnomski, F.B. 123

Palestine: emigration of Jews to 168; Gandhi's view of Arab-Jews question in 130; homeland for Jews 132–133, 144, 147, 155, 164; Jewish refugees in 158–161, 168
Pankhurst, Richard 79
Papers Concerning the Treatment of German Nationals in Germany, 1938–1939 (*Papers*) (confidential British document) 108, 109, 110, 119
Pedler, Mr. F.J. 93
Peel, W.G. 145
Peregrino, Jacob 34
Peregrino, Manuel 34
persecution of Jews 26, 103, 108, 112, 176; *see also* anti-Semitism; Holocaust
Plaut, Martin 1–2, 77
pogroms against Jews 20, 93–94, 126; *see also* Holocaust
Poland 61, 77
Polish Jews 102, 108, 123, 125, 162, 176
poll tax on Jews in North Africa 22
Portugal, anti-Semitism in 31

Prussin, Labelle 19, 30–31, 35, 37
Ptolemy I 19

Queen of Sheba 18

racial equality/inequality 76, 91, 94–95, 136
racial theories of 1920s 46–47
racism 59, 61–65, 95, 129, 175; *see also* Nazism
Randall, A.W.G. 160
reconversion of Jews 23
research criteria on Holocaust perspective of Africans 12–13
Roberts, Z.B.H. 67
Roman rule in North Africa 19–20
Roma people, persecution of 1, 102–103
Roosevelt, Franklin D. 85, 132, 148
Rovner, Adam 145, 147
Ruger, Adolf 64
Russian Jews 30, 120, 144–145
Russian news sources 120

Sabine, Noel 93
Satloff, Robert 4, 9–10
Sawyerr, Mr. Akilagpa 95–97
Scheck, Raffael 4–5, 7–9
Schmeling, Max 7, 55–56, 57
Second World War *see* World War II
Selassie, Haile 44–45, 68–69, 78–79, 133, 157
Senegal 8–9, 31–32, 37
Senghor, Leopold Sedar 6–7
Sephardi Jews 21–22, 25, 33–34, 36
Serer people 33–34
Shadle, Brett 145–146
Shain, Milton 26
Sheba, Queen 18
Shepherd, F.M. 116–117
Shoah 104–105; *see also* Holocaust
Shuckburgh, John Evelyn 88
Sierra Leone 32, 106–107
Sinclair, Sir Archibald 64
Sinti people 1, 102–103
slavery 66–67, 89–90, 107
slave trade, trans-Atlantic as framework for implications of German rule of Gold Coast 89–90
Smallbones, R.T. 113–115
Smidt, Wolbert 67–69, 78–79
Smythe, John Henry 55, 91, 93
social justice, World War II and conversations about 93–96
Solomonic dynasty 28

Solomon legend 18, 27
Songhai 29
Souls of the White Folk, The (Shadle) 146
South Africa 25–27, 108; *see also specific country*
South America 112
South Tyrol 79
Southwest Africa (present-day Namibia) 62
sports, Hitler's view on race and 55–56; *see also* Olympic Games (1936)
Stannard, David E. 103
Star of David patch 10, 111, 115, 117
Steffen, Hans 78
Stephany, Mr. 153
Stewart, Andrew 77–78
Stoler, Ann Laura 14, 165
Suez Canal 23, 25
Sultan of Fez 21
Sunday Express (British newspaper) 123
Sunday Referee (London newspaper) 59
survival of the fittest concept 48–49
Syrian refugees 168–169
Szlapak family 30

Table Bay (now Cape Town) 26
Tafla, Bairu 67–69, 78–79
Tanganyika (present-day Tanzania) 52, 54, 62–64, 107, 148–149, 161–162, 178
Tanganyika Herald (newspaper) 120
Taylor, C. Frederick 66
Temple, William 126
Thevet, Andre 32–33
Third Reich 60, 63, 67, 105, 132, 136
Thomas, J.H. 147
Tibebu, Teshale 28
Tiller, W.H. 145
Times of London (newspaper) 54
Tirailleurs Senegalais 6–7
Togoland 52–53, 62, 64
Trajan, Emperor 20
trans-Saharan trade period 31
Treblinka concentration camp 123
Tsibu Darko, Nana IX 80, 90
Tubman, William V.S. 66, 85
Tunisia 10

Uganda 162–164, 178
Uganda Herald (newspaper) 106, 120, 130, 163–164
UNESCO 104
United African Company 93
United Nations (UN) 1, 104

United States: Blacks in, Kesting's study of 9; emigration of Jews to 29; Ethiopia and 159; fascism and, attitude about 78; Germany's invasion of Europe and 78, 80; Liberia and 65, 67, 85
United States Holocaust Memorial Museum (USHMM) (Washington, D.C.) 13, 104
University of Monrovia library 13
University of South Florida Library (Tampa) 13
Upper Volta (present-day Burkina Faso) 55

Versailles treaty 60
Vichy France 9–10, 24
vom Rath, Ernst 108, 110, 113, 127, 176

warfare, "history" of 75; *see also* World War I; World War II
War Refugees Board 132
weaving in West Africa 35
Weimar Republic 64
Weld, Kirsten 14, 165
West Africa: assimilation and 37; colonialism in 62, 64; cultural similarities between Jews and 29; emigration of Syrian and Lebanese refugees to 168; German colonialism in 52; gold mines in 35; historical perspective of Jews in Africa before Holocaust 29–31; Holocaust and 12, 106–107, 129; Hull's study of 18–19; integration of Jews and 33, 37; Jew in before Holocaust 29–31; Jewish refugees in 164–169; Nazism in 53, 76–77; status of Jews in 36; weaving in 35; World War II and, attitude about 81, 83–85, 87; *see also* Africa/Africans; Gold Coast; *specific country*
West African Medical School 167–168
West African Pilot (newspaper): "Christianity Today" serial in 60; enlistments advertisement in *82*; Gandhi's view of persecution of Jews and 131–132; German Blacks' treatment 124–125, 130; German colonial claims and 57, 62, 101; Holocaust and, information about 119, 122, 124–133, 136–137; *Mein Kampf* advertisement in *61*; Nazism and, information about 66, 127; Olympic Games of 1936 and 56; racism as world problem and 129; vom Rath's murder and 127; World War II and, information about 76–77, 88
West African Students Union of Great Britain 136

"What Hitler Wants" (Lorimer) 60
white supremacy 46–49, 56, 59; *see also* Nazism
Wilelm II, Kaiser 68
Williams, Johnny 6–7
Williams, Joseph J. 29
Williams, Mrs. Lukya 163
Wilson, John 89–90
Wolny, Jan 123–124
Wolof people 32–36
World Jewish Congress 125
World War I 25, 45–46
World War II: African attitudes about 81, 83–88, 96–97, 176; African interest in, promoting healthy 88–93; African soldiers fighting in 1, 71, 90–91, 122; Africans' opinion of Nazism before 44–45; Africans in prisoner of war camps during 4, 7–9; Allied Powers and 1, 85; appeasement diplomacy and 62, 76, 83, 127, 176; colonialism in explaining 80–81; education of Africans and attitude about 80–81, 83; enlistment advertisements 81, *82*; fascist invasions during, two 77–79; German prisoner of war camps during 4, 7–9; Germany's invasion of Europe and 78, 80; Gold Coast's attitude about 80–88; Gold Coast's support for 80–81; human decency conversations and 93–96; Italian invasion of Ethiopia and 77–78; liberation of Auschwitz-Birkenau camp 1; Liberia's attitude about 85–86; literature relating to Africa and 1–2, 10–11; Nigeria's attitude about 88; outbreak of 78; overview 75–76, 96–97; signals of oncoming 76–77; social justice conversations and 93–96; as war against Jews 2; as war with Germany 2; West African attitude about 81, 83–85; *West African Pilot*'s information about 76–77, 88
World Zionist Conference 144
Wyman, David S. 101

xenophobia 25

Yad Vashem Holocaust Resource Center (Israel) 104–105
Yemen 28
Yoruba people 29
Young, Mark 62–63, 107, 149

Zegeye, Abebe 28
Zionist Congress 144

Made in United States
Troutdale, OR
08/14/2023